GREEN DEVILS

—

RED DEVILS

GREEN DEVILS

———

RED DEVILS

Untold Tales of the Airborne
Forces in the Second World War

by
Edmund L. Blandford

LONDON   NEW YORK   SYDNEY   TORONTO

This edition published 1993
by BCA by arrangement with
LEO COOPER
an imprint of
Pen & Sword Books Ltd,

CN 1840

Typeset by Yorkshire Web, Barnsley, South Yorkshire
in Times 11 point

Printed by
Redwood Books,
Trowbridge, Wiltshire

To Andrew

who knew carefree student days
before his transformation into
a 'red beret',
then, through suffering, to a greater role

CONTENTS

ACKNOWLEDGEMENT

I would like to record my thanks for the assistance given by both British and German ex-airborne soldiers, without whose recollections this book would not have been possible.

Introduction

Everyone familiar with the history of parachute troops will recall the 1930s film and stills of Russian soldiers emitting from a giant transport plane. The pictures were impressive from some points of view: the size of the aircraft, the men exiting in seemingly haphazard fashion, even sliding off the huge wing of the plane.

It seems remarkable, but the sport of parachuting had been taken up in the Soviet Union in the 1920s, and, with State support, the *Osswiachim Club* members were spread across Russia, and eventually by the outbreak of the 'Great Patriotic War' in June, 1941, one thousand villages were supporting such organizations.

By 1928 the Red Army had begun to organize parachute troops, and this move received the full support of its C-in-C, Marshal Tuchatschewski. In 1930 the Red Army held its annual manoeuvres – and sprang a surprise: a Lieutenant jumped with one platoon south of Moscow and 'captured' a high level staff who were taken completely unawares. This was the first known use of paratroops.

Six years later the Soviets lifted their usual curtain of secrecy and invited a host of foreign military attachés to their war games. A clutch of transport planes droned over the field and disgorged 1000 paratroopers who descended before the astonished gaze of the foreign observers. These paras were quickly followed by a further 5000 soldiers who landed in assault transport planes. One officer who witnessed this impressive demonstration was Britain's General Wavell, who was to gain fame in World War II. To his government he wrote:

'If I had not witnessed it myself, I would not have believed that such an operation was possible.'

Nevertheless, neither Wavell nor his superiors felt pressed to follow up such experiments.

Yet by 1940 the Germans' use of the airborne weapon made such an impact that fear of the sudden arrival of the enemy by parachute permeated Britain more than anything else. This led to all kinds of absurd rumours, the standard one being that of Hun parachutists disguised as nuns. Even the seemingly unflappable, erudite J. B. Priestley allowed himself to be swayed by foolish tales, so that in one of his famous radio broadcasts (9 June, 1940) he referred to :

'those half-doped, crazy lads they call parachute troops.'

The first part of his comment refers to one of the many tall tales that abounded in that slightly hysteria-ridden period of dead German paras being found with green-tinged faces. The British media seized on this as being evidence that the enemy needed pills to sustain their courage.

Similar stories appeared in print concerning the bodies of *Luftwaffe* aircrew, the green shade on the faces said to be the after effects of drugs — unless they had died in a green funk.

There was nothing clinically crazy about the trained German paratrooper; suicidally courageous at times perhaps, yes. The reputation of the German airborne soldier remained second to none in World War II.

Compared to them the British were slow starters, but once in the saddle the red berets proved they could ride with the best.

There are no soldiers equal to élite paratroopers, yet we should not forget the bravery and courage of the men who rode into battle in flimsy gliders, often paying with their lives for that very reason, men who in the main were impressed into such service; it seems only a few felt the urge to gain a coveted red beret via the easier route.

Although it has been necessary to place them in historical context, the main intention of this book has been to present the experiences of 'other rankers' as told in their own words. In the context of paratroops it is hard to refer to even the most humble private as a 'common soldier', for the very act of leaping from an aircraft marks down any human being as rather more than just 'ordinary'. And to do so without a reserve 'chute and often into the arms of an enemy intent on ensuring their early demise sets these soldiers well apart from all others. This was especially true in the early 'forties when all was very new in airborne warfare.

The fact that such men had conquered fear in leaping into space, relying on equipment which could never be 100% certain ensured them a morale and fighting spirit second to none, which was why German paras were able to survive and triumph on Crete, and why the red berets became fighting demons at Arnhem.

British or German, it was usually the daredevil spirit of youth which prompted most of these men to step forward as volunteers for parachuting; the glamour of belonging to something special came later. For those older ones such as some officers an even greater effort was required.

But whether ex-Hitler Youth or 'Nazi fanatics', as they were seen by some in wartime Britain, both German airborne and the Red Devils who made such an outstanding impression on their enemies were of the same breed.

Edmund L. Blandford

The Parachute

It was Leonardo da Vinci who first mooted the idea of an 'envelope' made of linen which could, he foresaw, enable a man to descend from a great height in safety. His original sketch depicted a hollow cloth pyramid, made rigid at the base, with cords attached to each corner to which the jumper could cling.

Three hundred years later, in 1785, the French pioneer of ballooning, Jean-Pierre Blanchard, made a small model of such a 'parachute', and, taking a dog with him in his balloon several hundred feet over Paris, he strapped the envelope to the animal and dropped it over the side of his basket. The dog descended safely, barking as it landed in good shape, to scurry away and not be seen by Blanchard again. The dog was therefore the world's first successful parachutist. Since there was apparently no rush of volunteers to take up this remarkable invention the idea lapsed.

But in time the crowds who had flocked to watch trapeze artists performing tricks by hanging from balloons grew tired of the novelty, so the carnival promoters had to come up with a new attraction. They recalled the parachute or life-saving umbrella. A number were made and a few daredevils paid to leap from balloonists' baskets. Beyond this entertainment there seemed no practical use for the invention.

The early parachutes consisted of cloth or linen fixed to a rigid frame, but these provided anything but a gentle, gliding descent. An Englishman, Robert Cocking, invented an alternative: in essence it was an inverted type, the designer reasoning that if air was allowed to escape at the top it would permit a much easier descent. His drawings resembled an inverted umbrella, using tin hoops, the largest of 34ft diameter at the top, all of them connected by wooden spars, the structure covered in Irish linen. Beneath the umbrella was suspended a wicker basket to carry the 'aviator'.

Cocking's would-be mentor was an impresario named Fred Gye who put on shows at London's Vauxhall Gardens where balloonists and parachutists were a regular part of the entertainment. But Gye declined Cocking's offer to demonstrate his new-style parachute over the Gardens as he did not consider the existing balloons strong enough to take the extra weight. Cocking would not be put off, however, and two years later Gye agreed to allow him to use a strengthened balloon to lift the inverted umbrella and jumper over the paying crowds at Vauxhall. Cocking had offered to make the first descent free of charge, but jumps thereafter would earn him 20 guineas per jump, rising to 30 guineas if success continued.

It was the evening of 24 July, 1837, when Cocking was released from 4000 ft above an anxious crowd who gaped as the rays of a setting sun caught the strange contraption and its inventor descending gently towards them. But then disaster struck, and swiftly, for the tin and wood structure was not strong enough to take the stress of weight and wind, the members snapped, tearing open the linen covering and allowing the hapless inventor to plummet to his death.

It was almost another half century before further serious work was done to develop a more practical parachute. The American Baldwin brothers set about designing a type that could be stowed on the person; in other words, it no longer utilized a rigid structure. There is a story that the brothers sat in a restaurant discussing their ideas, and in due course borrowed a table napkin from a waiter, tied four pieces of string to its corners and, using a wine cork as a weight, dropped it out of a nearby window. They reasoned that a full-scale version could be folded and strapped to the back of a jumper, but they did not proceed with their idea for several years; when they did it worked. The parachute was folded up, with a sandbag as weight and dropped from a balloon, and on 30 January, 1887, Tom Baldwin himself made the first successful descent by modern parachute from a tethered balloon from 5000 ft at Golden Gate Park in San Francisco. It had been the weight of Baldwin's body which had pulled the 'chute from its container, the whole apparatus secured to him by ropes and opening in five seconds.

Whereas ballooning had been the great spectator sport of the early Victorian era, parachuting now took over as the big carnival show attraction in America where there seemed to be no shortage of daredevils — both men and women — to take up the sport.

But it was the rapid development of aircraft which next produced a spurt in parachute design as the number of aerial disasters caused by poor design and structural failure grew rapidly. It was an obvious solution for pilots to save their lives by the magic umbrella. But although the Baldwin 'chute had proved excellent, its use by a pilot in an aeroplane was another matter. The problem was one of stowage, for although the parachute envelope itself had been perfected a satisfactory method of carrying one in a plane had not.

One early parachute bag was a conical container made of tin, designed to be fitted beneath the fuselage and attached by lines to the pilot, the idea being that in an emergency he would drop through the bottom of the plane and thus pull the 'chute from its container. Other designs made use of bulky canvas bags but it was the cone designed by Leo Stevens which was used for the first successful parachute jump from an aircraft. Albert Berry leapt from the wheel axle of a Benoist pusher biplane over Missouri on 1 March, 1912, descending safely to land near the mess hall of Jefferson Army Barracks.

But when war came to Europe two years later little or no thought had been given to the saving of military pilots from crippled aircraft, though the warlike possibilities of aviation had been realized. The advent of air fighting led to the deaths of hundreds of aviators, for most of the pilots and observers whose machines were disabled crashed to their deaths when their planes caught fire or fell apart, though some preferred to leap from their cockpits rather than be burnt alive. It seems an obvious solution now in an age of ejector seats, but in those days there seemed to be cogent reasons why aircrew should not be provided with parachutes. For one thing, some air leaders imagined that their airmen might be encouraged to flee from a fight by parachute, and in any case no ready supply of suitable equipment was available.

Meanwhile, another American, Charles Broadwick, had designed an ingenious 'parachute coat', a sleeveless garment containing the 'chute within its back, the designer selecting his adopted daughter for a demonstration before officers of the US Army in April, 1914. The girl is reputed to have been a professional jumper since the age of fifteen, a wife and mother, thrilling crowds across America since 1908. As 'Tiny' Broadwick, she had been the first woman to jump with a parachute, leaping from a hand-made Glenn Martin biplane over Griffith Park, Los Angeles on 21 June, 1913. A year later her official demonstration saw her landing almost at the feet of General Scriven and his amazed staff. Yet the US Army never adopted the Broadwick para-coat.

The use of observation balloons was common to both sides during the Great War, and owing to their vulnerability to air attack the crews were provided with parachutes which were carried in bags or cones and strapped to the balloon baskets; in some German balloons they were stowed in a rack over the heads of the crew. These balloon observers went aloft wearing harness containing hooks which could very quickly be attached to the parachutes in an emergency. The balloons themselves were filled with highly inflammable hydrogen gas and were therefore very vulnerable to gunfire. When fighting aircraft attacked balloons it was customary for the crews to hook up and leap out at once, for the enemy pilots could hardly miss their fat targets and the incendiary bullets used soon reduced the gas bags to a flaming mass which fell quickly to the ground. The balloons were, of course, stationary targets, tethered to the ground and usually protected by a ring of anti-aircraft machine guns which invariably failed to protect their charges from attack. In some cases a fake pass by an enemy pilot out of ammunition would be enough to send the balloon crews over the side.

But it was the pilots and observers in the fighting and observation aeroplanes who suffered most, and not until May, 1918, when the war was practically over, were the first parachutes issued to military aviators, and even then only the Germans received them. The equipment was hardly ideal, the pilots wearing a body harness which was attached to a separate container which needed to be thrown out of the disabled machine before the airman followed, using the static line method of opening the container and 'chute. The famous ace Ernst Udet owed his life to the parachute, bailing out on two occasions and surviving to become a General and one of the pioneers of the later *Luftwaffe*; he committed suicide in 1941.

It is impossible to say how many Allied aircrew lost their lives in that war because of the failure of their leaders to supply them with parachutes. But following the war they became standard equipment among airmen of those nations possessing air forces, though not of course for crews or passengers of airliners.

Airborne Soldiers

The notion of placing troops in the enemy's rear was hardly new, but, until the advent of the parachute, difficult to accomplish. As noted, the earliest experiments with para-soldiers appear to have taken place in the Soviet Union, for the Russian Government had become alarmed by the Japanese invasion of Manchuria and ordered the modernization of its armed forces. The Japanese had clashed with the Russians before, though only at sea, and had inflicted a heavy defeat on them. Extreme right-wing régimes were coming to power in Japan, Italy and Germany, so precautionary measures on the part of all nations, especially communist ones, were justified.

In 1931, the year the Japanese incursion into East Asia began, volunteers were taken from the Soviet 11th Rifle Division in Leningrad to form the world's first parachute infantry unit. Yet, despite this early start and the subsequent impressive demonstration of such units in the mid-thirties, the Soviets allowed development to stagnate. They do not appear to have had any firm plans for paratroop units above the size of a battalion. When war came such units were only used in comparatively small-scale actions, usually in support of partisan operations behind the German lines.

There can be little doubt, however, that the leading European military powers had been impressed by the Soviet experiments, and by the early winter of 1935 both the French and the Germans took steps to set up parachute infantry units. The French Army set up its jump school at Avignon in October, 1935, and by April, 1937, it could boast two trained units of paras, the 601st and 602nd Air Infantry Groups. Then the Italian Army under Benito Mussolini opened its own parachute training school at Tripoli, the capital of its Libyan colony.

Meanwhile, no plans whatever had been put forward in Britain or America for the inclusion of such forces in their armies, although discussion papers had appeared in military journals.

The prime use of parachute troops has always been to disrupt the enemy's defensive system by landing within or behind it, causing chaos and alarm, as part of a larger offensive. The seizing of vital communication centres, bridges, and key airfields were part of the general strategy, while comparatively small bands of hard, well-trained men could exact further toll by laying ambush to supply convoys and rail networks, eliminating staffs and generally spreading confusion.

Obviously, owing to their nature and their method of transport, they could only be lightly armed — with pistols, rifles, light machine-guns (especially sub-machine-guns) and grenades. In due course light and heavy mortars, anti-tank guns and even vehicles were added to their impedimenta as better transport planes became available. In Western armies at least paratroops were never seen as expendable; they were too highly trained to be sacrificed, but the Japanese may have thought otherwise when they themselves used such troops on a small scale in the Second World War. Operations planned for the new arm had to be very carefully conceived and carried out.

In general, airborne forces in the Second World War were used as a kind of shock advance guard dropped at key points before the main army's advance; in other words the lightweight paratroops would leapfrog ahead to prepare the way for larger ground formations. But, without heavy weapons it was essential that they be relieved within a day or two of being dropped, for no matter how much shock or success such units at first achieved behind the enemy's front, once the defenders were given time to recover they could launch heavy assaults to eliminate the threat before relief came to the invaders. Obviously, the loss of such élite forces would be a serious setback to an attacker, and in more than one sense, for such troops cannot quickly be replaced.

To secure the kind of objectives named earlier required the forming, training and employment of at least a battalion, though more ambitious plans would need a regiment or even a division. A single battalion of say 600 men would be sufficient to seize a vital river crossing and hold it for perhaps half a day, but quite insufficient to attack and hold a town already infested with the enemy. A similar sized formation could secure an airfield in a surprise assault, and much smaller units could fatally disrupt a traffic artery for a while. The use of sub-units, platoons or even squads, to carry out special missions also came up in the Second

World War, as exemplified by SAS operations and the daring rescue of Mussolini from his mountain prison in 1943 by a German troop landed by glider. The kidnapping or elimination of important enemy generals or even political leaders also cropped up, as evidenced by the German attempt to capture the Yugoslav leader Marshal Tito, which nearly came off. The most notable British attempts in this direction − the bid to get Rommel in Libya and the kidnapping of General Kreipe on Crete — did not come under the heading of parachute operations.

But such ideas, or the use of whole parachute divisions, did not come up at all in the early days, when the whole concept of delivering troops by air and specifically by parachute was seen either as a novelty or a limited ploy by some, while the more daring and free-thinking among military commanders and strategists envisaged grander schemes. The majority of the military on both sides were always conservative by nature and did not favour the forming of élite units; when paratroops did gain success their admiration was grudging, and when failure or disaster came, the long-time doubters shook their heads in confirmation of established views. For most the use of paratroops could only be seen in terms of small-scale tactical surprise.

It was the successes achieved by the German airborne forces in Holland which in due course brought about first the creation of Britain's own airborne units and later those of the United States. It also brought about an expansion of the German airborne corps and the conceiving of bolder schemes which only a short time before would have seemed ludicrous. During the execution of these larger plans the vulnerability of airborne troops was well demonstrated and serious lessons learned at a high cost in lives. The very costly German victory in Crete, the Allied disasters in Sicily and at Arnhem and the casualties incurred in the Rhine crossing in 1945 all seemed to point to the futility of using such troops. Such reverses, however, did not lead to their abolition, though on some fronts, most notably in Russia, airborne forces were reduced to the role of line troops in a defensive capacity, much to the disgust of both leaders and men.

GREEN DEVILS

Soldiers With Wings

By 1936 the German Army, the 100,000-man force permitted under the 1919 Treaty of Versailles, had been reorganized. Gone was the old *Reichswehr*; the *Heer* (or Army) became part of the new *Wehrmacht*, the old force of veterans having been in effect an army of officers and NCOs who would act as a huge cadre for a greatly expanded army being swelled by conscription, the first recruits entering the service in 1935. This solid backbone of professionals would prove its worth in the testing times to come.

As noted earlier, the Germans were much impressed by the Soviet paratroops, but, by all accounts, it was not the German Army which initiated such a formation for the new *Wehrmacht*, but General Göring, Hitler's right-hand man, ex-WW1 air ace and now head of the *Luftwaffe*. He, in consultation with his Reichsminister for Aviation and C-in-C of the Air Force, General Milch, decreed that Germany should have its own paratroops.

The first troops had a curious origin, the men having been part of a mobile police unit, the Prussian *Landespolizeigruppe General Göring*, a regiment-sized formation designed to provide escort protection for Nazi leaders, especially Göring himself, during various tours and engagements before and after their election triumph of January, 1933. Once this need had passed, the unit was redesignated a military formation and with effect from 1 April, 1935, it became the *General Göring Regiment*. In September of that year its commander, General Jakoby, was ordered by Göring to transfer his unit en bloc into the *Luftwaffe*. As from 10 October General Jakoby commanded a regiment of 'non-aviation' origin and indeterminate function, but this was not to last, for almost at once he received orders to form a cadre of paratroops.

It is notable that even at this early stage Göring was intent on seizing control of everything that was "of the air", so that even the infantrymen, once conceived as air-transportable, were seen by him as his property. His axiom that 'if it flies it belongs to me' would in due course result in a clash with Grand Admiral Raeder of the *Kriegsmarine*, who wished to retain control of the air patrol and reconnaissance squadrons maintained under his command. Though to some degree getting his own way and taking over a whole naval squadron, who thereafter flew Heinkel bombers, Göring was obliged to allow naval officers to continue to fly among the *Luftwaffe* aircrews who manned the North Sea patrol planes. It is certain that he went ahead and inaugurated his own parachute infantry without any agreement, and probably no discussion, with the Germany Army. Such a situation would be impossible in Britain or America where clear divisions of responsibility were well established. It is difficult not to be amazed that in late 1935 both the *Luftwaffe* and the German Army were each organizing quite separate units of paratroop infantry. If Göring had made the first move, it was to be the German Army which made the first impression.

The first "Göring" paratroops-to-be are said to have come together in November, 1935, but the executive order for such a formation was not signed by General Milch until 29 January, 1936. Marked 'Secret', it laid down that a mere fifteen officers and NCOs of the *General Göring Regiment* were to form the cadre of a new parachute training and packing course, for every paratrooper would be responsible for his own 'chute. The soldiers would undergo an eight-week course, half devoted to ground instruction and the rest to airborne practice, to include six jumps, at the conclusion of which the successful candidate would be declared a fully-fledged parachute soldier and entitled to wear the *Fallschirmschutzen abzeichen*, otherwise known as the *Fallschirmschutzenschein*, or Parachute Rifleman's Badge, which had yet to be designed and made. All volunteers needed to be under the weight limit of 85 kilos (187 lbs) and naturally not afraid of heights.

This newly constituted *Luftwaffe* regiment was transferred to the Altengrabow training area to act as an experimental unit in the formation and training of paratroops. Everything was new: there were no existing guidelines for a course of instruction in military parachuting, or indeed any facet of their employment in war. The regiment was then sent to another training base at Doeberitz to watch a display of parachuting, but the single jumper was injured on landing and taken to hospital. At this stage the men were still only militarized policemen in *Luftwaffe* blue; they had not been co-opted into becoming paratroopers. Nevertheless, despite the unfortunate demonstration they had witnessed, over 600 men stepped forward that day to volunteer and were soon organized into the 1st Parachute Battalion. But during reorganization of the regiment the parachute element was re-titled the 4th Parachute Battalion and continued as such until 1 April, 1938, when it was re-designated the 1st Parachute Battalion of the 1st Parachute Regiment. One of the company commanders was a Captain Reinberger, of whom more later.

The remaining battalions of the Göring regiment were developed into an élite motorized infantry unit, its members entitled to wear a sleeve ribbon *(General Göring)* in the German manner, the letters stitched in aluminium gothic style on a royal blue ground and worn on the lower right tunic sleeve. The parachute unit's German title was *1 Bataillon/Fallschirmjäger-Regiment 1*, its own sleeve ribbon would be *Fallschirmjäger Rgt 1*, the silver lettering embroidered on bright green. The old unit gained new equipment, containing motorcycle and engineer companies as well as light flak, and when later expanded would go on to become well known in Tunisia, Sicily and Italy as the Hermann Göring Division, though by 1943 it bore the curious official title *Fallschirm-Panzer-Division Hermann Göring*. It was considered an élite unit and received the best equipment, which before its commitment to the Mediterranean theatre included SS-type camouflage clothing. The unit has no place in this history, since, despite its grandiose designation, it was not a parachute formation.

Karl Baumer was one of the original volunteers:

"I had been a policeman in Berlin-Brandenburg and I believe it was about 1932 that we were detailed to become part of a special unit of the Prussian Order Police who would be provided with vehicles to act as a protection squad for Göring and other leaders in that period.

"I had no special political convictions, but like most I suppose I just wanted some stability in the country and saw the Nazis as a rather rough but strong force who might be able to pull our nation together. This was the prime wish of most, to make Germany a self-respecting and respected member of Europe. We saw nothing of aggressive intent as far as the Nazis were concerned, at least, not towards making another war.

"In my case, as a policeman I had to follow orders, so I found myself detached with others from my local neighbourhood and part of a much larger unit called the Göring Regiment. That is what we came to be called, although our official title was something much larger. We went around to various places in that part of the country and I saw Göring on many occasions and he always struck me as a good natured but rather blustery sort of character but with two sides to him: one part was laughing and boyish, but the other was much harder, perhaps as a result of his experiences in the war.

"I think that it was later in 1935 that we were told that our old duties were over, for by then the Nazis had taken power and were reorganizing everything, including the police. We were still the Göring Regiment, but from then on we would be fully militarized, which we really were anyway; we always had rifles and pistols and carried them. And then, almost at once we were told that we would be part of Göring's *Luftwaffe*, and this was a great surprise to us all. We changed our uniform from green to blue, and wondered what would come next. My home was in East Berlin and when I went home I created a good deal of fuss in my different outfit. My parents and lady friend were amazed.

"But an even greater surprise came next, for our leaders told us that the *Luftwaffe* was forming a parachute troop unit and that we would be the first regiment. We were thunderstruck and wondered how on earth we could become paratroopers. We knew nothing at all of such matters, and were not even trained infantrymen. But we were sent at once to an Army training base and there we saw some soldiers demonstrating manoeuvres etc, and then we went on to Doeberitz and I'll never forget that day, the day we were told we would see a parachutist in action. We would then be allowed to decide for ourselves; there would be no dishonour in refusing, it would simply mean that we would become *Luftwaffe* soldiers. Well, we were all in a state of amazement by these developments, and when the afternoon of the demonstration came there was a lot of talk among the men, many of whom had no interest whatever in jumping out of planes, I can tell you!

"At that time I would say that we had up to 1500 men in the Göring Regiment, and we all came together on the airfield as the plane droned over, and at last a tiny figure appeared from it and soon a parachute opened. It was quite exciting to watch and all very new to us. The figure came down in a few moments but there was a slight wind and a gust must have caught the 'chute unexpectedly, as the man fell backwards at the last moment and hurt his back on landing. An ambulance quickly took him away. It was not a serious accident but not a good thing to happen in front of would-be volunteers!

"Our officers then took us to a large hangar and addressed us. We could volunteer for this new, special, élite unit of parachutists, or we could remain as we were — Luftwaffe soldiers to undergo military training. I think quite a few hundred men moved off to one side as invited to become paratroopers, and I was among them. I was young and swayed by a few daredevil friends in the unit. I had no great desire to become a paratrooper, but, being young, was susceptible to the blandishments of our officers who promised more pay, a special, élite status, and of course being a more glamorous unit more girls! Yes, one Lieutenant said, and I recall this exactly: 'You boys will have all the girls in Berlin after you in no time, I assure you! So come on, become a parachutist and you'll never regret it!'

"We volunteers were marched off and sorted into companies, and before long we travelled to Magdeburg and Stendahl, which was the new base for training parachutists. Everything had to be worked out; even the instructors there were learning in the matter of taking men up in Junkers and showing them how to exit from the planes. Some of the men were terribly nervous and in other cases full of bravado; in my case I tried to put on a brave face, but inside I was quaking. We had special uniforms, strange grey jackets with short trousers, high, lace boots and new style helmets with a neck strap at the back. We attended a lot of lectures on the parachute and in a large room watched how to pack them; we would have to do the job ourselves and many mistakes were made. I must say our instructors knew their job in this respect and were very, very patient. We were told that it was only right that we packed our own 'chutes as our lives depended on their being packed properly, therefore our lives were in OUR HANDS! No other person would ever pack our parachutes.

"At first we received the same pay as before, but this would go up a lot once we had completed six jumps. Our little barrack huts were quite comfortable, but the base itself was not exactly home from home. However, we were kept very busy indeed learning parachute packing and then how to put them on, how to fall, how to jump and all the rest of it. At the end of the day we used to fall on our beds exhausted, and that was before we had even begun jumping. At this stage of the para forces we had our own section of infantry training instructors, but I believe later on trainees had to attend an Army school.

"In this period, to our surprise, a company of Army paras also began training at Stendahl, and in fact our schedule had to be arranged with them, for it was not possible to have too many planes in the air at once. We did not see much of them or have any cooperation with them which must seem strange, but, as you know, eventually they came over to the *Luftwaffe*. When we finished our training and they theirs we went our separate ways.

"But then the great day came when we were to make our first jump, and some men dropped out — just a few. They were returned to the Göring Regiment at once and we never saw them again.

"We climbed into a Ju 52 with many other pupils watching us. We were not the first batch to go up but nearly so. I was almost trembling with nerves as I imagine most were. Our NCO and officer seemed quite calm and when we were up a few hundred feet shouted out final instructions. All we had to do was remain calm and remember all we had been told.

"To jump out of a plane requires all of one's courage, it is such an unnatural thing to do, for everyone is immersed in the knowledge of certain death to fall from a great height. We relied on that little piece of rope and hook at one end and connected to the 'chute at the other. If anything went wrong we were dead.

"I was the second man in line, and I wished dearly that I was the last. But I gritted my teeth and saw the first lad go out of the door. I was petrified, but the Sergeant slapped my back and shouted 'GO!' and I just dived out in a complete faint — or very nearly! I shut my eyes as the wind hit me, and then felt the great tug as the chute came out and pulled me into an upright position. I dared to open my eyes and saw the man before me just about to land, with an officer shouting at him from the ground. I felt a terrific thrill and actually laughed with relief and joy.

"From that time on everything was fine, my nerves were largely conquered and I completed the course. There were one or two accidents, but I did not see them — fortunately. We went on to complete our jumps, received our badges and certificates and then began combat exercises, and these at times included Army troops who we had to get the better of. But it took time for us to learn a few tricks and when we did we felt better than any of them.

"It was a long time before I was promoted to Corporal, and when the war came we wondered how we would be used."

The first base chosen for the school had been Neubrandenburg, but Milch changed the location to the existing airfield at Stendahl near the village of Borstel which is about 60 kms north of Magdeburg. There the 600 volunteers of Germany's first parachute battalion under their officers were required to act rather as guinea pigs, for only the Soviets possessed any force of standing and they were not about to pass on any expertise to others. In any case, the Germans preferred to plough their own furrow; they would develop their own tactics and methods for this novel new force.

The first problem to overcome had been that of the parachute itself, for those commercially available were unsuitable, the standard type pilot 'chute that Hermann Göring himself had sold as an agent after the earlier war when he lived in Sweden. These parachutes took too long to deploy. A falling body can travel a long way in a few seconds, especially as the smaller, guide 'chute had to stream out first. The whole principle of dropping paratroops rested on getting them to the ground in as short a time as possible; so the Germans set a maximum height limit for their peacetime training at 120 metres, or about 360 ft. This meant that the jumpers needed a parachute that would open automatically and be fully deployed within a fall of 50 meters or 150 ft.

In a short time the model RZ1 was produced, this to be followed later by the RZ16 and 36.

The trainee paratrooper at Stendahl was quickly introduced to his parachute and began learning how to pack it. His life depended on his doing it right; there would be no reserve 'chute. Apart from this instruction his first month was spent in learning how to jump, fall, and above all land correctly, for an injured para was no use to his unit. A part fuselage of a Ju 52 was set up on wooden trestles in a large shed and the troops were taught how to exit from its open doorway in the right manner on to a large mat. The German method was to dive headlong — they called it a 'pike dive', and in this they differed from the Allied methods which came along later. In another training hall the students were hung suspended in full rig-out in order to get the feel of hanging in space, as well as turning into the wind and other facets of control during descent, though photographs of German parachutists coming down give an impression of no control whatever; their harness to the rigging lines was different to that used in the Allied forces.

On the field they learned the forward fall and how to control their 'chutes during their most vulnerable moments on landing, especially in windy weather, and, as an aid to getting the feel of this, a "de-winged" aircraft was set up with its engine running to provide the necessary blast of wind. The static line method of jumping was devised with the new 'chute. Each man had a short length of rope with a metal snap hook to be secured to a steel bar running along the fuselage of the plane. Each Ju 52 carried a crew of four, including an officer or NCO supervisor *(Uberwacher)*, plus a jumpmaster *(Absetzer)*, but the cramped body would only accommodate 12 soldiers. It was an old-style airliner-cum-bomber, but the only suitable type available.

The man assigned to take over the new formation was Kurt Student. Born in 1890, he had entered military service at the age of eleven, being admitted to the academy at Potsdam as a cadet, moving on a few years later to the Yorck (Jäger or Infantry) Regiment, where he stayed until 1913 when he transferred to the new air corps. Student became a fighter pilot and by 1916 commanded the 9th Staffel which was attached to the Army Group "Crown Prince". Following the Armistice in 1918 he continued his service career as a Secretary of Technical Development in the aviation department of an army without any air force. As such he was responsible for new materials and this involved him in much travelling. By 1929 he had returned to the infantry, first as commander of the 2nd Company in the 2nd Infantry Regiment, moving on in 1931 to take over the 1st Battalion of the 3rd Infantry. In 1933 he returned to the Aviation Ministry and eventually as a Lt-Colonel took up an appointment at the flying test centres at Rechling and Travemunde. Here he came into contact with parachutists and when he was made Inspector General of *Luftwaffe* Schools the new parachute training centre at Stendahl came under his command.

The staff at Stendahl had had to formulate and put into practice a set of rules for the carrying and dropping of paratroops from the Ju 52. It ran as follows:

The twelve soldiers were seated facing each other, the 'chutes strapped to their backs tending to force them forward so that knees were touching, such was the lack of room in the plane. On approaching the drop zone the supervisor would shout, "*Fertigmachen!*" (Get ready!); the soldiers would stand up and "hook up" to the bar above them and face the exit door on the port rear side of the plane. On the command "*Fertig zum sprung!*" (Ready to jump!) the first trooper shuffled forward to the doorway, holding on with both hands to the side rails until a klaxon horn sounded, at which point he sprang out head first, with the jumpmaster beside him to see that he went. As he sprang clear so the next man in line moved forward to take his place at the doorway; it was essential that the whole troop jumped as close together as possible so that they could quickly come together on landing. Too much wind or even a few seconds delay could mean dispersal on landing. During these first years the German paratroops only carried pistols and relied on recovering rifles, machine-guns and grenades from the containers which were dropped with them. The first eight weeks were devoted solely to jump and parachute instruction with no combat training whatever.

Konrad Seibert completed college and, at the age of eighteen, wanted to become a scientist, but like other youths who faced inevitable call-up decided that if he volunteered first he would perhaps get a greater choice:

"My parents were aghast, but they had no choice, for the war would claim us all. I was a Berliner and from a fairly good family; we had plenty to eat as father owned a restaurant! So when I went with some of my friends to the *Luftwaffe* recruiting office we were offered the choice which we had hoped for. Two of my friends were very keen to fly, but I myself had a certain interest in the military side of things, including weapons, although I was in no way a militarist and had no idea of a career in the forces. I had already done Hitler Youth and Labour service training so was already disciplined. I saw a poster in that office for the paratroops, and they at once struck me as something different. I had no idea if I could find the courage to jump from an airplane, but I thought that if the worst came to the worst I could opt out. So I put down my name for the paratroops with one other fellow who I did not know, and went home to tell my parents. They were very concerned I could see, but said little. I had one older brother who was already in the army in the tank corps, but when I saw him he told me that he did not care for his vocation, but it was too late to change it!

"Not long afterwards I received my notice to report to the *Luftwaffe* barracks in Berlin-Lichterfeld, and there I found I was with some other fellows including the one who had joined with me. We were inspected and then dispatched to a training school for infantrymen which was actually run by the Army. This was something I had not bargained for, but it was quite hard at times. The NCOs were not bad fellows, but inclined to bully and tease us, especially as we were not really in the Army. We had ordinary grey working clothes all the time, and never saw a *Luftwaffe* uniform until we went to Stendahl."

Konrad spent some eight weeks being trained as an infantryman before being transferred to the *Luftwaffe*. They packed up and moved out at once, being driven away in *Luftwaffe* trucks, back to the barracks at Lichterfeld where they were fitted out with their new uniforms. After one night in barracks they were shipped out to begin the course at Stendahl.

Karel Weise was a German-Czech who lived with his family in the disputed territory of the Sudetenland, and when the area was annexed under the Munich Agreement of 1938 he found himself eligible for call-up into the Wehrmacht:

"I did not mind this as my heart, I'm afraid, embraced the 'New Order' as did most I knew, for we only knew what our leaders wanted us to know. I entered the German Army as a private, but as I had a university education I was invited to become an *Antwarter* or cadet officer. At this time I heard about the paratroops and as I had always had some interest in aerial matters I decided to try and transfer to the *Luftwaffe* and the paratroops. This was not easily done, but at last I succeeded and went over to the *Luftwaffe*. By that time I had done some infantry training, but I had to undergo further instruction in arms drill and tactics before I was sent on to Stendahl."

Heinrich Pabst took a rather different course into the paratroops:

"I joined the paratroops from the *Luftwaffe* at the beginning, though I was not one of the Göring Regiment. I had a certain amount of experience as an NCO, first with transport planes, and then as a learner in parachuting; we had done a parachute course as part of the curriculum, but when I heard of the new para unit I volunteered and found myself delegated to teach what I knew about parachuting. It was all very new in 1936-7, and the rules and regulations had only just been devised."

Karl Pickert was unusual in that he was one of the very few to have served in the German Army Parachute Battalion:

"I had been in the Hitler Youth as had most German boys and done some eighteen months labour service which had hardened me physically, but I had no special desire to go to war, but by 1938 things were very difficult and it appeared that war would come. I worked in a steel mill as an apprentice in Essen, which was full of war factories making guns and ammunition and tanks etc. I thought, as did my family, that it might be a danger zone if war came.

Colonel-General Kurt Student,
'ther' of German airborne forces in
cond World War.

2. German paras make an impressive
showing on Hitler's birthday parade
20 April, 1939.

3. Paras assemble after a practice drop during which they were armed
only with pistols.

4. **Top Left:** General Student congratulates the victors of Eben Emael.

5. **Above Left:** Paras emplaning into the cramped confines of a Ju52, an obsolete transport which nevertheless served Germany well throughout the war.

6. **Above Right:** Oberleutnant Becker briefs his men after the one-battalion drop in Norway.

7. **Right:** This dramatic leap was not the usual style of exit practised by German paras.

"I had two sisters, and a younger brother who was very keen to go into the air force when older. I'm sorry to say that he got his wish and was killed over Britain as a gunner. But in 1939 I was called up and went into the Army where I found some choice open to me. I could become a common infantryman or perhaps go into a workshop trade as I had some knowledge of sheet metal work. Perhaps I should have listened to my father's advice. He was an old soldier and knew the ropes from the previous war. But I met an old friend who had joined the *Luftwaffe* and he told me all about the paratroops and what good fellows they were, and all that sort of thing. He himself had actually volunteered for this force and he asked me why I did not do the same. I told him that it was too late, but he assured me that the war in Poland was almost over, and that he could guarantee me a quiet war after that! It all sounds very silly now, but we were young and a little foolish. I must admit that after we had had a few drinks together I began to get used to the idea and agreed to ask for a transfer.

"When I went to see our officer in the training battalion he thought I was a real nuisance. He told me off for wasting his time: how dare I join the Army and then ask for a transfer to the Air Force! It was stupid, insane. When he heard that I wanted to join the paratroops he said:

'Oh! I see. Why didn't you say so, then? We have our own paratroops you know. I'll see what I can do."

"Well, some weeks went by and I heard nothing more and decided that I had been a fool anyway. By then I was well into the usual Army training that everyone had to undergo before moving on into a more specialized branch or staying in the infantry. But one morning the officer sent for me, and when I presented myself to him he looked at me and said:

'You are a lucky man. I have here a transfer order sending you to the parachute school at Stendahl!'

"I could hardly believe my ears, and my stomach turned over, I was that surprised. I had almost forgotten about becoming a paratrooper and had lost all my enthusiasm! Like an idiot I stammered something to this effect and the officer shouted at me — 'Are you insane? Here are your orders! See the Sergeant-Major and he will give you your travel documents. Now get out of my sight!'

"Well, I clicked my heels and saluted in the approved fashion and beat a hasty retreat. The Sergeant-Major took sympathy on me and when he gave me my documents at the orderly room he also managed a short leave pass, so off I went to Essen and my family for a day before leaving again for Stendahl. I can tell you I was in a terrible state of nerves! I knew nothing about flying, my parents thought I was a little mad, my sisters made fun of me, and my young brother could not understand why I was not in the flying branch. I wondered how I had ever got myself into such a position, and when I eventually reached Stendahl and saw some men jumping from planes I felt quite sick. There were other new boys just arriving and we compared notes and I found I was alone in not wishing to join the paratroops after having volunteered! It must sound very silly, but that was my situation. I had got cold feet!

"All of us had done some Army training, and after a little testing on the parade ground and some weapon training we were issued with our equipment. I must tell you that this was the German Army part of the establishment, for at this time the parachute force was divided into both *Luftwaffe* and Army, but later they all came under the air force. But once we had put on our jump clothing we looked very much the same as the *Luftwaffe* lads except for our insignia.

"Well, there was no backing out and I could never have faced going back to my unit and that bullying officer; I would have been a laughing stock."

Karl Pickert entered the standard training curriculum, spending a month on ground lectures and instruction in much the same as did the *Luftwaffe* trainees across the field. So the German Army's *Fallschirm Infanterie Kompanie* gained one rather unwilling and terrified recruit, but one who, as will be seen, would go on to fight with his comrades in the hell of Crete.

An extraordinary situation had developed in 1936 when the German Army Command decided that it too should have a paratroop unit, and accordingly organized a volunteer *Fallschirm Infanterie Kompanie* to be equipped not only with small arms but machine guns and mortars. Since there was but one base offering training facilities, the Army students were despatched to Stendahl where they were provided with the same jump smocks, helmets and boots as the airmen, though they wore the Army-style eagle and swastika. It is difficult to ascertain how much rivalry existed between the two battalions, but the school commandant was a *Luftwaffe* Lt-Colonel, so obviously a degree of cooperation had to be maintained. When the Army paratroopers completed their course, which was most likely of similar duration to that of the air force men, they were awarded a certificate and metal badge to be worn, as with the *Luftwaffe* paras, on the left tunic pocket, though the Army insignia bore a different style of eagle. The jump certificates were, incidentally, good for one year only, and to remain valid needed to be renewed by fresh jumps.

The parachute school enjoyed visits from a succession of bigwigs, especially on open days when members of the public and civic dignitaries were allowed to enter military bases, much as did the public in Britain on Empire Air Day and during air pageants such as the famous shows at Hendon. Visitors at Stendahl included the Army Commander-in-Chief, Colonel-General Freiherr von Fritsch, who was soon to be ousted, and the well-known aviator Hanna Reitsch.

On German Thanksgiving Day in 1937 the Army's Parachute Infantry Company was shown off in public at Buckeburg, and during manoeuvres so impressed the Command that expansion to battalion size was authorized. At this time the unit was designated a *Zerstör-Bataillon*, or Raider Battalion, and, like the *Luftwaffe* paras, lived in modest barracks, while the men of the Göring Regiment were moved off to super-modern accommodation in Berlin, complete with the latest swimming pool. On 4 November the Army paras moved into the Rosalie barracks at Braunschweig and in a parade presentation received their new colours, given by the Inspector of Infantry to the unit commander, Major Heidrich.

Konrad Seibert found Stendahl very different to his previous camps, but the discipline was strict. When the new recruits saw the Junkers flying over and men jumping from them they felt frightened, but excited:

"We were not quite so keen. We received our para smocks and boots and helmets and found beds in the barrack huts. We were given an address by the school commandant and told that we would be the élite of the whole Wehrmacht, and that great days lay ahead of us.

"My early training was very interesting, until we reached the actual jumping part from the Ju's! I had never been up in a plane, so when we climbed aboard that Ju we were all very thrilled as I doubt if any of the others had flown either. It was noisy and we did not go very far, just to a few hundred feet in a big circle. The ground seemed very far below and the wind whistled past the open door. We lined up, our stomachs turning, hooked up as ordered, and the first man went to the open door. I was the third in line, and all too quickly the command came and out went the first man without hesitation. The second man moved forward and out he went and I recall his face. He looked terrified!

"I had no time to consider my past life or feel anything, as the NCO gave me a slap and out I went, diving head first into the wind that took my breath away. The roar of the plane's engines vanished as I was hurled about for a second or two, but the 'chute opened quickly and then I was in heaven! The relief was tremendous. I looked around me and saw those who had gone before. The first was just landing and it would only be seconds before I too hit the ground. I braced myself and I believe made a perfect landing. The feeling was indescribable, I was terribly thrilled and felt on top of the world. We all gathered up our 'chutes and said what great fellows we were. As you know, we had to pack our own 'chutes and the NCOs soon told us to pull ourselves together and get over to the waiting truck as we had only just begun to work. But we were not downhearted by this bullying because we realized we had got over the worst hurdle. I myself could hardly wait to write home to tell my parents what I had done.

"The very same day, in the afternoon, we went up again, but this time we were less frightened. Even so, one man was ill and refused to jump. Without delay, the officer and NCO bundled us out of the plane in double quick time so that the infection would not spread.

"We did six jumps, just to get the feel of getting it right, and then began to use weapons and containers and learn tactics in combat. It became very hard work as we were now doing long marches during which we sang our para anthem — *Rot Scheinnt die Sonne* which you may know, and many other songs, and not all of them military I can tell you!"

Karel Weise had plenty of confidence in himself but when he thought of jumping out of an aeroplane his heart sank, but he went on with his ground training, feeling that there was yet time to change his mind.

"When we had completed this I felt it was time to make a move if I really was too scared to start leaping from a plane, but in the event I mastered my nerves and began the airborne phase of our course. When we entered the plane I was very apprehensive like the rest, although we tried to make light of it.

"In a few minutes we were up in the sky and our instructors told us to get ready. The first man was full of bravado and leapt out before receiving the signal and the NCO was furious. This meant that a delay took place, and when the rest of us went out our foolhardy friend was already on the ground receiving a good telling-off from an officer.

"I must say that I surprised myself and mastered my terrors quite well and had a magnificent drop and felt absolutely marvellous by the time I got down. From then on it held no terrors for me and by the time we had completed the course I felt a fully fledged parachutist. We were quite well paid, and when we went on leave had a riotous time. My parents had moved back into Germany and I had a brother who seemed to look on me as a hero. Looking back, I suppose I was a little big-headed, but it was such a great achievement to become a paratrooper that I really did feel superior to all other beings!"

As noted earlier, Heinrich Pabst was one of the instructors, and mentions that mistakes made cost one or two lives at Stendahl:

"This came about because the parachutes were not packed properly by the men concerned. I recall one incident which is vivid in my memory. I was with a squad of men and we went up in a Ju on a fine morning. At the required height of 4-500 ft we made ready. It was my job to see them out of the plane and at first all went well, three men leaving in the approved fashion. But when the fourth man went out I could see at once that something was wrong, for his 'chute case did not open properly and he went down to his death. All of his equipment was his own responsibility, but I felt that I should have made a closer inspection and resolved to do so thereafter. The rest of the men left the plane quickly, and nothing was noticed until later. It was a tragedy, but inevitable at the time.

"There was one other incident that I recall. This occurred when two men collided in mid-air, and one of these fell to his death. Again, this should not have happened at all and was the result of the pair leaving the plane too close to each other."

The reluctant recruit Karl Pickert completed his ground training and reached the dreaded day when the first jump was scheduled:

"The plane's engines were ticking over and I climbed aboard and sat down with the rest. We were all very nervous but put on our best smiles. We were not used to flying — at least, I had never been up — and the noise of the three engines was terrific, so that we had to shout to be heard a little. The NCOs looked at us and grinned and then we were off. It was very uncomfortable sitting on the wooden bench seat with our 'chutes on and we could not sit well, nor could we look out of the windows.

"I know I had never felt so sick and weak and continually told myself what a fool I'd been. At last we were high enough and the order came to stand up and clip on our hooks. We moved to the rear and in a short time the order was given and out went the first man who was a very big fellow — but I'm sure quite terrified! I was about the sixth in line, and when it came to my turn my legs would hardly support me, I was so scared. But the NCO laughed at my expression and said something like, 'You'll make a fine officer I can see − OUT!' And he gave me a hearty shove and I almost fell out rather than dived. I screwed up my face and tried not to look, but the wind was terrific and at first my eyes seemed to be torn from their sockets for some reason. But it was over quickly and I did not have time to faint from sheer terror. The 'chute came open with a big, hard jerk and I was swinging freely, and suddenly I thought, 'My God! Is it really me?'

"I managed quite a good landing, and felt a tremendous relief to be alive. But back on the grass my first thought was that I did not wish to repeat the expericnce! Yet within the hour we were up again, and I was just as scared, but did not hesitate. We had one or two accidents and I thought, 'You're a fool and may have to pay the penalty!' But all went well and I finally became much calmer and more blasé about this new experience, and in a short time I was able to take it as routine. I was rather surprised at my change of attitude and quite pleased with myself. We were given our badges and a raise in pay and by then the Polish business was all over, and soon afterwards came the amazing news that we were to be transferred to the *Luftwaffe*. My best memory of that period is going home on leave and seeing the look on my younger brother's face when he saw my new uniform. I was now a fully fledged *Luftwaffe* paratrooper, and a little bewildered how it had all come about. I did not feel that I was in control of my destiny somehow. There I was, quite the proper soldier, but inside of me I was not really interested. I could now see that with a few drinks in me I was ready to volunteer for anything! I had no lady friend, but I can tell you that once you had some of the right sort of badges and insignia one became very popular with them. In fact I soon found a young lady during leave in Essen and we agreed to keep in touch."

By that time Hitler's eastward march, the so-called *Drang nach Osten* had begun. Austria had 'agreed' to be welcomed into the

Greater German Reich, the *Anschluss* having proved by plebiscite that the population were overwhelmingly in favour of it, and the Munich Agreement in September had assured the German occupation of the most fertile and industrially rich areas of Czechoslovakia, the Sudetenland, containing many German inhabitants. The German Army parachute battalion had taken part in this occupation, but Göring's agitation had borne fruit, for the unit was actually placed under *Luftwaffe* control, and on 1 January, 1939, it was officially absorbed into the *Luftwaffe*, becoming the 2nd Battalion, 1st Parachute Regiment. By that time the airborne soldiers had been expanded into the 7th Airborne Division, with the former Army Major Heidrich in command of the 2nd Regiment.

Until the implementation of General Student's ideas on the employment of paratroops, considerable controversy took place between the German Army chiefs and the *Luftwaffe* as to their usage. Student had been appointed commander of all German airborne forces effective 1 July, 1938, and at once began his fight to establish principles more radical than those currently favoured and certainly far bolder than those of the German Army High Command, with whom of course he was obliged to coordinate his military doctrines. The generals had seen their paratroops as useful for seizing bridges and vital points such as road junctions just ahead of the main army's advance, but, as will be seen, Student had much bigger ideas.

On 20 April, 1939, the young German paratroop units took part in a big military parade in Berlin in celebration of Hitler's fiftieth birthday; the soldiers looked very impressive as they marched past, clad in their unusual attire, which included parachute harness over jump jackets, gauntlet gloves and rifles and bayonets slung over their shoulders. Among the thousands watching were the usual clutch of foreign military attachés and diplomats who were always invited to such events.

II

A Year of Triumph

The so-called 'Munich Agreement' of September, 1938, which resulted from the crisis engendered by Hitler's demands on Czechoslovakia secured vital time for the western democracies to move forward their war preparations, for, whatever Prime Minister Neville Chamberlain claimed on his return from Germany, there was not to be 'peace for our time'. By August the following year war seemed inevitable, Hitler had not only violated the Agreement by sending his forces to occupy all of Czechoslovakia, but now presented demands to the Poles. Even though they were already poised for an attack on Poland, on 26 August the German Government announced that it had 'mobilized' its armed forces.

Following the carefully staged incident on Germany's eastern border with Poland, Hitler ordered his troops to invade and the western allies declared war. The news that an international conflict had begun reached the German paratroops during a motorized journey along the Berlin-Breslau autobahn in Silesia, and the troops moved into airfields around Breslau, anticipating their first airborne operation, though the existing Army plans did not make provision for any. The same airfields had been occupied by the paratroops the previous March when war with Czechoslovakia seemed imminent, the plan then being to leapfrog over the strong Czech border fortifications near Freudenthal. But the Agreement signed at Munich resulted in the Junkers landing their troops quite peacefully in stubble fields; they were thus able to take part in the neutralization of the Czech forces before returning to Germany. But in March, 1939, when Hitler decided he could safely take over the rest of the country, the airborne troops were again alerted to occupy vital points, including airfields. In the event a snowstorm prevented the operation, so that the parachutists once more made an unopposed landing in their transports, this time at Kbely Airport, near Prague.

This kind of frustration was to occur again and again during the war, especially to the British.

For the paratroops of the *Luftwaffe* the coming of war in September, 1939, seemed to signal the opportunity to prove their worth and put into practice all they had learned. But at this time Hitler wished to save his trump card; for he felt sure that the use of paratroops would come as a great shock to the enemy, even though everyone knew that the *Wehrmacht* possessed them. Indeed, knowledge of them spread beyond the routine reports sent home by the military attachés in Berlin. For example, the new British weekly *Picture Post* had featured the German paras in training before war broke out, though it would be a while before the public at large began to appreciate their potential.

But at this stage Hitler had not yet taken on the mantle of Supreme Commander and did not insist on overseeing every aspect of military planning as he did later. So, initially at any rate, the German generals' plans for the subjugation of Poland included airborne drops by a whole regiment, who were in fact held in reserve. The 7th Airborne Division stood at readiness in bases in the Liegnitz area, the Army's intention being to drop them behind the Polish lines. No less than three successive operations were detailed, and at one point the troops were actually in their planes ready to go when a cancellation order came. The first drop was to have been near Dirschau, the second to capture a bridge over the River Vistula at Pulawy, the third to establish a bridgehead on the San at Jaroslaw. Hitler was to state later that he himself had deliberately refrained from disclosing his 'para hand' in Poland. It had in fact been the rapidity of the German armoured advance which had proved the paradrops superfluous, but some accounts allege a reluctance on the part of the German High Command to unveil its 'secret weapon', which seems to confirm Hitler's later claim. But the effect on the paratroops' morale and on that of the leader, General Student, was serious, with a number of officers and NCOs allegedly considering transferring. Student himself was furious over the Army's dithering, and later saw this period as the start of the 'sell out' of his airborne forces.

However, the airborne troops did see action: the entire 7th Air Division rolled forward into Poland in its own transport and on 14 September the first clash between airborne soldiers and enemy forces occurred when the German 3rd Battalion encountered Polish units. In fact, the invasion of Poland was no walk-over, even though it has often been quoted as the first Blitzkrieg victory of the war. A serious situation arose on the Bzura front which resulted in the 7th Division's only air-landing troop (16 Infantry) being flown in to join the battle; it was this order which particularly incensed Student, especially as his parachutists were not committed. "We might as well have spared ourselves the effort of training them," he said.

Then, on 24 September, towards the close of the campaign, the 2nd Battalion of the 3rd Parachute Regiment had a tough fight against Polish troops cut off near Wola Gulowska, the Germans suffering 'painful casualties'. The division's units went on to occupy airfields and other key points as the Polish forces collapsed and finally surrendered. By mid-October all the airborne troops had returned to Germany, leaving their first war casualties behind, buried in the fortifications of Demblin. A few weeks later Major-General Student awarded the Iron Cross 2nd Class to the 1st Parachute Regiment's 2nd Battalion commander, Captain Prager, as well as to several other paratroopers of the same unit.

The men of the 7th Division spent the winter months of the so-called Phoney War in training.

Konrad Scibert:

"When we went on leave to our homes we felt very, very proud to be parachutists and wear the special badges, etc, on our uniforms. For my part, I felt I had really accomplished something and did not mind if the war continued to be a quiet one! Then we had some quite difficult exercises in the New Year and rumours began of a big German attack in the offing in the west. The paratroops had hardly been used in Poland, and we had heard some ugly stories that the commanders were in revolt over the treatment given to our branch of the service.

"Then one day we were called together in a large hut and told we would take part in the invasion of Holland. We were stunned and did not understand how this could be, as we had no quarrel with the Dutch. But there was some talk of the British being involved in the country which I'm sure was nonsense, but in any case we had to accept orders and knew it was all part of a larger plan. We had not taken part in the operation in Norway but had heard some disastrous stories of things going wrong, but as you know we won in the end! But obviously some lessons had been learned, and I doubt if I or those with me were ready for that kind of thing anyway, though by May, 1940, we were keen to get on with it.

"The operation in Holland went like clockwork for us, but not for others. We dropped near a bridge and captured it without a fight; all we had to do was wait for the Army to come up to relieve us. It was, as I believe you would call it, a 'piece of cake'!

"But when we returned to Germany and found we were again unemployed we felt a sense of anti-climax and boredom; it is very bad when special, highly trained troops stand about with no work, especially in a war of course. They tried to keep us busy, but we knew it was a ploy to stop us getting into mischief. We all had girlfriends and some even had wives and we liked to see them on leave, but our masters were determined to keep us in top-notch condition, so it was a case of one exercise after another."

Although Hitler's designs had always been focused on the East, the surprise intervention of the western allies and their refusal meekly to accept his absorption of eastern neighbours led him to consider ways of eliminating them as a menace to his rear.

As the Phoney War lingered on, Hitler ordered his generals to produce a plan for a grand offensive to so damage the French Army and the British Expeditionary Force that neither would be able to interrupt his plans Hitler was convinced by his knowledge of the French that they were ripe for collapse, and that their much vaunted Maginot Line would prove no obstacle. But, as a safeguard, he decided to secure his right flank by the bold and novel use of airborne forces to seize vital points in neutral Belgium. In a risky venture glider troops would land on or near the 'impregnable' forts at Eben Emael, which dominated one portion of the Albert Canal, while other airborne units would seize crossing points over the Canal.

The Germans had long practised the manufacture and use of gliders. The great expansion of sailplane clubs had come about in part through the encouragement and instigation of the secret *Luftwaffe* before the Nazis took over in 1933 and the clubs were organized on military lines. In 1932 the firm of Rhön-Rossitten Gesellschaft had produced a high-wing glider of broad span for meteorological use at high altitude. This was the model taken over by the German Institute for Glider Research (DFS) and heavily used for gliding courses under the instruction of several experts, including Heini Dittmar and Hanna Reitsch, who was towed aloft for the first time by a Ju 52.

It was the ex-WW1 fighter ace Ernst Udet who, though now a civilian, saw the military possibilities in the DFS glider, and in 1937 the type was redesigned and put into production for the *Luftwaffe's* airborne corps. The fuselage was constructed of steel frame in box shape and covered with canvas, its wings braced and a landing skid fitted under its belly, this latter the result of Udet's own experiences in landing gliders on Alpine glaciers. The DFS weighed 16 cwt unloaded and could carry ten men with their weapons, but was in truth a rather cramped and primitive craft.

Some of the *Luftwaffe's* airborne commanders had realized that part of the surprise effect of paratroop landings was lost as soon as the enemy heard and saw the transport aircraft flying over in formation, whereas in certain circumstances gliders could make a virtually silent approach and landing. Expert pilots could set down gliders within a few feet of an objective, the troops within could jump out in a tight-knit group ready for action and able to seize strongpoints in short order, providing the circumstances were favourable. Gliders seemed the obvious choice for assaulting the Belgian forts at Eben Emael.

Hitler was impatient to start the offensive, but various hold-ups due to the weather put off the attack until early 1940; that winter was the worst in living memory. Then an unexpected bombshell meant that the whole plan had to be revised, though in the end it proved to their advantage.

On 10 January the paratroop company commander, Major Reinberger, was due to attend a conference in Cologne. His intention was to try and clarify the relief by Army troops of the parachutists to be dropped in Holland, for by then Hitler had decided that it was imperative that the whole of the Low Countries be secured as part of his strategy to eliminate the West. Reinberger carried a yellow briefcase containing the plans of the coming offensive, and he accepted the offer of transport from Munster in a Messerschmitt 108 Taifun (Typhoon), a light plane to be piloted by the base commander himself, Major Hönmanns. But after take-off the weather closed in and the pilot got lost. With his plane icing up and its engine failing he landed in an open field; the pair soon discovered they were in Belgium.

Major Reinberger was obliged to borrow a cigarette lighter from a Belgian farm worker in order to try and destroy his secret papers, but gendarmes quickly arrived and arrested the two, confiscating the documents. At the police station Reinberger made a brave attempt to grab the papers and put them in a stove, but was again frustrated. It was not long before the plans were in French and

British hands, but the Allies were not convinced of their authenticity, and in any case the chief facet of the German scheme seemed to be a thrust through Belgium, as in the earlier war, and this was exactly what the Allies expected. But they were unaware of one very important part of the German plan — the assault on the Belgian forts by airborne troops which was considered so secret that it had never been committed to paper. In fact, every soldier detailed for the operation was sworn to secrecy on penalty of death and two men were actually charged and sentenced for minor infringements of security, though the penalty was later revoked.

Nevertheless, the loss of the general plans for the offensive was a tremendous blow to the Germans. It caused Hitler to fly into a rage and four high-ranking *Luftwaffe* officers were dismissed.

But all this was over when a different aspect of the war opened up in April, 1940, and this was one that would provide the airborne corps with its first real opportunity to get into action.

Tension had been rising in Scandinavia for some time, for the Allies were concerned over use of the Norwegian port of Narvik by German and neutral shipping transporting Swedish iron ore to enemy ports. The British, with Winston Churchill as First Sea Lord, were not over-concerned with Norwegian neutrality, as shown in the famous action when the destroyer *Cossack* was sent into a Norwegian harbour where British sailors boarded the German prison ship *Altmark* to rescue seamen who had been taken from merchant ships intercepted by German surface raiders in the Atlantic. The British Government warned both the Swedish and Norwegian governments that it would take suitable measures to prevent the use of Norwegian waters by German merchant ships (ie, the use of Royal Navy warships), and despite Norwegian protests that its neutrality and sovereignty were being threatened, the Supreme Allied War Council drew up plans in February, 1940, to land four divisions at Narvik in order to occupy the Swedish-owned ore mines. Hitler had pledged at the outbreak of the war to respect Norwegian neutrality — providing the Allies did the same. In the event both sides began preparing to land forces in Norway in the same week. On 8 April the Allies began laying mines in Norwegian coastal waters, their intention being to follow this up by landing troops at the four principal ports in western Norway, including Narvik.

Behind all the bluster, threat and counter-threat lay more facts not made public at the time, for whatever pledges Hitler gave were only valid so long as it suited him, and in December, 1939, he had already received the Norwegian fascist and German sympathizer Vidkun Quisling in Berlin to assure him that when the time was ripe he would occupy Norway and install him as its puppet leader.

On the Allied side there had been a rash commitment to aid the Finns who had been resisting Soviet invasion for some time. Despite the Russian alliance with Germany in occupying eastern Poland Hitler was of course in sympathy with the Finns, but unable to assist them because of the Nazi-Soviet Pact. For its part Britain assembled some bombers and crews as a prelude to the landing of a Franco-British force at Narvik which would march across the country and aid the Finns. The sudden cease-fire and agreement between Finland and Russia cancelled the Allied plan, but the land force was already in being to land in Norway and stop aid to Hitler, even though in the event the whole attempt turned out to be an ill-planned affair.

This was the rather convoluted background to the next German operation involving airborne troops.

Four airfields were to be captured by paratroops so that a follow-up force of infantry could be landed to secure staging posts for the main attack on Norway, and in one case as a defence base against attacks by the British fleet, this last in the south-west of Norway. It is a surprising fact that even at this early stage of the war the *Luftwaffe* had already built up a formidable force of transport aircraft, some 500 in all, mostly Ju52s, but including a few Junkers 90 and Focke-Wulf 200s.

Inevitably, Denmark would have to be occupied first; then the base at Fornebu was needed for a rapid occupation of the Norwegian capital, Oslo, and just two companies of the 1st Parachute Regiment were detailed for this task. The two airfields at Aalborg (West and East) in northern Denmark were to be captured by only one platoon of paratroops, for some of the soldiers had been diverted to seize the key bridge linking the Gedser ferry terminal with Copenhagen; two more platoons were ordered to capture the three-kilometer-long bridge intact.

Twelve Ju52s of 8/KGzbV1 (a Bomber Group for Special Duties) took off for Denmark but all other units were delayed by fog. Just after 0700 hrs the paras dropped on Aalborg and captured both airfields without a fight. The other platoons under Captain Gericke landed near the vital bridge on the isle of Masnedsund and at once set up machine-guns to cover the approaches; there was a Danish coastal fort not far away. But some of the German paratroops did not wait to collect the heavy weapons which had floated down in the containers nearby, they rushed the fort brandishing pistols and captured the sentries and garrison without a fight. Another German detachment found some bicycles and by some fast pedalling overtook the Danish guards before they could fire a shot, and shortly afterwards the advance troops of the 3rd Battalion 305th Infantry reached them, having crossed the water by ferry from Warnemunde. The troops entered Vordingborg and took the bridge connecting Masnedo island with Seeland. The whole operation was completed in little over an hour and was the first paratroop assault in history.

But elsewhere the weather and Norwegian resistance completely upset the German timetable.

Over the stretch of water known as the Skagerrak the fog bank stretched from almost ground level up to 2000 ft, and aboard the first wave of Junkers transports visibility was reduced to about twenty yards. Two of the planes vanished. Oberleutnant Drewes was anguished — should he go on or turn back? Even reversing course in the thick murk could prove hazardous. At 0820 he signalled his operations HQ in Hamburg that he was forced to turn back for Aalborg. This smelled of disaster, for another wave of Junkers was already en route for its objective, the airfield at Fornebu, the planes full of Army infantrymen. To try and land at an airport not yet secured could spell suicide.

Göring had ordered that if the paratroops failed to drop for any reason then the transport planes following must turn back, but in pursuing this order Lt-General Geisler met stiff opposition from the squadron commander, Freiherr von Gablenz, who refused to pass on the order, believing that his pilots would carry out their assignment in spite of the weather and the Norwegians still in occupation at Fornebu. Despite the two officers arguing in Hamburg, the leader of the Junkers formation, Captain Wagner, had already decided to push on, and when his planes reached the target area they found it free of fog. But all was not well, for the Norwegians were fully alerted. German Messerschmitt 110 "Destroyers" were circling the field and two planes could be seen blazing on the ground. Worse, flak began to shoot up at the Junkers and Captain Wagner plus others in his plane were wounded.

While the Junkers battled their way through the fog an air battle had been in progress, the eight Messerschmitts had been attacked by nine Norwegian Gloster Gladiators, obsolete biplane fighters supplied by the British, and two of the German aircraft had been shot down. But the Me's had destroyed two Gladiators on the ground and shot up the flak defences. The Messerschmitt crews believed the Junkers to be carrying paratroops and were amazed when the first transport came in for a touchdown, only to be driven off by Norwegian fire.

Then an amazing thing happened. The fighters were down to the last of their fuel, while three of the remaining six had each lost an engine. The formation leader ordered one of his pilots to land on the airfield. This was Lieutenant Lent, who had already shot down five enemy planes including one of the Norwegian Gladiators. Lent tried to slip down while his comrades continued to shoot up the defences, but as his wheels reached for the runway Lent saw with horror that a Ju 52 had appeared from nowhere and was attempting to land on the second runway which gave both planes an excellent chance of collision. The other Messerschmitt crews circling the field watched in amazement as the two aircraft on the ground neared each other, but the Messerschmitt's greater speed carried it past the intersecting point of the two runways first and a collision was avoided. But Lent's plane careered off the short runway, ran on down a boundary slope and lost its undercarriage, so the rest of the German fighters now landed and were so placed by their pilots as to afford some covering fire from their cannon and machine guns, while the Junkers 52 disgorged the paratroops signals section.

Around 0915 some more Junkers arrived, and as soon as the troops had emerged the Messerschmitt commander, Oberleutnant Hansen, directed them to clear up the remaining Norwegian defence posts. Suddenly the Germans were amazed to see a car drive up from which a German diplomat emerged. It was the air attaché and he had come to inform them of the serious situation elsewhere. The Norwegians were resisting fiercely and an Allied expeditionary force was on its way; Hansen sent a signal to HQ in Hamburg that the Fornebu airfield had been captured by his fighter squadron.

By that evening reinforcements of paratroops and infantry had arrived and the airborne men marched into Oslo, the first capital city to be captured by such troops.

The paratroops sent to capture Stavanger airbase were likewise put out by fog. Not one man of the 3rd Company had been provided with a lifebelt and the risk of collision and a fall into the icy waters off the inhospitable coastline was very real. The whole transport squadron was swallowed up in thick cloud, but at last the planes emerged into brightness, though they had been scattered in the murk and it took half an hour to regain some cohesive formation — except for one Junkers whose pilot had got lost and flown back to Aalborg. But they had suffered no losses, unlike the Oslo operation, where the two missing planes had crashed into the sea.

Even so, the flight was rough, the planes hugging the ground at less than fifty feet as they flew inland towards Stavanger. One hundred paratroops leapt from their planes from a height of 400 ft, and as soon as they were clear the pilots took their planes back down to a lower level to escape possible flak fire. This precaution was justified, for even as the planes droned away the descending parachutists were fired upon by Norwegian machine-gunners. But just as suddenly two Messerschmitt 110s appeared on the scene and proceeded to engage the defences with cannon and machine-gun fire. There should have been eight fighters, but two had gone missing in the bad weather and the rest had turned back.

But the paras got down and in half an hour it was all over; Stavanger was in German hands.

By 14 April the Allies had begun landing their own forces, so once again the German parachute troops were alerted, and the same evening the 1st Company under Leutnant Schmidt was dropped eight kilometers south of Dombas to try and prevent a link-up between British and Norwegian forces north of Oslo. It was a risky business owing to the darkness and the rough, snow-clad terrain, and only 61 men of Schmidt's company assembled on the ground. This group blocked a vital road for four days before running out of ammunition and 34 survivors were forced to surrender to the Norwegians five days later.

General Dietl's mountain division became trapped in the Narvik area, assailed by the Allied force, which however hastily assembled, had more than managed to hold its own with the aid of some very effective support from the Royal Navy. The only way the Germans could give aid to Dietl was by the use of paratroops to try and relieve the pressure, but again the mountainous terrain and deep snow made such an operation hazardous. Nevertheless, the 1st Battalion of the 1st Parachute Regiment was dropped later in May, the difficulties added to by the extreme range of the objective from the nearest German-held bases. Extra fuel tanks were built into the Junkers' fuselages, but this restricted the number of troops carried, which was small enough anyway. It took many days to transport the Walther Battalion, for example. Surprisingly, but because of the emergency, some of the mountain division's reserve was rushed through a parachute course and included in the drop.

These reinforcements enabled the pressure on Dietl's men to be eased, but it was not until the German armies attacked in the west on 10 May that the Allied forces in Norway began to withdraw. In fact, despite the intervention of the paratroops, the Germans themselves were on the point of withdrawing from Narvik under cover of their almost total air superiority.

The Walther parachute group was only able to occupy Narvik on 8 June.

As shown, outside factors such as the weather could seriously disrupt planned airborne operations, the other crucial factor being intelligence on enemy dispositions. One German ex-paratrooper has commented on the lack of information provided for most of the German airborne battles of World War II; it was obviously vital that the lightly armed troops should not be dropped into a hornet's nest, and never against an enemy thoroughly alerted to their coming.

The capture by the Belgians of the German plans for an offensive on the Western Front necessitated a complete revision by Hitler and his staff of their intentions. Although the coup-de-main against the forts at Eben Emael had not been committed to paper, there existed in the original plans now in the possession of the Allies a much larger airborne attack. Four battalions of the 7th Air Division, plus troops of the 22 (Air Landing) Division, were scheduled to drop on the fortified zone of eastern Flanders preparatory to the main advance of the German Army, spearheaded by its armoured columns. This plan had now to be abandoned, and instead Hitler adopted "Plan Sickle", a scheme put up by General Manstein which laid emphasis on a bold armoured thrust through the Ardennes; added to this was Hitler's decision to include Holland within the offensive, and this part of the plan, because of the special difficulties it presented, necessitated the inclusion of the 7th Airborne Division.

The principal objectives of the airborne troops in the Dutch operation would be airfields and bridges, the latter were especially important because of the nature of the country which was criss-crossed by waterways. There were three vital airfields around

The Hague to be seized by parachute battalions, with air transported infantry to follow them in. The airbase at Waalhoven was the most important, and 28 Heinkels of the 4th Bomber Wing were assigned the task of neutralizing its defences before the paratroopers arrived. The bomber leader, Colonel Fiebig, hoped to catch the Dutch by surprise, but in the event the defenders had been expecting a German attack for over a week, and newspapers in the Allied Press had abounded with rumours of an impending enemy offensive, including an attack on Holland.

Fiebig's bombers took off from three bases in Germany on 10 May, their crews expecting to cross the frontier by 0530 hrs, but the formation leader decided to try and fox the Dutch defenders by approaching the target area from the west. The Dutch were not fooled, however, and were fully alerted to German tactics following the invasion of Scandinavia; they stood ready to meet both air and parachute attack.

As the Heinkels began their bomb run on Waalhoven airfield the Dutch flak guns opened up a heavy barrage, after which the Germans found themselves under attack by fighters. Colonel Fiebig's bomber was shot down and he was forced to take to his parachute and made prisoner on landing.

The 3rd Parachute Battalion had orders to capture the airfield by direct assault, and this they now attempted to do, jumping from their planes into the direct fire of Dutch troops on the ground – the Queen's Grenadiers. It was the first time that paratroops had dropped into the arms of a well-prepared enemy and a classic error. For some twenty seconds or more the German paras swung helpless in the air over the field where the hangars were ablaze from the bombs of the departing Heinkels – and it was into these fires that some of the parachutists now fell. Yet most of the troops managed to land unscathed near the edge of the field, scrambling out of their harness to race to their weapon containers. The Dutch troops' fire had been confused and erratic, and even as they switched their aim to the German paras on the ground they were bewildered by the sight of more Junkers coming in to land, full of infantrymen – the advance guard of the 16th Infantry Regiment. One of the transports was hit by flak and an engine caught fire.

The soldiers poured out of the planes before they had stopped taxiing and joined the paras in hemming in the Dutch defenders who still greatly outnumbered them. More and more transport planes arrived, making dangerous touch-downs among those aircraft already on the ground, some of which were now burning wrecks.

The Dutch infantrymen called in heavy mortar and artillery fire as the battle began to go against them, intending to withdraw under cover of the bombardment and regroup outside the airfield for a counter-attack. But then they saw green signal flares shoot up from the German positions. This was the Dutch troops' own signal to stop artillery fire! Obliging and unknowing, the Dutch gunners ceased fire. Their guns were sited near Rotterdam and they were unaware of the true situation. This error cost them the battle.

But the most important objectives in the German invasion of Holland were the bridges over the Rivers Maas and Waal on the south-eastern side of Rotterdam. The orthodox plan was for the 3rd Battalion of the 16th Infantry to fight its way through the city streets in a race to reach and secure the bridges before the Dutch defenders had a chance to blow them. This was too much of a gamble, and so was born perhaps one of the most original and amazing ploys of the whole war.

One company of the 16th Infantry, including engineers, were air-transported from the large lake at Zwischcnahnsee near Oldenburg, using obsolete twin-engined Heinkel 59 floatplanes which, although old and mainly used for air-sea rescue work, had spacious bodies large enough to hold 20 soldiers. These old biplanes flew in two groups of six, laden with 120 infantrymen. One group flew in from the east, while the other curved round to come in to its objective from the west. The German pilots flew along the course of the New Maas river until they were well into the heart of Rotterdam itself, then landed on the water close to the Willems Bridge, taxied to the north bank and disgorged their troops. The soldiers paddled ashore in rubber dinghies, and within minutes had secured the Leeuwen, Jan Kuiten and Willems bridges, as well as a nearby railway viaduct, setting up machine guns to cover all main approaches.

Holland was a defender's paradise, with myriad water obstacles, canal systems and dykes; the Dutch were prepared for conventional attack, but less so for a determined airborne assault. The totally unorthodox approach of a mere 120 men of the 16th Infantry must be unique in the annals of modern war.

The Dutch troops in the south side of Rotterdam were thoroughly alerted, but too late, for detachments should have been set up to cover and destroy all the main bridges. They did mount a counter-attack against the audacious men who had arrived in their midst, and a ferocious fire fight erupted as the German infantrymen sought cover and attempted to hold on to their gains. It would only be a matter of time before the overwhelming strength of the Dutch wiped out the two small German bridgeheads over the Maas, for there seemed to be no hope of quick reinforcement.

Then a second, but unplanned, miracle took place, and once again dashing innovation saved the day for the Germans. Dutch and Germans locked in combat were startled by a sudden clanging of bells as a convoy of street trams and other vehicles drove into sight from the south. The motley collection of vehicles contained fifty paratroopers of the 11th Company, 1st Parachute Regiment, led by Oberleutnant Horst Kerfin. This special detachment had been dropped on the stadium and, knowing the urgency of their task, had commandeered any transport they could lay their hands on in order to dash to assist their comrades at the Maas bridges.

The trams crossed the river, the troops joined the battle for the northern bridgehead and the fight raged on. But the 3rd Battalion of 16th Infantry which had unloaded on Waalhoven airfield suffered heavy casualties as it tried to fight its way through the streets to the Maas bridges. This battle was to go on for several more days, and the paratroops and infantry already in possession of the Willems and other crossings were gradually whittled down to just sixty men.

Meanwhile, the 9th Panzer Division had been ordered to drive fast over the frontier on the first day of the assault and head direct for the southernmost bridge over the Maas near Moerdijk in order to relieve the paratroops. It was this facet of the operation which had most concerned Major Reinberger when he set off on his ill-fated flight to Cologne in January.

Only one company of the 3rd Battalion was dropped to capture the bridges over the Old Maas river at Dordrecht, but in the battle the Dutch retook the railway bridge and the German commander, Oberleutnant von Brandis, was killed. Reinforcements consisting of more parachutists and infantry were rushed from Waalhoven, but the fight was to continue for three more days.

The bridges at Moerdijk had been assaulted by paratroops of the 2nd Battalion who dropped on both sides of the river following a precision attack by Stukas on the Dutch flak and other defensive positions. These bridges were modern structures built of steel box girders set in concrete piers. The highway bridge was 1200 meters in length, the rail bridge 1400 meters. The former was defended at its northern end by Dutch troops ensconced in a large concrete box bunker, but they were overwhelmed in one attack by paratroopers of the 5th Company led by Oberleutnant Straeler-Pohl, while Leutnant Tietjen was later awarded the Knight's Cross for the decisive part he played in the attack.

The bridge leading directly into the heart of Rotterdam was likewise a modern steel and concrete structure, and the sixty German soldiers surviving on the north bank of the New Maas were trapped by large Dutch forces, while elements of the 3rd Battalion, 16th Infantry, were holed up on a small island in the middle of the river and under the bridge structure. The Germans were under heavy fire from all arms, including heavy artillery, while other Dutch troops tried to assault the bridge in motor boats. 'Not even a mouse could cross the bridge by day or night,' commented one post-war historian; the main German force on the southern bank included the 9th Panzer Division, but neither these nor the accompanying infantry could make any progress over the bridge to rescue the trapped paras on the far bank.

The German officer in charge of the battle was Lt-Colonel von Choltitz, and as he stood under cover with his staff surveying the scene in frustration he was surprised to see two civilians appear on the southern end of the Willems bridge; the men were waving white flags and were allowed to approach the German positions. One man was a vicar, the other a merchant, and they offered to cross the bridge in order to ask the Dutch commander, Colonel Scharroo, to give up and save further bloodshed. Von Choltitz allowed them to go, but when they returned the Germans learned that the Dutch commander would only deal directly with the enemy. Since they were clearly in the ascendancy, it is not easy to understand why the Dutch were in any mood to parley at all, but in any case this delay was to lead directly to the tragic bombing of Rotterdam which was to have dire consequences for the Germans from the propaganda point of view, apart from the severe loss of life caused.

As usual in such situations the High Command were pressing for the battle to be concluded. Hitler, especially, was anxious for the operations in Holland to be brought to a speedy conclusion so that the forces involved could join the attacks now in progress in France and Belgium. Already it was becoming normal practice to call up "air" when ground troops were held up, and on 14 May a combined air and artillery assault was ordered to precede a tank attack over the Willems Bridge with the express proviso that the bombers take every care to avoid unnecessary bloodshed among civilians.

A similar situation had come about when the German armies reached the area of Warsaw during the Polish campaign. The Polish commander had ordered the capital turned into a fortress and had refused calls to surrender. Consequently the city was heavily bombed, a perfectly 'legitimate' event in terms of war and perhaps brought about by the Poles' obstinacy, but then they were defending their country against a brutal invader. Inevitably, civilians died and an outcry resulted of German savagery; thereafter the propaganda media of the democracies would refer again and again to 'Guernica-Warsaw-Rotterdam'. The exact circumstances and train of events which led to the breakdown of communications and the bombing of Rotterdam were not, of course, known to the Allies during the war and they have not been well publicized since.

The German commander sent a final demand to the Dutch to surrender and the two sides actually met to discuss possible terms. The German demand was for an honourable capitulation before the city environs were bombed and shelled. The Dutch had until 1800 hrs to decide, but in the event proved evasive, as well they might. They had bottled up the remnants of the paratroops and infantry and barred the way to the main German force on the southern bank of the river; they felt they could afford to wait until the paras surrendered, for the men were almost out of ammunition and supplies.

But events were moving inexorably to a disaster, for the Germans were determined to force the issue: the Heinkel bombers of Kampfgruppe 54 had taken off, their commander, Colonel Lackner, very carefully briefed to attack only a small triangular area on the north bank of the bridge in Rotterdam where the Dutch forces were concentrated and, of course, aware of the small knot of German paras still hanging on close by. The raid had already been postponed from 1500 hrs, and a flaw in the *Luftwaffe* communication net ensured that disaster would follow.

The likelihood of a Dutch surrender meant a postponement of the air attack, but Colonel Lackner and his crews were already in the air and the warning message relayed from the airborne troops HQ at Waalhoven airbase to 2nd Air Division was delayed by an interrupted wavelength. In fact, the Heinkel leader had been warned before take-off that surrender negotiations were likely, but to watch out for red Very lights if they were successful. As the bombers flew in towards Rotterdam they saw light flak erupting from the Dutch defences below; the city was also enveloped in haze and visibility was not good. But the coloured, winking lights below did not all originate from the barrels of the Dutch flak gunners, for even as the Heinkel bomb aimers took up position over their sights the German officers by the river were frantically firing off red Very lights to warn them off. But the lights were lost in the haze and flak fire and unseen by the bomber crews.

The drama now unfolding was added to as radio operators at 2nd Air Fleet HQ also tried to reach the Heinkels, while the Air Corps for Special Duties (the transport group HQ) had also picked up the postponement signal from its base in Bremen and passed it on. While all these desperate calls were in progress the operations officer at 2nd Air Fleet HQ raced out to an Me 109 fighter and took off in a last frantic attempt to divert the Heinkels to their alternative targets — British and Belgian troops in the West.

The leading Heinkel droned on, now approaching the old part of Rotterdam where Dutch soldiers and guns were inextricably mixed in streets still housing civilians, for the military had not evacuated the area. The German paras were squeezed into a small enclave against the Willems bridge, with the few Army infantrymen still huddled on the tiny spit of land in the middle of the river. It was a tough assignment for any bomber crews.

The lead observer in his Heinkel delayed until the last possible moment, his bomber piloted by Lt-Colonel Hoehne, who was finally forced to give the signal. But even in those last, vital seconds as the bombardier triggered the bomb release Hoehne thought he glimpsed red warning lights below and at once called his radio operator to signal the last of the Heinkel formation to abort. But it was too late. Fifty-seven bombers released their loads on Rotterdam, dropping 158 500 lb bombs and 1150 100 lb, in all 97 tons of explosives. As a result many fires sprang up which the city's civilian volunteer fire brigade was quite unable to quench with a handful of fairly modern fire appliances and one very ancient two-wheel hand pump. Next day the Germans themselves despatched a modern fire fighting regiment to help douse the flames.

Within hours of the bombing a great outcry rang out in the Allied and world Press and radio: the treacherous Germans had razed Rotterdam in a terror attack and killed 30,000 civilians. In fact, 814 lost their lives, while 78,000 were made homeless. The dazed Dutch commander surrendered at once, and the country followed suit. The German paratroop survivors emerged in tattered condition, still carrying the swastika flag they had displayed to identify their positions. The tanks of the 9th Panzer Division rolled into the city, followed by the infantry of *SS Leibstandarte Adolf Hitler* who in their enthusiasm to clear up any remaining pockets of Dutch resistance opened fire on a house containing the newly established HQ of General Student. As he leapt to the window to stop them he was struck by a bullet and seriously wounded.

At Rotterdam the German forces had triumphed for small loss in lives, though politically it had been a disaster, and in a sense this soured the successes of the airborne corps.

It had been the German intention to capture the Dutch royal family at The Hague on 10 May, and to this end parachutists had been ordered to take the three airfields at Valkenburg, Ypenburg and Ockenburg. But things went awry: at the first base near Leyden, north of The Hague, the paras leapt out of their still-moving planes which then sank up to their axles in spongy ground. Unable to take off, they proved easy targets for the Dutch defenders, so that by the time the next wave of Ju 52s arrived the field was cluttered with burning aircraft and they were forced to turn back.

At Ypenburg, north of Delft, an even greater disaster overtook the attackers, for of thirteen Junkers in the first wave all but two were shot up by flak and came down in flames. The Dutch, well aware of German airborne tactics following the invasion of Scandinavia, had strewn their landing grounds with obstacles, with the result that even those Junkers which managed to squeeze in onto the debris-strewn fields impaled themselves and caught fire. The dazed and shaken soldiers who survived were unable to hold out for long against the Dutch surrounding them; the few planes left of the transport group, with the Army's Major-General Graf Sponeck aboard one of them, were forced to divert to the airfield at Ockenburg, only to find a similar situation. The Divisional Commander's own aircraft was blasted by flak as its pilot desperately sought a place to get down; his task was a forlorn one, for everywhere they looked the ground seemed to be filled with wrecked and burning transport planes. In desperation, some German pilots had even landed on the Rotterdam-Hague motor road. British newspapers were soon displaying pictures of the wrecked German planes littering the area.

That evening the Divisional Commander managed to get through to Kesselring at 2nd Air Fleet HQ to report the disastrous assault on The Hague; he was ordered to call off the operation, collect as many men as possible and march on Rotterdam to aid the German troops battling for the city. The survivors so ordered numbered one thousand, and were harried en route by the elements of three Dutch divisions, but they reached the outskirts of Rotterdam during the night of 12-13 May.

Thus ended the northern part of the German operation, the subjugation of Holland, wherein it was shown quite decisively that an attack by airborne forces on a well-armed and prepared enemy could prove a costly business. Of the 430 Junkers 52s engaged in the operation around 290 or two-thirds were lost. Perhaps the more serious loss to the German airborne corps was the wastage of instructors who had formed the bulk of the transport crews and had been withdrawn from the training schools for the operation. It is said that this particular loss affected the recruitment of bomber crews later, and it was to be compounded by the heavy losses suffered in the Battle of Britain.

For the Battle of France the German airborne troops were assigned two roles: to neutralize the frontier fortress of Eben Emael, and secondly to seize three vital bridges to the north-west on the deep Albert Canal. As pointed out, although the Allies had their hands on the captured German plans, these did not refer to the planned coup on the forts. The main German offensive, they believed, would thrust north of Brussels, whereas the main weight of the attack would be put into General von Kleist's armoured fist on the southern flank.

A glance at the map showed every German staff officer and armchair strategist on both sides that two serious water obstacles would bar the path of their armies, the River Maas and the Albert Canal, and as such they must have figured in dozens of academy and staff exercises for decades. Both were comparatively straightforward objectives for airborne assault, but the forts at Eben presented special problems. For one thing, troops landed too far away would give the Belgian defenders too much time to site and fire their weapons. This meant that any air-dropped troops would have to be placed as close to or even on the objectives themselves.

The forts consisted of a series of heavy concrete bunkers, some with retractable, round steel turrets mounting guns, some of them twin-barrelled cannon. The Germans had been able to carry out a certain amount of reconnaissance with their high-flying Dornier 17P aircraft using super-lens cameras, but no amount of aerial photography could tell the whole story. In the event a lack of more precise intelligence led to some of the troops being assigned the wrong objectives. But few plans work out perfectly in war and a certain degree of improvisation is always necessary.

The forts at Eben Emael were situated three miles north of Maastricht, close to the Belgian-Dutch border, and sited to dominate the Albert Canal, all the bridges of which were prepared for demolition. The defensive emplacements were dug into a hilly plateau running nearly 1000 yards north-south, and 700 yards east-west. They had been conceived and built in the early 1930s and were part of the general belief in many static-minded military circles in defence lines constructed to withstand assault and bombardment from any known enemy, but specifically the Germans. They were, their designers believed, the last word in such forts and on a par with the much vaunted French Maginot Line. Certainly the armoured casements with their rotating steel capsule turrets containing 75 and 120 mm guns appeared a formidable proposition. The north-eastern and north-western flanks faced an almost sheer drop of 120 ft into the Albert Canal; to the south the Belgians had dug broad anti-tank ditches and a 20-foot wall. The walls and defence cuttings were provided with additional concrete pillboxes and searchlights, the whole system connected by three miles of underground tunnels. Everyone agreed that the network had been cleverly designed and appeared invincible. No enemy force could possibly pass that way − or could it?

It was certainly a tough nut to crack, but the German airborne planners knew a way. To them it was the obvious and only one; they would 'drop in', out of the sky, right into the enemy's laps.

Sturmabteilung Koch was split up into four segments:

Section "Granite", commanded by Oberleutnant Witzig, comprised 85 soldiers with small arms and explosives to embark in 11 gliders; their mission was to put the outer defence works at Eben out of action until relieved by the Army's 51st Engineer Battalion.

Section "Concrete", commanded by Leutnant Schacht, comprised 96 men and command staff in 11 gliders, assigned to capture the high concrete bridge over the Albert Canal at Vroenhoven.

Section "Steel", commanded by Oberleutnant Altmann, 92 men

in 9 gliders to seize the steel bridge at Veldwezelt, some 3¾ miles north-west of Eben.

Section "Iron", under Leutnant Schächter, with 90 men in 10 gliders, their target the bridge at Kanne, to be secured until the arrival of Army troops.

The entire training and execution of the operation was under the command of Captain Koch and great secrecy surrounded the troops when they were briefed and trained in the Altvater area of Czechoslovakia where suitable fortifications lent themselves well for rehearsal. As from 2 November, 1939, the men lived in virtual quarantine, for the German offensive, it will be remembered, had been mooted by Hitler at an early stage but put off by the harsh winter.

Kurt Seiler was one of those detailed to take part in this hazardous mission. Although he came from Magdeburg, he never went to the Stendahl parachute school, being called up into the German Army in 1937 and undergoing the usual infantry training. At this point the men were addressed by an officer who invited them to volunteer for a new air-landing unit; they would fly in gliders into enemy territory in the event of war.

"This, I felt, was something different. I had often watched gliders soaring in the sky, but had never had the courage to take a trip. Now I could ride as a passenger. A few volunteers were forthcoming and we were at once sent away to a school where such troops were trained. This was at Hildesheim, but first we received some instruction in the tactics of glider landing. I was very surprised at the small size of the DFS glider, and when we were loaded — six men with equipment — there was no room to move at all or stretch out.

"But we were committed and by now members of the *Luftwaffe* and received the same kind of clothing as the paratroops. Then came our first flight. We crammed inside and the flimsy door was closed. We had our knees drawn up and were very apprehensive as the thing began to move at the end of a towrope pulled by a Ju. Then the scraping and rumbling stopped and we felt we were in flight. It was quite an eerie sensation and rather pleasant at first. But then it began to get more bumpy. The glider rose and fell as if we were at sea and we all felt sick and miserable and I wondered how I could have been such a fool as to have ever volunteered for such a job!

"When the rope was parted our pilot soared down in a very steep dive and suddenly we were scraping along the ground. Then the Sergeant threw open the door and we scrambled out in rather undignified fashion and rushed away to lie flat on the grass with weapons at the ready. We were using live ammunition and shot it off in that exercise which was quite fun, but we did not know the objective, if any. The war was about to erupt and we wondered what kind of fate lay in store for us. We soon found out."

It is believed that officers in the German Air Ministry (RLM) had always been opposed to the formation of glider troop units, believing that such formations could do nothing that the paratroops could not do. For this reason no large orders had been placed with the Gotthar vehicle factory for the DFS glider, only some 28 pre-production models having been delivered by the end of 1937. However, by the end of 1938 an experimental glider troop commando had been formed and included in the *Luftwaffe*'s 7th Air Division, later being combined as an assault force in the XIth Fliegerkorps. By early 1940 the glider enthusiasts had prevailed. They felt that the cadre formed had proved by experiment and demonstration that assaults by glider troops were a real possibility; as a result production of the DFS 230 model was put in hand and the 1st Group of the 1st Air-Landing Wing formed. This was the formation that included Kurt Seiler, and its expansion or demise would depend on what kind of show they put up in the coming offensive.

"Within a few weeks we began to receive serious training in landing near or on obstacles — forts, trenches and even airfields. These were mostly carried out in Germany, but a little while later we were sent into Czechoslovakia where we were shown some strong fortifications and told that these were to be our next exercise. Our job was to land on or near to the forts which were in some cases only seen as turrets sticking out of the ground, or otherwise concrete bunkers surrounded by barbed wire. We wondered what the enemy would be doing when we dropped in on them.

"By then we had made so many drops that we had mostly got used to it, but one man could never get over his sickness and he left the unit. I myself was nineteen years old and I had a young wife in Berlin while my parents still lived in Magdeburg, so I was quite anxious to stay alive!

"Then, after many rehearsals, we were told that we would be part of a big German attack in the west and that we had the most important job of all and would spearhead the attack by capturing some Belgian forts. It sounded very exciting and also very dangerous. The gliders we used were very flimsy, you could almost put a finger through the sides. The [fuselage] tubing was made of steel, but it was only a crude framework. Those machines were, I must say, very primitive compared to those designed later.

"There was a very great deal of secrecy and we were all called together one day and shown a paper pledging on oath that we would never breathe a word of the coming operation to anyone, and had to sign it. We were not allowed out and had quite a miserable few weeks, until at last we went by train across Germany to the Cologne area and onto an airfield where we received final instructions and a pep talk from our officers and NCOs."

There had been several false alarms, but by 9 May the assault gliders and their crews, plus the Junkers 52 transports, were assembled on two airfields near Cologne, Ostheim and Butzweilerhof. Forty-two Junkers had been assembled for the operation. The total strength of the force, including the glider pilots, was eleven officers and 427 NCOs and men. The toughest task had been given the Witzig group, and, appropriately, all the soldiers, apart from the glider pilots, were trained combat engineers. As to their opponents, it was thought that the forts were manned by some 1200 Belgian soldiers under the command of a Major Jottrand, the exact tally of weapons at his disposal standing at: twelve 75mm howitzers in casements; four 75mm howitzers in rotating, armoured turrets; two 120mm howitzers similarly placed, all the turrets having an all-round (360°) firing capability, being supported by 17 infantry positions equipped with anti-tank and machine guns, plus seven anti-aircraft emplacements. All-round observation was maintained from separate cupolas.

At exactly 0430 on the morning of 10 May the take-off signal was given to the Junkers pilots on the two airfields as they sat in their cockpits with the planes' engines already ticking over. The first three Junkers trundled across the fields and were soon lumbering into the lightening sky, dragging their loaded gliders behind them. The rest of the *Ketten* (flights) took off at 30-second intervals, and at last all the planes were airborne. To aid navigation, despite the blackout, a string of beacon lights had been lit, pointing the way to Aachen near the frontier, which was where the towropes would be unhitched, leaving the gliders to soar down to their objectives. The route was simple and the offensive would be launched at dawn; previously the Army's High Command (OKH) had proposed beginning the attack at 0300 hrs, before the sky began to lighten, but Captain Koch had pointed out that his own operation should coincide with the Army's zero hour and had to go in with the first light of dawn.

One hitch occurred as the fleet formed up south of Cologne: the pilot of the Ju towing the last glider of the Granite detachment suddenly saw the exhaust glare of another plane on a collision course and dived to avoid it — his tow-rope parted and the glider behind went down to land in a meadow near the Rhine. This was unfortunate, for inside it crouched the leader of the Witzig group, the Leutnant himself. Scrambling clear, Witzig ran to the nearest road where he stopped a passing vehicle and drove to Cologne-Ostheim airfield, hoping to find another tow plane. But none was available, so he was forced to telephone the base at Gutersloh. Only twenty minutes remained before his unit's zero hour!

"Some of us had made our wills and then we tried to get some sleep," relates Kurt Seiler. "But I could not get any rest at all, and I believe many of the lads were the same. We were up long before dawn and got everything ready and at last went out onto the field where every glider crew had received last-minute instructions. As you may know, not everything went according to plan, and one of the leaders lost his tow and had to land and come on later. We flew into the early morning and at last realized we were over Belgium which was of course still neutral. I had qualms and felt sick for the first time in a year or so, but then someone shouted, the signal had been given and we felt a lurch as the towrope parted. Down we dived and I could see the pilot peering out, trying to make sure of his objective.

"We came down with a terrific thump and one of our wings broke off and out we went. We could see the forts and tunnels and heard a machine gun firing near us. Two men carried explosives and we rushed with them towards a great round turret which had a large gun sticking out of it."

The German aerial convoy had stretched for some 45 miles across western Germany and when the Granite team were released to glide down into Belgium they were unaware that part of their detachment were back on land in Germany. A further hitch had arisen en route when twenty minutes into the flight and at 5000 ft one glider pilot saw his tow plane waggle its wings and blink its navigation lights, which was the signal to release the towing cable. Baffled, the pilot cut the tow and came down in a field near Duren. Furious, the men leapt out to find a road and commandeer vehicles and begin a frantic race to the frontier to join up with the Army units about to begin their attack.

Granite was now left with nine gliders as the formation came to the final beacon which was a searchlight, and the pilots prepared to unhitch. But the weather had proved unreliable, the following wind had blown them ten minutes early, and the planes had yet to reach their operational height of 8500 ft. As a result the Junkers flew on into Dutch airspace, the tow pilots hoping to make good the error. But in doing this they alerted the Dutch defences, and as the gliders were released so the Dutch flak gunners opened fire. The glider pilots jinked this way and that to avoid the red tracer shells shooting up at them. The gliders swooped down silently on the plateau and forts of Eben − five minutes early. Major Jottrand, the Belgian commander, had been aroused from his sleeping quarters just after 0300 hrs by his superiors of 7th Infantry Division, and as a result had ordered his garrison at Eben into an increased state of alert. But when, two hours later, the drone of planes and the sound of flak from the Dutch seemed to indicate a possible German air raid which then petered out the Belgians relaxed again.

But suddenly the more alert of the Belgian defenders saw black-winged shapes diving down on them. Alarmed, the sentries tried to alert the gun crews, and very quickly some of the howitzer barrels were depressed and opened fire. But just as swiftly the winged silhouettes vanished from view, having struck the ground nearby or landed on the forts themselves. Incredibly, one of the German gliders actually severed one of the Belgian machine-gun barrels, dragging it along the ground. Within seconds, soldiers rushed out of the glider firing submachine-guns and hurling grenades into the embrasures of the nearest fort.

"The men were going to spike the guns," Seiler continues, "but as we got near them there were shots and bullets started flying around us. We had to dive to the ground and I heard someone calling out as they were hit. We crawled forward into a dip in the ground and tried to see where the fire was coming from, but it was very hard. At last our Sergeant told us we must make a move, so we leapt up and rushed at the big turret, firing in all directions as our two expert explosives men began fixing charges to the turret and down the gun barrel itself. We dashed away, and by the time the charges exploded we were under cover.

8. Crete. A flimsy DFS glider with some of its dead occupants alongside.

9 & 10. **Below Left:** These pictures illustrate the heavy cost in transports; Ju52s lie wrecked and burning on Maleme airfield.

11. **Below Right:** The heavyweight boxing champion Max Schmeling jumped with the 1st Battalion 1st Para Regiment on Crete.

12. **Top:** Surviving paratroopers survey the graves of fallen comrades on Crete.

13. **Above:** Despite their pyrrhic losses the German units took part in victory parades on returning to Germany, here at Stendahl.

14. **Right:** A craftsman completes the German para memorial on Crete.

"There was a lot of shooting going on and we could hear men calling and crying out. Our Sergeant then led us off to a bunker entrance but it was closed up tight, so we hurled grenades through a gun aperture and then the door flew open and some Belgians ran out with their hands up."

All nine of the Granite gliders had touched down in the right place, no mean feat in the circumstances, but the defenders had reacted swiftly and machine-gun bullets tore between the forts as the Germans debussed from their gliders and ran into action. The Belgians had been hampered, however, by the restricted range of vision from within the actual turrets, and fired inaccurately. The explosive experts with Seiler and the other teams had brought a new innovation with them, 100 lb hollow charges especially designed to deal with steel and concrete fortifications, and while these were being applied other troopers destroyed the periscope sights on the turrets and other bunkers, leaving the defenders blind. But even the special explosive charges failed to destroy the steel cupolas, causing cracks and holes, so that the German glider troops resorted to firing their weapons into the Belgians' gun embrasures.

Some of the toughest-looking forts and turrets which had shown up in aerial photographs turned out to be tin dummies. But from a wooden shed used as a billet Belgian troops opened fire with machine guns, causing casualties among the attackers. After some ten minutes of rushing around Eben the Germans had succeeded in putting ten of the Belgian positions out of action, and with them most of the defenders' howitzers. Seiler stood guard over their prisoners, but the battle was far from over. There was plenty of shooting going on and it was obvious to the glider troops that it was not to be an easy victory.

"We were obliged to lie flat with bullets flying about and one of the prisoners was killed by Belgian fire. Then I was detailed to watch over the rest of the prisoners while the rest went off to join in the battle. The Belgians seemed very shaken and frightened and said nothing.

"At last it was fully daylight and we were very much in control of the situation and saw a lot of our planes going over on bombing raids, but we were waiting for the Army to come and relieve us. This took some time. Meanwhile, we were still under fire and had not managed to clear all the forts which were very well built and mostly underground."

In fact, the Belgian commander, Major Jottrand, had been

observing the progress of the battle from his own command bunker not far away, and now ordered down artillery fire to catch the attackers in the open and destroy them. This sent the Germans into whatever cover they could find, preferably the captured bunkers. At about 0830 hrs both defenders and Germans were amazed to see a single DFS glider swoop out of the morning sky, to land near fort No 19. Out of it leapt Lieutenant Witzig and his men, for he had managed to arrange another tow plane which had somehow collected his stranded glider from the field outside Cologne. Under his leadership the German airborne troops resumed the assault, dropping small charges into the Belgian gun barrels, blowing up the surrounding tunnels and isolating enemy sections from each other. When they turned their attention to fort No 17 they were obliged to suspend their charges on ropes as the Belgian position was set into a 120 ft wall on the western side of the Albert Canal.

"Some hours went by and I took my turn in shooting off all our ammunition, and we ran out of supplies. If the Belgians had counter-attacked then I believe they would have won, but they didn't, and we remained in control; but a number of the enemy refused to surrender and stayed underground."

Captain Koch learned by radio that the Army relieving force had been delayed by the enemy's successful destruction of some of the bridges over the River Maas, one had collapsed at the very moment Iron detachment landed. But the assaults at Vroenhoven and Veldwezelt had succeeded, the bridges were secured by the Concrete and Steel detachments, though all the German bridgeheads came under heavy Belgian artillery fire. Yet the glider troops held on, aided by the 88 mm guns of a flak battalion and repeated raids by old Henschel 123 biplanes of a Battle Wing. All the German airborne bridgehead units were relieved the same day by Army troops, long before the Granite detachment, which was forced to fight on until 0700 hrs next morning, 11 May, when the relieving assault engineers finally reached them. A stalemate had ensued because the glider troops were out of ammunition and other supplies, but the Army's arrival signalled a final assault on the last stubbornly held positions at Eben Emael. Even then the Belgians did not surrender until 1315 hrs when a single trumpet blast indicated that the defenders had had enough. Some 1200 soldiers came out into the daylight with their hands up; their comrades who had fought above ground lost 20 men, while the Granite detachment lost six killed and 20 wounded.

"It had not been an easy operation," Seiler commented, "but was unique and I believe we made quite an impression on the outside world. We went back to Germany in trucks and received a few medals and were visited by many high-ranking officers. Hitler met our commanders and gave them the Knight's Cross. I believe they were the first awarded in the war. I myself received the Iron Cross II Class, as did my comrades, and we were allowed to go home on leave. My wife went to Magdeburg and we had quite a family celebration. I was treated like a hero but did not feel like one. A sort of reaction set in and I felt I was lucky to be alive. When my wife told me a child was on the way I was overjoyed and wanted to leave my dangerous profession."

One other new ploy was employed by the Germans on 10 May, one the Allies would themselves adopt later in the war. The same Junkers 52 transport planes made a further flight, going on some twenty-five miles beyond Eben Emael to drop dummy paratroopers made of straw and fitted with self-igniting charges to simulate battle noises. The Belgians at first thought they were being attacked in the rear and the episode may have made some small contribution to the prolonged myth of Germans parachuting down in disguise, the most absurd variation being that they could be seen as nuns.

The atmosphere in Germany was euphoric. The nation celebrated the amazing victories which had surpassed even Hitler's expectations. In a lightning campaign the Wehrmacht had conquered a huge segment of Western Europe, and for comparatively few casualties. They controlled the coastline from Norway to the Spanish frontier; the British Expeditionary Force had been, by a miracle, snatched from total annihilation by the Royal Navy and an armada of small craft, and for the British this was something to celebrate, though few among them realized the scale of the defeat, or worse, the dire state of the defences against a now possible invasion.

Although much of the BEF had been rescued, along with thousands of other Allied soldiers, most of their equipment had been left behind at Dunkirk or other points along the French coast. British losses in equipment, amounting to several months of production, were as follows:

> 7,000 tons of ammunition
> 90,000 rifles

2,300 guns
120,000 vehicles
8,000 Bren guns
400 anti-tank rifles

The bells rang out throughout Germany, and in Berlin a huge victory parade was organized by Goebbels, attended by thousands of troops and applauded by millions of people, especially when the architect of it all appeared in his armoured Mercedes, escorted as always by his personal SS bodyguard. The cheering crowds were heard by radio throughout the Reich and beyond. The Führer had conquered Czechoslovakia, Poland, Denmark, Norway, Holland, Belgium, France and Luxemburg, apart of course from bringing Austria back into Greater Germany. It only remained for the stubborn and stupid British to admit defeat and throw in the towel as their French allies had done and peace could be declared. The Führer could afford to be magnanimous, he respected the British and was prepared to guarantee their Empire. But his vaguely worded radio appeal was coldly rejected by the British, to Hitler's genuine disappointment, and for more than one reason. He always wished for a better working relationship with the British, but never more so than now, for despite the fact that his people saw the war as virtually over, as was proved by the return of some servicemen to civilian life, Hitler's mind was already turning back to his fundamental problem, the quest for *lebensraum* in the East. In no way did he relish a thorn in his back when he began making preparations for the *Drang nach Osten*.

Konrad Seibert:

"Many weeks went by, and with the great victory over France, and England we thought beaten, we wondered if we would once again become civilians. We then heard that there were plans to invade England, but when the Autumn came all that was forgotten."

The ex-Army para Karl Pickert had been in a reserve unit while the offensive in the West took place:

"By the time it was all over we had done nothing but read about what our comrades had done in the Netherlands and Belgium. In fact we had seen some of them afterwards, and the medals they wore and begun to feel a trifle envious. Even so, I had no wish to stick my neck out and felt content to stay as I was. The victory in the West was so stirring that I felt it very probable that the war

56

would be over, as did we all. I saw myself returning to civilian life covered in a dubious kind of glory — reflected from those who had done the real fighting."

Karel Weise had not seen any action in Poland but after a hard winter's training took part in the 1st Parachute Regiment's drop near The Hague:

"It was not all honey and we had a few casualties, but I remained unscathed. Then, after we had completed a little clearing up and the guarding of prisoners we went back to Germany and once again felt that the war was as good as over. We had quite a good life, training and leave, more training and leave, until at last we could see that the war was far from over."

Heinrich Pabst had helped train several hundred paratroopers at Stendahl, but when war broke out applied for a transfer to a combat unit:

"In truth I was becoming bored and longed for a more active role. I was assigned as a senior NCO to the 1st Parachute Regiment, and not long after that we entered Poland but saw no action. When we returned to Germany it was to more training, and I was then promoted to Lieutenant and given command of a company. It was then that I took part in the attack on Holland — on the Moerdijk bridge where we did some fighting but nothing serious. After our return to Germany we tried to analyse our failures and omissions, and certain recommendations were made. We had a long period of exercises which grew very boring, but I recall some very pleasant interludes at my home."

Any restlessness and boredom felt by the German paras was soon to be dispelled in drastic fashion.

Karl Pickert was involved in the Norwegian operation:

"I will not describe it in detail. We went over in dense fog in our Ju's, but had to turn back, the weather was so bad. Our troops did have some successes, but overall it was very experimental and many lessons were learned. First of all, the weather was always a very big factor, and secondly, the enemy had to be taken by surprise, otherwise disaster could occur. When the Dutch operation came up I was in reserve and took no part in it. So 1940 went by with great victories for Germany and we felt a certainty that the war was over. However, we were sent into France and began to receive briefings for a possible landing in England. But this all came to nothing and very soon we were back in Germany on leave."

Kurt Seiler was another German airborne soldier detailed for the invasion of England:

"A very great victory was won in France. Everyone thought that it was the end of the war, but I myself felt that with England unbeaten we still had a long way to go. In fact, before long in that grand summer we were being briefed for a possible landing in England. We airborne men were to drop in Kent and Sussex near the Downs, and fan out to take the British beach defences from the rear. But exciting as it all seemed I could not see it coming off, and that's what happened. It all fizzled out and before long our billets in France were left empty and we returned to Germany. Yes! We were actually allocated airfields from which we would take off for England, but we were not there long. When we went back to Germany it all seemed very peaceful and the war seemed far away. Everything was left to the *Luftwaffe*, and I had a very fine time at home until fate overtook me in 1941."

In the summer of 1940, which turned into what Churchill dubbed the "Battle of Britain", the German radio and press became filled with bombast and songs of victory, but as the weeks went by following the Italian declaration of war the attention of the world was subtly but unmistakably switched to the Mediterranean, for there the grand schemes of the Italian fascist dictator were already crumbling as his navy and army in Libya were defeated by the British. Following these humiliating reversals to his dreams of empire Mussolini, somewhat irritated and jealous of his more powerful Axis partner, Adolf Hitler, decided to invade Greece; what he could not accomplish in North Africa he felt could perhaps more easily be done in the Balkans. After all, Italy had already managed by guile and intrigue to oust all British influence in Albania and virtually take over the country which was conveniently situated alongside his next target, which meant that Italian forces had but to move aside the frontier posts in order to march in. Or had they?

As the winter of 1940-41 got underway so the invading Italians were rebuffed and met with continual defeat in the mountainous passes at the hands of the numerically inferior and less well equipped Greek Army. This further embarrassment to a degree reflected on Hitler, who was already irritated by this eruption of conflict on his south-eastern flank, coming as it did just as his plans for the huge attack on Russia were nearing fruition. Hitler reserved all rights to extend the war in an easterly direction, for there was ever the potential threat of some British intervention in the region, beyond the dominance they had already achieved in his partner's *Mare Nostrum*. That this should be the case was itself extraordinary and an indication of Hitler's failure to subdue Britain, which having survived the threat of invasion was ever ready to nip Hitler's tail in the so-called 'soft under-belly of Europe', a region which would once again become one of Churchill's pet themes, as it had been in the earlier war.

British attempts to undermine Nazi influence had been in hand long enough in Rumania for example, but were finally thwarted when Nazi agents and then military advisers, soon followed by troops, helped to strengthen the powerful fascist element as both a move to eliminate British subversion and warn off Stalin's Russia. Stalin, supposedly Hitler's ally, had already confirmed his untrustworthiness by taking over Latvia, Estonia and Lithuania, these moves followed by a demand to Rumania that it cede Bessarabia. Hitler advised his Rumanian friends to comply and bide their time, for in due course he would settle accounts with Stalin and the Rumanians would share in the spoils. There was, of course, the question of the Rumanian oil supplies which were vital to Germany, so German protection in the form of troops and flak guns was justified, or so Hitler felt.

Hitler's fears of a growing British involvement to protect their long-standing interests in the Mediterranean were confirmed by the British occupation of Crete the very day after the Italian attack on Greece. As the Italian offensive in Greece bogged down, so Hitler admonished his friend as a tutor might an erring pupil, pointing out that he had now practically invited the British into south-east Europe, but neglecting to point out the real basis of his fears which was that these unexpected developments now threatened to upset his timetable for Operation "Barbarossa", the attack on Russia.

Hitler also told Mussolini that if he had known his plans he would have offered the use of a German airborne division to secure the island of Crete, an obvious and vital strategic bastion which the Italians ought to have taken over before attacking Greece.

So, as early as 1940, soon after the official 'conclusion' of the air battle over Britain (disregarding the night blitz), the German staffs were considering the taking of an island from the air. But Hitler would not allow his plans to be upset unless it became absolutely necessary — and this it did. By early 1941 the Italian Army had made no progress in its Greek venture, and indeed continued to suffer humiliating reverses. Mussolini and his fascist government became the laughing stock of the world, which made their German allies increasingly angry. Then, in March, Hitler's worst fears were realized: the British had the audacity to land troops and RAF units in Greece itself. Although it was a political move by the British, Hitler could not tolerate a return to the continent by his enemy; but, specifically, he feared RAF bombers based in Greece might strike at his precious Ploesti oilfields in Rumania. A further excuse for German intervention came when in the last week of the month young King Peter of Yugoslavia renounced the treaty the Prince Regent had just signed with the Axis Powers; Hitler struck south-east to clear up the growing mess before starting his Russian adventure, sending in the *Leibstandarte SS* plus army troops and strong air forces who subjugated Yugoslavia in a swift campaign.

British and Commonwealth forces had meantime moved into northern Greece and these also came under German attack. Whatever weakening had occurred in North Africa, where a certain General Rommel was beginning to make his presence felt, the British intervention in Greece paid dividends in drawing off German forces from the build-up for Barbarossa and thus upset Hitler's timctable. Furthermore, the Germans now felt obliged to send *Luftwaffe* units of the Xth Air Corps to Sicily to assist their Italian allies in the Mediterranean.

All these complications, quite unforeseen by Hitler, were to bring about the demise of Hitler's élite airborne forces.

III

Disaster on Crete

It is an extraordinary fact that the actual operational life of Germany's élite force as an airborne corps lasted a little over one year of the six years known as World War II. It is also a fact that it was one man, Mussolini, who can be seen to have brought about their destruction, for the reasons given in the previous chapter. It may well have been that in any case no further great opportunities for their employment would have come up, but this is speculation. The fact is that German forces were drawn into the Balkans in the Spring of 1941 by the mad schemes of Mussolini.

Apart from the diversion of considerable numbers of troops and the resulting casualties, there was much wear and tear on vehicles when the German columns were obliged to drive south-east over difficult terrain, not to mention the great amount of fuel consumed. However, the forces employed were fairly rapidly re-deployed once the campaign was over, though it did mean an ever-increasing use of garrison troops in the whole area, and these had to be greatly augmented over the coming years as the national guerrilla armies became organized.

But before the affair in Crete which was to end in the death of so many of Germany's finest there was one small job that needed to be carried out, a small operation which brought both success and failure to the airborne soldiers engaged.

By the end of April the decision to extract the British forces from Greece had been taken and was being implemented. The British commander, General Wilson, was battling under increasing difficulties in trying to move his expeditionary force to the southern tip of Greece and its ports of evacuation. The German forces were pressing his men hard, and they were heavily assailed by the *Luftwaffe* which had dominated the air from the start. The few RAF planes scraped together to fight in Greece included obsolete Blenheim Is and a few Hurricanes and were being reduced to nothing by air combat and attacks on their bases which were hopelessly unprotected by flak or ground units. In fact, it was this problem which led to the forming of the RAF Regiment.

The British units were streaming south, leaving rearguards to cover their withdrawal; it was, it seemed, yet another ignominious retreat. To cut off this line of withdrawal and perhaps even trap Wilson's forces it was necessary for the Germans to capture the bridge over the Corinth Canal. The 2nd Parachute Regiment was therefore ordered to drop nearby and seize the crossing. The assigned units were: 1st and 2nd Battalions plus divisional engineers, one light artillery battery plus signals and medical companies.

The troops moved to Larissa and took off in their Junkers transports at 0500 hrs on 24 April, 1941. In the van was the engineer unit, their mission to rush the bridge and prevent its demolition. This is what happened:

By 0700 the German sappers had landed, overwhelmed the bridge guards and removed the explosives. At the same time other paratroopers had landed on both sides of the canal to set up bridgeheads. It seemed like a copybook operation, but then disaster struck. By an extraordinary fluke, an unexploded British anti-aircraft shell fell on the demolition charges which had been removed from the bridge by the German engineers; the charges exploded with a roar, demolishing the bridge and sending the broken structure into the water below, thus effectively blocking the canal. A German photographed this event at the second the explosion took place.*

The German 2nd Parachute Battalion, meanwhile, had moved on to capture the airfield, but as some companies advanced beyond it they were ambushed, but eventually prevailed and forced the enemy to surrender. By the time the German Army troops reached the canal the para engineers had constructed a new and temporary crossing.

It has been suggested that if this airborne operation had taken place two days earlier then the bulk of General Wilson's force would have fallen into German hands. On the other hand it had gained the Germans little and had given away the fact that German airborne forces were in Greece and not near the projected eastern front.

Oddly, this operation is alleged to have been carried out without

---

* This is the German version; but two British officers are said to have been trying to ignite the demolition charges by rifle fire. They may have succeeded.

General Student's knowledge, but this may have been because he was still recovering from the wound suffered from an SS bullet in Holland.

May, 1941, can be looked back on as the most sensational month of the whole war.

It was the month in which the *Bismarck*, the mighty German battleship, was destroyed after much effort and grievous loss by the Royal Navy, with some crucial help from RAF Coastal Command. Of perhaps even greater sensation was the flight of the Deputy Führer, Rudolf Hess, to Scotland, which itself coincided exactly with the biggest and by far the worst *Luftwaffe* air raid of the war on London.

Then came Crete.

General Student, 'father' of the German airborne forces, did not enter the picture until 20 April, five days after General Lohr, commander of the 4th Air Fleet, had put it to Göring that the island of Crete could prove a thorn in Germany's southern flank, and could be eliminated by airborne troops of the XIth Air Corps. This organization had just been formed to take in not only the airborne troops but also the transport plane component. Lohr, an Austrian, was responsible for air operations in the south-east sector and had overseen the *Luftwaffe*'s heavy contribution to the Balkan campaign which had included Stuka units based in Bulgaria, a country in a sense linked to the Soviets but politically tied to Hitler. Bulgaria would be excused from putting troops into the huge package of allied forces, which included Italian, Rumanian and Hungarian troops, that Hitler was assembling to invade Russia, but the free use of bases and other aid given to the Germans hardly cemented closer ties with Russia.

Student returned to duty from his long convalescence to be appointed chief of XIth Air Corps, not a mere formality, for previously he had not actually been in direct control of the air transport groups. He embraced the plan for Crete, expanding on it and working up a detailed scheme which he put to Göring, who passed him on to Hitler, with the support of his Chief-of-Staff, General Jeschonnek. These men conferred with the Führer on 21 April, the day that Greece capitulated to the German-Italian forces.

For Hitler the situation was something of a paradox: on the one hand his timetable for the attack on Russia had been seriously compromised, though how seriously he did not then know, with

German military strength being dissipated around the Balkans. On the other hand, he was flushed with the victories gained over Yugoslavia and Greece. He had successfully inveigled Rumania and Hungary into an alliance, as well as seducing Bulgaria out of any thoughts of tying in with Stalin. Above all, he seemed to have stabilized the theatre and eliminated British influence. The fact that his domination of the whole of southern Europe (with an even chance that Turkey would grant him favours) irked the Soviets did not concern him in the slightest, for Stalin and his government seemed to be doing their utmost to fulfil their part of the trade pact between the two countries, even though the Germans had deliberately reneged on their portion for obvious reason. The Russian Bear, the Soviet bolshevik colossus, would collapse as soon as the might of the German *Wehrmacht* and its allies was unleashed on it.

There remained two problems, albeit of comparative insignificance, to be taken into consideration: Crete and Malta.

Under Mussolini the Italians had come to regard the Mediterranean sea as their rightful heritage. Its southern periphery lapped the shores of their North African empire, Libya and Tripolitania, where Italian settlers and colonists had set up homes and enterprises on a modest scale, and with military help dominated the indigenous population and its fragile economy. (It was, of course, long before the days of Libyan oil.) But war with Britain, an ill-considered move, had ruined everything and placed the whole shaky Italian colonial set-up in jeopardy. Their 'Grand Army', which had launched a much-trumpeted entry into Egypt, had been smashed by a far smaller British force under Wavell, while its Navy was bottled up in port, under quarantine by the Royal Navy. It had been galling to be forced into accepting even modest German help in the area.

The key to British dominance lay in the island of Malta, and for once the head of the German OKW, General Keitel, was correct when he suggested that this should be the target of a German airborne assault. Once in German hands it would not only deny the British use of the Mediterranean, but act as an invaluable sea and air base for the invasion of Egypt, thus cutting off the British from their vital oil supplies in the Middle East and demolishing one bastion of its Empire once and for all.

But Student, Lohr and the rest saw it differently, as did Hitler, for although he recognized the importance of Malta, he was soon persuaded that Crete, being close to and part of Greece, posed a greater threat to his southern empire. Practically all the British and Commonwealth plus some Greek troops had been evacuated there, but how many and how well they were organized was not discovered by German intelligence and never suspected by the commanders, an omission that would be paid for with the lives of the German airborne troops.

On 25 April Hitler issued his orders for Operation "Mercury", having given the proviso that only one parachute and one airborne division should be used. This suited General Student perfectly, for he was convinced that his men could do the job without further assistance; but had he been aware of the enormous difficulties facing the troops even before they began the operation or indeed what was to come on Crete itself he would certainly have blanched.

The airborne corps had twenty days to prepare itself for action; the units were alerted at their home bases in Germany and told to proceed with all speed to launching sites in southern Greece. The sorry tale of their journeyings is a saga in itself and if such details had been known to the British it might have coloured their growing belief in German thoroughness and military invincibility.

The whole of XIth Air Corps had to be shifted from Germany to southern Greece under the cover name of "Flying Dutchman" which seems singularly inappropriate as the movement consisted of an enormously long winding column of assorted transport which became more and more snarled up the farther south it progressed. Some 4000 vehicles tried to thread their way through the difficult and at times almost impassable roads of the Macedonian mountains. For a start one of the parachute assault regiments found it was 220 trucks short, which meant that most had to travel by train. It took them several days to reach Rumania, where enough vehicles were scraped together for the 1000-mile drive to Athens. During this time those airborne units travelling by road were held up three whole days in the mountains because the 2nd Panzer Division had priority in the narrow passes and was urgently needed to join the build-up for Barbarossa.

The 22nd Air-Landing Division also reached Rumania after being held up in the hopeless road system. The German Army Command had its own problems trying to cope with the enormous logistics involved in the attack on Russia, trying, in addition to much else, to mesh the allied forces into the invasion plan. Because of the great delays suffered, the 5th Mountain Division under General Ringel was called upon to take over the role of 22nd Division, still stuck fast in Rumania. This should not have posed any great problem, for any well-trained infantry force was capable of stepping in and out of a fleet of transport planes. Even so, the men of Ringel's mountain force had never set foot in planes before and certainly not been set down in the middle of an enemy.

"Mercury" would involve all of our witnesses, and provide them with a scarring experience. Heinrich Pabst was in one of the advance parties:

"I tried to make the journey a little easier, but even with good transport there was nothing we could do about the road system which grew worse as we progressed. When we arrived in Greece we were rather demoralized, but as an officer it was my job to inspire the men, and this I tried to do."

Karl Baumer had thought his unit might be transferred to Africa:

"Instead we motored down into Greece in an interminable journey and eventually emerged in airfields near Athens. There we were told that the beaten British troops were setting up a base in Crete and this was a danger to Germany; so we, the élite, would go down to rout them out and put a stop to it!"

The ex-Army soldier Karl Pickert mentions that after reorganization and more training his hopes of a quiet war were dashed:

"I was to be put into the firing line after all. We went down through the Balkans and in a short time were ready to jump on Crete. We had very little knowledge of the island or its location, being ignorant, so we were well surprised when shown the maps and discovered what kind of place it was. Someone had a few photographs, but apart from that our orders were simply to go in fast and get the job done double quick! We were told that there was a rather disorganized collection of Allied troops who had just taken a beating in Greece and would be no match for the German airborne. Well, I was as confident as the rest but many of us had not seen a shot fired and although there were veterans of the Dutch thing they said little."

Karel Weise:

"We were sent down through Greece in a long and tiresome journey which frayed my nerves. There we were told that the island of Crete had to be conquered as it was now a British bastion and intolerable off the coast of German-occupied Greece. It seemed a very big gamble and nothing like it had ever been tried before."

Kurt Seiler would be one of the first to land on Crete in a glider:

"We were alerted and had a terrible long journey through the Balkans into Greece and a field near Athens. There our Ju's and gliders were made ready and we received a briefing. We were to crash-land on the island of Crete and help to nullify the AA defences and help capture the airfield at Maleme. We were also told this: the British and Empire forces were beaten and resting on the island and were second-rate as far as we were concerned. We might have some fighting to do, but it would all be over in a day or two. That was exactly what our commanders expected, and in this I include Student himself."

Konrad Seibert had this recollection of those days:

"Our useless Italian allies were becoming more and more involved....We were alerted and told to pack everything into trucks as we were leaving Germany. It was supposed to be secret, but soon after we started off everyone knew we were going to Greece. It was all a grand adventure which we enjoyed from the travel point of view, but terribly slow, with many halts on the way. The roads got worse and worse and I felt we could go faster on foot. We crossed the border into Rumania and then into Greece and finally reached a camp outside Athens which we could see clearly. At once we were told that the great event had come. The British had been driven out of Greece into Crete, a large island essential to Germany's security — and we would take it! Just like that. It was an operation unparalleled in military history, and we wondered if it would go as planned. Some officers came round with large maps and someone built a model, but it was rather crude."

Karel Weise:

"The airfield nearby was packed with Ju's which sent huge clouds of yellow dust flying into the sky. It was all very exciting but rather worrying as we had no idea how it would turn out. We had no special equipment at all, only the same we had used in Germany; but a few men had developed camouflage clothing and this was to become general use later on. We moved into the dust laden airfields which were quite unsuitable for our Ju's and everyone cursed our luck."

Karl Pickert:

"When the great day came for my baptism of fire it proved a terrible, chaotic fiasco, the like of which we had never seen or expected. The airfields were totally unsuitable and full of choking dust. The aircrews and staffs were having a terrible time to sort out the muddle and we were amazed that German efficiency could be so low. It was all a great improvisation, for there were no proper airfields to operate from. I felt in despair that we could survive on that dreaded field and was almost relieved when we finally got into the air."

Kurt Seiler:

"The airfields were hopeless and we had a big job trying to sort out the chaos caused by the climatic conditions. But after a few days we were ready to go. Our aim was to subjugate the island of Crete as a British base by occupation."

All this is confirmed by Heinrich Pabst who adds that the German troops were assured they would not have to remain on the island.

Despite all the difficulties, the last of the airborne troops reached their Greek base by 14 May. By an oversight, during the rail transport arrangements the 1st and 2nd Assault companies were overlooked and were obliged to make their way as best they could by road from Hildesheim in north Germany.

Yet the Germans' problems in preparing for Mercury were only half over, for the huge air transport fleet needed to be moved into position, and in this lies one statistic which throws even more light on the great cost of Hitler's southern diversion.

The special transport plane group comprised some 500 Junkers 52s, so obviously the fleet had been brought up to strength following its heavy losses the year before. However, many of the aircraft had already been engaged in supply operations in the Balkans and needed servicing. As a result the whole force of aircraft had to be flown back to bases in Germany and Austria on 1 May, and such was the urgency of the task that all other aircraft maintenance work had to be dropped. The huge job took two weeks, and included complete overhauls and engine changes for some of the planes, so that by 15 May 493 Ju's could be flown south again to the clutch of dust-laden airfields around Athens.

But this was only one segment of the problem. The next hump to be negotiated was the airfields themselves, for the only modern bases available were already occupied by the bombers of Richthofen's 8th Air Corps. What, then, remained?

"Nothing but deserts!" complained one air transport commander. He was referring to the totally inadequate fields allocated them which were little more than a few sandy wastes. The heavily laden three-motor Junkers would, he reckoned, sink up to their axles in the soft ground. The unfortunate officer had been allocated a field already ploughed up by the Army — "to make it more level"! The nature of the landscape was such that in rehearsal the aircrews discovered that dust clouds were thrown up to a height of 3000 ft, blotting out the sun. Each take-off meant a wait of over fifteen minutes before the next plane could get airborne. The field looked as if a huge sandstorm were in progress. Every airstrip allocated the air transport squadrons was the same, and chaos resulted. How could an operational schedule be kept to in such circumstances?

Yet even this bugbear was of lesser intensity or urgency than the fuel situation. There were 1479 thirsty aero engines to satisfy in the transport fleet. Each plane would need to make three sorties to transport the whole airborne force to Crete — about 650,000 gallons of petrol. The logistics were staggering: all this effort just to ferry two divisions. The basis of the problem lay in the poor capacity of the Ju 52, which although so affectionately regarded by its users (Auntie Ju), it was no more than a rather antiquated airliner from a past era, and not comparable for example with the Douglas DC3 Dakota.

A tanker carrying the aviation fuel was despatched from Italy, but by 17 May, three days before the planned operation, not one can of petrol had been delivered to the servicing crews on the Greek bases. This was due to the fluke destruction of the bridge over the Corinth Canal. It lay in the waterway and blocked the tanker's passage. Divers had to be rushed from Germany to clear the canal so the petrol could get through. All this was favourable to the Allied forces on Crete; it gave them more time to prepare.

Hitler's directive had stipulated that the attack on the island should be made no later than mid-May, but the various difficulties had already postponed the operation until 18 May, and because of the fuel situation it was now put off for a further two days. The tanker finally arrived at Piraeus and the transfer of its precious cargo began in feverish haste. Yet even by midnight on 19-20 May the Junkers transports were still not all tanked up and the airborne troops themselves were called in to assist in the task. For many of them it would be one of the last jobs they would do in this world.

There was one final problem to be overcome before the planes could take off: trucks went around the airstrips spraying water over the ground in an attempt to lay the dust, but even then fortune did not seem to favour the Germans, for even as the pilots began taxiing and assembling their fully-laden planes at one end of the fields ready for take-off the wind changed 180 degrees and the whole procedure had to be restarted. All the transports taxied back to the other end of the airstrips, raising huge dust clouds and bringing more chaos. But at last the first planes began rolling at 0430 hrs and were soon vanishing into the dusty fog of the pre-dawn darkness; 53 Ju's towing their gliders containing the 1st Battalion of the Assault Regiment.

"On the morning of our take-off it was like a thick fog, but yellow, and when we finally got off large clouds blotted out all sight of our tow plane. It was as if we were suspended in yellow murk. Only when the rumbling ceased did we realize that we were in the air. And finally we escaped into clear sky and it was a great relief."

That was Kurt Seiler's impression of the fateful morning as he and his comrades sailed off for what was to be the hell of Crete, well in front of the rest of the participants named here. The men were demoralized even before they started out, as Karl Baumer recalls:

"It was a terrible place to be. The heat and dust got into our clothes, eyes and mouths and it seemed as if we would never get into the air."

Konrad Seibert recalls marching out to the waiting planes in choking dust clouds wondering how the Junkers would ever get off the ground. "It was an experience I would never want to go through again. We sat in the plane for a long time in terrible heat, until at last we were moving off, and it was all a shambles, with very little order."

Karl Pickert says that getting into the air only led to more confusion, with the planes trying to form some sort of formation but hampered by the clouds of yellow dust. The Junkers towing the glider-borne troops vanished over the Aegean Sea, heading due south, while the next wave of planes carrying 5000 paratroops attempted to form up over Greece. This first wave was to hold their ground until reinforced that afternoon. This forming-up process took a whole hour and used up much precious fuel. The air crews had no idea if more fuel would be waiting for them on their return to pick up the second wave.

What were the thoughts of these young German airborne soldiers as they winged their way south towards their objective? Certainly, a few like Heinrich Pabst had their doubts, but all had been assured that they faced only a few thousand ill-equipped and demoralized British and Empire troops who had only just escaped a gruelling campaign and retreat in Greece. They would be, admittedly, the first British and Commonwealth troops the German airborne had come up against, discounting the comparatively small action at Corinth. For once the *Luftwaffe* had failed to gain sufficient aerial data through its reconnaissance flights on which the airborne chiefs could base any clear assessment. Good intelligence is the one essential precursor to any attack, and this was the one thing the Germans lacked. The air photographs did not disclose the cleverly hidden, camouflaged positions of the New Zealanders and other Allied infantry, the rifle and machine-gun pits, or even the handful of Matilda tanks which were waiting for the expected assault. All the German commanders were certain of were the obvious AA and artillery positions which were easily discernible in the pictures. Obvious too were the vital airfields, and one of these — Maleme — had to be captured on the first day so that the planes could bring in the 5th Mountain Division.

German Intelligence under Admiral Canaris had also failed. Given time they might have produced something, but this is doubtful, for the Cretan population was as a whole violently anti-German. They were part of the Greek nation which had been attacked first by Italy and then Germany; their men had fought with the Greek Army and many were missing on the mainland.* It would have been well nigh impossible to infiltrate agents into such a close-knit community, and despite the *Luftwaffe* the Royal Navy still enjoyed considerable command of the sea and patrolled the slot between Crete and the mainland.

The aerial photographs had also failed to disclose the horrendous nature of the terrain on Crete, which for the most part consists of small, rocky hills quite unsuitable for the landing of airborne troops. In short, this was the worst of several failures of intelligence the German airborne force suffered, as mentioned by one survivor earlier, and it was to cost them dear.

By great contrast, British Intelligence knew perfectly well what the enemy were planning and the nature of the threat. This has been made even plainer by the most recent disclosures. Apart from the usual spies and radio monitoring, the "Ultra" set-up had procured its own bonanza of information and this had been passed to the Allied commander on the island, the tough New Zealand veteran, General Freyberg. But Freyberg was bound by the absolute need to preserve the Ultra secret, so instead of

---

* The Greek King had called on the population to rise up against the invaders.

concentrating all or most of his forces around the three airfields he left many troops stationed in packets around the island. To do otherwise it was felt might have tipped his hand to the Germans. With hindsight this seems very unlikely, but at the time no chances were being taken, so in a sense General Freyberg was depressingly aware that in preserving his intelligence source he was also quite likely throwing away his chance of victory. To put it another way, the enormous advantage of advance intelligence available to the British was thrown away.

In fact, only a political and military idiot could have overlooked the fact that, having conquered Greece, the Germans' next step had to be the taking of Crete. In this both Hitler and the British concurred, but in any case the *Luftwaffe* had begun an aerial blitz on 14 May, though on the face of it this could easily have been interpreted as an attempt to neutralize the British forces and their installations without any thought of a landing on the island. Relays of Dorniers, Heinkels, Stukas and Junkers 88s roared and howled over the island, paying special attention to the flak posts around Suda Bay and the airfields, as well as bombing any ships in the harbour, which was a Royal Navy and supply ship anchorage. These bombing raids were interspersed with attacks by Messerschmitt 109s and 110s who raked the hills with fire in the hope of knocking out possible Allied troop positions, but so well hidden were these that much of the enemy's effort was wasted. But it was the incessant air attacks which most told against the Allies on Crete.

As Winston Churchill was to remark later in his memoirs, there were unique aspects of the contest. Nothing like it had been seen before; it was the largest use of airborne troops to date. Churchill looked on them as the 'flame of the Hitler Youth movement' the 'ardent embodiment of the Teutonic spirit of revenge for the defeat of 1918.'* As he saw it, the German paratroops were 'valiant, devoted, and ready to lay down their lives on the altar of German glory and world power.' For all his greatness, Churchill erred at times; it is very doubtful if any of the Germans involved quite saw it that way; they were simply young men caught up in a war as soldiers, carrying out orders as all soldiers do, anxious to stay alive and, though believing in their country, were in the main certainly not the 'fanatical Nazis' so beloved of British propaganda. But Churchill was right in seeing the battle as an intense clash between

* *The Second World War*, Cassell, 1950

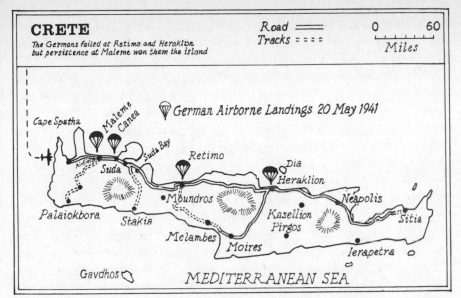

CRETE

The Germans failed at Retimo and Heraklion but persistence at Maleme won them the island

Road ====
Tracks = = = =

0   60

Miles

Cape Spatha

Maleme
Canea

Airfield

Suda Bay

Suda

Palaiokbora

Stakia

Moundros

Retimo

Dia

Heraklion

Neapolis

Sitia

Kasellion
Pirgos

Melambes

Moires

Ierapetra

Gavdhos

MEDITERRANEAN SEA

German Airborne Landings 20 May 1941

Germany's finest troops and the men of the British Empire, though one must remark that few if any troops can equal the élan and fighting spirit of parachute troops.

The German 8th Air Corps had available for its assault: 280 bombers, 150 Ju87 Stukas, 180 fighters, 40 reconnaissance planes, 100 gliders, and 530 Ju 52 transports, of which 493 actually operated.

The British, fully in the know and expecting the invasion, had already allocated a code-name for the battle: Crete was "Colorado" and the German attack was to be called "Scorcher". However, despite all its intelligence gathering capability, the British did not know the actual strength of the invading force, though believing that two to three divisions of airborne and Army troops could be involved. Over 30,000 Allied personnel had been evacuated from Greece to Crete, but the garrison was short of artillery, including flak, possessed few machine guns and had little transport. It also had nine worn-out "Infantry" tanks, Matildas armed with one small-calibre 2-pounder gun and one machine gun. The few thousand Greek soldiers on the island were under-armed and half-trained, and most useful in guarding the six thousand Italian prisoners, who also needed to be fed, as did the civilian population.

Of 27,000 tons of ammunition sent to the island in the first three weeks of May only 3000 tons had been landed, owing to *Luftwaffe* intervention, 3000 tons being lost. About 2000 men of the Mobile Naval Base Defence Organization were rushed to Crete, but over 3000 were retained in Egypt. These men brought with them one light and one heavy flak battery to defend Suda Bay.

By the end of April the Generals (Freyberg and his chief, the Middle East C-in-C, Wavell) were in agreement that the island could only be held with full support from the Royal Navy and RAF, while Churchill, in one of his frequent cables, suggested to them that the battle would present a fine opportunity to kill German parachute troops. The Prime Minister also assured the commanders that he was making extreme exertions to reinforce them by air. In fact, nothing could be done in this direction, at least, not in time. There were not enough planes in Egypt or Libya where a small German corps under General Rommel was pushing eastwards. The threat of invasion of Britain had long ceased, and it seemed to be common knowledge that a German attack on Russia was imminent, yet many hundreds of fighter planes and their pilots remained in Britain, most of them inactive, when they were desperately needed in the Mediterranean theatre, and most especially on Crete. The actual number of planes available on the island early in May was: twelve Blenheims (possibly including Mk1s), six Hurricanes, twelve obsolete Gladiators, and six Fulmars and 'Brewsters' of the Fleet Air Arm. (The reference to 'Brewsters' was Churchill's; he may have meant Brewster Buffaloes, a totally inadequate American aircraft.) Of this paltry few, only half were serviceable, and the only way to reinforce them was either by shipping them in pieces for reassembly in the usual manner at a staging post in West Africa, and then flying them to Egypt, where they needed to be transported by sea again as they had not the range to reach Crete, or else simply send them on the top deck of an aircraft carrier. (They could not be stowed below as they had no folding wings.) Either method would take weeks to organize and execute. In the event the few usable planes on Crete were flown out to Egypt on 19 May. This left the defenders on the ground feeling very helpless against the ceaseless enemy air attacks, and also no doubt bitter that once again the RAF had let them down.

Although some German historians have quoted the Allied garrison on Crete at 42,000, this is almost certainly an exaggeration, and even the British figure of 33,000 gives a wrong impression. A number of 'odds and sods' had found their way to Crete, among them a few characters such as the humorous amateur soldiers so marvellously portrayed in Evelyn Waugh's famous novel *Officers* *and Gentlemen**. For a different view of the Crete battle this book can hardly be bettered, spiced as it is not only with humour and eccentric gentlemen officers but a heavy leavening of fact, based on the author's own experiences with the commandos who landed on the island. But one line says much: 'No air cover. The RAF have packed up in Crete.' He is, of course, quite wrong. The few airmen there had barely escaped from Greece and really had nothing to put in the air. These were among the non-combatant personnel who could do little but take cover when the fun started.

Heraklion was defended by two British and three Greek battalions; at Retimo was the 19th Australian Brigade with six Greek battalions; at Maleme the New Zealand Brigade, with a second brigade further east. These were the main defence forces available on Crete. There were also a few scratch units and a commando group was landed later; Churchill quoted an active force of 28,000 men.

On 5 May, despite the almost total lack of air support, General Freyberg cabled Churchill that he could not understand 'nervousness'; he was 'not in the least anxious about an airborne attack'; he felt he could cope adequately with the men he had. However, at that stage Freyberg was still counting on total naval help and a few more fighter planes. All he received from Wavell was six more 'I' tanks, 16 light tanks, 18 AA guns, 17 field guns and one battalion. But further reinforcements were proposed, possibly including the Polish Brigade from Egypt, though landing any forces was proving difficult owing to the *Luftwaffe* supremacy. Only at nightfall could men and supplies be smuggled in. The Poles remained in Africa.

The British problem was of course that no long-term preparation had been made for such eventualities, the necessary men and equipment were not available in the Middle East, and organizing and despatching them by sea was too slow. When emergencies cropped up commanders were obliged to make do with what they had. The German intervention in Libya and a revolt in Iraq had further stretched Britain's resources to capacity.

But in mid-May General Wavell himself visited Crete to inspect the state of preparation, afterwards wiring Churchill that he had been greatly impressed and encouraged by all he saw; the troops were fit and in high morale and had extended their defences,

* Chapman & Hall, 1955.

including the laying of wire; there were now 45 pieces of artillery in position with adequate ammunition; two tanks had been allocated to each airfield and more Bren carriers and transport had been successfully landed, as well as the 2nd Battalion of the Leicestershire Regiment.

The German plan called for a four-pronged attack on four locations on the first day, the paratroops being divided into three detachments: Group West would capture Maleme airfield and the high ground behind it (Hill 107) from where they would be able to control the airfield. Group Centre would seize the administrative town of Canea, Suda Bay and Retimo airfield. To Group East was given the task of taking Heraklion and its airfield.

By 0700 hrs on the morning of 20 May the *Luftwaffe* bombardment had been in progress for one hour, its chief object to force the defenders to keep their heads down and into further demoralization. When the German fighters swept in again their pilots hoped that the clusters of tents dotting the hills contained Allied soldiers and shot them up, as well as anything that looked like encampments or troop positions. In fact, the garrison was on full alert and had been for days and in some cases – notably the New Zealanders – had actually been practising anti-airborne exercises. They were ready and waiting in well-concealed dugouts.

The first Junkers 52s droned over the sea in a southerly direction, having rendezvoused over the island of Kithira into one big but trailing formation from the various bases. When the leaders reached a point due west of Crete they turned their planes eastwards into the rising sun, heading straight for the island. The sky over Crete was now clear of German warplanes, and there were no Allied fighters left to intercept the transports which would have proved sitting-duck targets.

Seiler:

"The flight was quite smooth, and at last our pilot warned us to be ready as we were approaching the island. Then the rope parted and we heard the most infernal din of firing and a great shock hit us! We had no idea that this would happen. There were bullets actually zipping through our glider in the few seconds it took us to get down. Of course we could see nothing at all from our cramped positions, and then we hit the ground in a terrible crash and the pilot was killed. We fell out of the wreck and were enveloped in shooting; there were bullets flying at us from all directions and two men were hit at once, and their cries soon ceased. We could not move, but there were bushes near us so we decided to get to cover. But as we rushed out from our position more fire came in and two more men went down, never to rise again. I myself felt a bullet or splinter hit my left ankle and I fell down into the bushes. I found I was completely alone, with the shooting now sporadic. Then I heard the sound of our planes attacking and wondered what to do next. I drank my water and felt terribly exposed and helpless, and I lay like that all morning."

This was to be a typical welcome experienced by many soldiers of the glider-borne *Sturmregiment* on that fine morning.

The first glider had been released at 0710 hrs and had soon crashed down onto the rough ground beside Hill 107. Its passengers comprised Major Walter Koch and the battalion staff of the 1st Assault Regiment, but things went wrong at once, for the gliders had been released too high over the sea. The rising sun was in the eyes of the pilots, smoke from bombing also impairing their vision. The objective for most of them was a dried-up river bed just beyond Maleme airfield, but by the time the glider pilots had spotted their target they were obliged to make steep, twisting descents, and began to lose their combat cohesion. In other words they became separated, and this error was at once compounded by the many small hills which abounded in the area, the pilots simply losing sight of each other, landing their troops in penny packets, scattered among the rocky mounds and out of touch with each other.

As Kurt Seiler has described, from within the cramped fuselage of the glider it was almost impossible for the troops to see anything, so when they scrambled out − those who were still able to − and into the murderous fire directed at them, they were surprised to find themselves not on flat terrain but shut in by rocks and hillocks, interspersed with a few small trees and bushes. They flung themselves down in the scrub as a hail of bullets swept around them, those that missed their human targets striking rocks and stones and sending damaging splinters flying which also caused wounds. The great problem for the German troops was to know exactly where the fire was coming from. Until they identified their targets they could not shoot back.

But these men were made of stern stuff. Major Koch rallied enough men to try and rush the tented camp of the New Zealanders on nearby Hill 107, dodging into and around the many bomb craters. But the charging Germans found no enemy to assault. So Koch urged his men on up the hill, his intention being to set up a commanding position near or on its crest from which he could direct the battle for the airfield. They had barely begun moving again when a fresh deluge of bullets cut them down. Koch was hit in the head, and others killed or wounded.

The hillside before them was terraced, like many on Crete, and the New Zealanders had simply burrowed into the shelved ground, adding camouflage, waiting for the Germans to arrive.

Yet elsewhere things went according to plan. The 3rd Company of the Assault Regiment landed smack in the river bed and as soon as the troops cleared their gliders they opened fire on the Allied AA posts on the nearby airfield. Two sections of airborne attacked the flak posts to the east and west and put the crews out of action or took them prisoner.

At this point, with many of the glider troops lying dead or wounded, the first Junkers carrying the parachute troops droned in over the island. Flying at 400 ft, disgorging their loads, the crews were pleasantly surprised that not one flak gun had fired at them. At least this is how one historian has described it, but the German contributors to this account found things otherwise, which probably points to the fact that they were in the second wave, though this is uncertain. Konrad Seibert:

"In due course we were told to get ready as the objective was near. The plane wobbled its wings and we knew that this was the signal to stand up and hook up. We were very nervous, but even so confident that we could do our job. We had faith in our officers and NCOs who were hard men we could rely on.

"At last we came over the island and I could see the flak bursting. I had never seen any before, and as the first men went out I could quite distinctly see the tracer bullets coming up at us. This was very different to our experience over Holland, but we had no time to dwell on this as we went out of the plane and fell towards the brown earth below. It seemed an age before we hit the ground and I will never forget those moments. There were bullets zipping past me and some of my comrades were hit coming down and cried out horribly. It was very frightening to be hanging there and be unable to do anything but wait for the earth to come up or be killed. There was a great deal of noise going on, the planes coming over and the guns firing below, and I also heard Stukas waiting to come down to assist us. In those seconds I did wonder if any of us would be alive when we hit the ground.

"At last I was down. I lay absolutely still, hardly daring to raise

my head as all the fire was erupting around us. I could hear
shooting and even whistles blowing and more of our Ju's coming
over. Then Messerschmitts came over, strafing the English
positions which I could not see, but there were bullets and shells
flying everywhere, and it felt as if they were all directed at us. At
last I turned my head and saw a few of my comrades, and after a
lot of wriggling managed to join them without being hit. We were
at a loss as our officers and NCOs were missing and could only
have been killed or wounded. We were near the airfield at
Maleme and knew that our task was to secure it, but we had too
few men to do the job. It was a nightmare situation, heat and
thirst, and our small rations soon gave out. We had not been able
to recover all our weapons and in fact only had a few rifles
between us."

Karl Pickert never forgot the bright morning sunshine as they
flew over the sea towards Crete. His officer and NCO were
confident, but he felt as ignorant as the rest concerning the kind
of reception awaiting them:

"In a few moments we were at the door and jumping and at
once realized that we were in for a bad time. As I came out of the
plane I saw many flashes on the ground among the hills, near the
harbour, in fact all over the brown landscape. Men were calling,
shouting and crying out in pain, and I was quite terrified. I tried to
hunch myself up to make a smaller target. I even tried to make my
'chute collapse a little to get down faster. It seemed a very long
while but in reality was only about twenty seconds, and by the
time I landed I could not understand why I had not been hit, for
shells and bullets were flying all around us. It was terrible. For
once I forgot about wondering how I ever became a paratrooper, I
was too busy trying to stay alive.

"I got out of my harness in an inferno of noise and ran away to
a little hollow where some of our lads were hiding. We had no
chance to recover our weapons, and that was one of the big
mistakes of that battle. All we had were a few useless pistols. We
had one NCO with us and he had no idea what was happening or
what to do next. Anyone who raised a head above the hole was
shot at once. We were completely pinned down. We just lay there
wondering what had gone wrong. I know I cursed the fools who
had told us what an easy job we would have, and myself for not
bringing more water and rations. The heat seemed terrific, and I
wondered how we would last the day.

"Meanwhile more planes came over, and some went down in flames. Others just blew up and some tried to land on Maleme. We watched and waited and had not fired a shot when evening came and it got quieter."

Karel Weise also commented on the beauty of the morning as they flew over the sea.

"I remember wondering what my family were doing at home in Germany as we came near the island and got ready to jump. I was a little nervous as we all were, but our commanders had assured us that the enemy were disorganized and we would win.

"As soon as we came into our drop we knew that things were not quite as expected. There was a lot of flak and one plane caught fire near us. The men jumped out and the Ju went down in the mountains. Then we were out of the plane and the noise coming up was terrific. Lots of lines of tracer bullets came from all directions, and I felt something hit my right leg and I cried out in pain. Other friends near me were hit and killed or wounded. We got down and went to ground in great fear of our lives. I had never been in such a fierce battle, and neither had my comrades. We could not raise our heads and only a few had managed to recover some weapons. I tried to rally some comrades to me, but the fire was so intense it was impossible for them to move. So I rushed to them and found that my leg wound prevented me from running. I fell to the ground and crawled the rest of the way.

"This was no good, I decided. We were not doing anything and making no progress. Heavy bombing and strafing by our planes was a hindrance as they could not really tell friend from foe. We managed to hold on for hours until it was dark, and that was the worst day of my life."

Karl Baumer was by then a Sergeant in command of a planeload of men, and recalls coming in over the sea in brilliant sunshine, the men in good spirits until the moment of jumping when all of a sudden a hail of flak came up at them.

"One of the plane's engines was hit and caught fire, but we all got out double quick, our hearts racing and senses reeling as all those tracers came up at us. I felt we were in a terrible trap and it took an age to get down in all the noise and death around me. I fell into a hole and thanked God, otherwise the bullets would have clipped me up. I could hear many cries of men being hit, and wondered how we could ever have got into such a mess. There was no question of moving, even to help the wounded. I tried, and a bullet grazed my helmet. I was stuck — a platoon leader without my men. This is how it went; men were being killed all around and I just had to lay there until darkness came."

The officer Heinrich Pabst had his doubts as to the success of the operation, but these he kept to himself, and when they approached the island hoped that all would go well:

"Our gliders had already gone before and we wondered how they had fared. When we jumped it was into the very great shock of multiple flak and infantry defensive fire and many men including some of my own never reached the ground alive. There was a veritable storm of fire, with planes burning and crashing and the cries of men in pain as they dropped around me. The noise was infernal.

"I managed to land intact and my first thought was to get some men together and try to attack the flak defences. But as I got out of my harness and made to rally my men I was struck by a bullet in my right arm and collapsed in pain. I tried to bandage it though the wound was not serious, but this was difficult. I could see that we were surrounded by machine-gun and rifle fire as the enemy tried to wipe us out. And they were succeeding. The shock to our morale was very great. Paras are useless when split into small parties. I tried to crawl away into better cover and succeeded in drawing more fire, but eventually I was in a little dip in the ground from where I could just see a few heads of other paras.

"At this time our Ju's were still coming over and paras were coming down nearby, but many were never to stand on their feet again. I could see that without a drastic change in the situation we would be annihilated. Then waves of Me's came over, strafing the enemy and I'm afraid us too. It seemed hopeless. All I could think of was to hold on until help came, or darkness when we could get together some men and make for the nearest hill.

"Then, as the day wore on I found that I was still losing blood. I had not succeeded in helping my wound. So I resolved that whatever happened I would reach some of my men, so after a pause to collect my wits I jumped up and ran and dodged across the terrible ground and managed to reach a dip where several of our men were huddled. The bullets had failed to catch me and I was still alive. A Sergeant made a good job of bandaging my wound, and then I assessed the situation. I had six men including myself, two of whom were wounded. We had about four rifles and pistols, so I decided that when darkness came we would get off that accursed ground and make for the hills, but being very careful as the enemy seemed to be everywhere."

Those aircrews who had escaped the flak flew back to Greece to report that the defences appeared to be cowed, which was very far from the case. But there had been some success on the ground, for some at least of the flak guns at Maleme airfield had been captured by men of the 3rd Company of the Assault Regiment and to some observers in the planes it gave the impression of a walkover. But as soon as the 3rd Company moved onto the airfield itself they were pinned down by machine-gun fire; neither could they make contact with Major Koch or his staff who were in any case lying dead or wounded or otherwise pinned down on Hill 107. Despite all this, hundreds of paratroops had now landed on both sides of the airfield and comprised the rest of General Meindl's Assault Regiment, their urgent assignment to secure the airfield in readiness for the arrival of the air-landing troops in the transports.

The 3rd Battalion of the Assault Regiment had arrived at about 0720 hrs, this wave being dropped from 53 transports, the Junkers pilots dropping the troops slightly further inland so that they would not be blown into the sea by the wind. In fact their exact drop zone was the beach, but the parachutists began floating in scattered fashion over the hills further inland. The aircraft pilots and the paratroopers had almost certainly believed that their drop would be trouble-free, but any such optimism was shattered as soon as the planes reached the island. A storm of small-calibre defensive fire blasted up at the aircraft from the many gun pits dug into the hillsides. The paras floated down into a hornet's nest that spelt death for many of them. As one record has put it: "The unit took such heavy losses that it was no longer combat effective."

Many of the soldiers were killed or mortally wounded as they swung helplessly downwards, gazing below them in horror at the New Zealand and Greek troops who were enjoying an easy pigeon shoot, picking their targets and knocking them off with rifles and machine guns. Many were wounded and then permanently disabled when they struck trees or rocks on landing. Those few that survived were pinned to the ground by a curtain of fire, unable to reach their weapon containers and virtually helpless. All the battalion officers were killed or severely wounded, the survivors held together by NCOs in small groups, clinging to the rocks and heat-baked soil, still clad in the same outfits they had worn at Narvik and the Netherlands a year before, running out of water and ammunition, desperately hoping they would still be alive by nightfall. When the merciful darkness finally came the survivors of 9th Company were able to make a move: led by resolute NCOs, they managed to infiltrate or fight their way through the enemy lines into the Tavronitis valley and some relief. Other parties of paratroops stayed where they were, in an increasingly desperate state, until they were relieved after two or three days.

Of the 3rd Battalion's 600 men, nearly 400, including their commander, Major Schuber, were killed.

The 3rd Parachute Regiment was dropped on the plain south-west of Canea, but attacks on the New Zealand posts were not all successful, so the assault on Suda Bay failed completely. The Regiment's 3rd Battalion was dropped right into the laps of the enemy and cut to pieces. The other two battalions suffered less, but were still too weak to push on to Canea, the administrative capital of the island. The town had been the target of Group Centre, led by Lt-General Wilhelm Sussman, but an accident had killed him and several of his staff. After taking off from their base near Athens their glider had suffered a near-miss by a Heinkel 111 which had so disturbed the fragile craft's equilibrium that it had reared up and disintegrated, the remains and the occupants crashing down on the island of Algina. They had been part of the glider force which had been dispersed by heavy fire and failed in their task.

For whatever reason, some New Zealand dugouts west of Maleme remained unoccupied, and it was there, just outside the Tavronitis valley, that the 2nd and 4th Battalions of the Assault Regiment were dropped and achieved some success. The valley was spanned by a bridge on the east-west coast road and this was captured by troops landed from nine gliders that crashed down at 0730. Despite the death of their leader, Major Braun, the Germans seized the bridge under heavy fire and removed the demolition charges. The Assault Regiment commander, Major-General Meindl, now gathered together sufficient men to make an advance on the airfield from the west, but progress was slow because of the machine guns firing down on them from Hill 107. Meindl's chief concern was to establish contact with Major Koch's group on this hill. So far he had been unable to do so, but he decided to try some kind of visual contact. He raised an arm holding a signal flag, but was immediately hit in the hand by a New Zealand sharpshooter, and then collapsed, hit by a burst of machine-gun fire. Yet he survived to direct an attack on the airfield from the front and south, his troops gaining ground yard by yard; but on the western side they could make no progress.

Five more gliders landed near a gun battery and became involved in hand-to-hand combat with 180 British troops; the 50 Germans rushed and overcame the position, but in a fourth assault were driven back from the British command radar station sited one hundred yards further on.

One of the best known German paratroop commanders was Baron Captain Friedrich-August von der Heydte, whose book on the Crete battle was published after the war, with its scholarly title *Daedalus Returns*. A handful of troops from three gliders had landed in Canea itself and attempted to attack the AA positions there, but were pinned down by fire. Their appeals for help over a portable radio brought a response from Heydte, who with his men of the 1st Battalion, 3rd Parachute Regiment, sought to relieve them, but were stopped a thousand yards short of their objective by intense defensive fire and Matilda tanks. The 2nd and 3rd Battalions were likewise driven back, the latter unit, commanded by Major Heilmann, 'broken up almost to extinction'.

While the remnants of the shattered German airborne troops were fighting for their lives on Crete, back in Athens their commander, General Student, had little or no idea of the true situation, for all attempts at communication had failed. What *was* known did not seem too bad. Only seven of the 493 Junkers 52s had been lost, but when the mass returned to their bases they found the same terrible dust clouds which caused more chaos. Planes had been forced to use up hundreds of gallons of precious fuel circling the airfields for hours until visibility improved on the ground and they could attempt a landing, and when they did many collisions occurred, causing damage and blocking the airstrips.

The total lack of news from Crete resulted in General Student despatching an airfield servicing team in a Ju 52. Led by a Major, they were to survey and hopefully land on Maleme airfield and radio back its condition, ready for the airlift of mountain troops. When the plane arrived its occupants peered out and saw a swastika flag displayed on the western edge of the airfield, which, the Major mistakenly assumed, indicated the field was in German hands. He ordered the transport pilot to land, but as soon as the plane came in low it was met by heavy fire which riddled it with bullet holes. The Major and his team barely escaped to fly back to their Greek

15. British paras of the then Special Air Service demonstrate their elan on Press day.

16. **Below Left:** Men of the 1st Parachute Brigade disembark at Algiers to begin their unsatisfactory experiences in Tunisia.

17. **Below:** A para sergeant demonstrates his 'jump ready' state in 1944. The Bren gun valise will be dropped by quick release and suspended 20ft below him during the jump.

18. An early photo of impressed glider infantrymen in the comparitvely spacious interior of an Airspeed Horsa.

19. One of the elite glider pilot-infantrymen en route to Arnhem 17 September, 1944.

20. Glider troops of the Border Regiment astride a road prepare to repel a German counter-attack west of Arnhem town.

base and were able to give General Student some indication of the real situation on Crete.

About this time the German command centre in Athens received a faint signal from the troops at Canea that their attack had been repulsed with heavy losses. Consternation now gripped General Student and his staff. Obviously their plans had gone wrong, but exactly how bad was the situation on Crete? How had the other units fared? Student agonized all afternoon as no further word was received. There were no German ships near the island who might have gone in close to make a proper observation, while air reconnaissance was too fleeting and unreliable.

Then, at 1615 a comprehensive report came through. The two heavy, long-range radio transmitters landed in gliders by the first wave had been smashed and it took hours for an Oberleutnant to piece together some kind of working transmitter from the undamaged parts. But any relief felt at XIth Air Corps in Athens was soon dispelled by the news received. The Assault Regiment commander was seriously wounded and German attacks were held up everywhere by strong enemy forces, including 'waves of tanks' on the airfield at Maleme.

The 1st and 2nd Parachute Regiments were to have been committed in the afternoon of the first day, 20 May, their objectives the other two airfields at Retimo and Heraklion, but owing to the disasters at Maleme, Student was now more inclined to reinforce at Maleme. This drastic change of plan would possibly add more confusion to a difficult situation and assist the enemy. If the German forces were concentrated at one end of the island it could prove easier to bottle them up. The Germans believed the Allies had some 42,000 troops on the island, quite enough to destroy an airborne force in need of relief within a very few days. The Royal Navy could assist in its destruction by offshore bombardment.

Meanwhile, even more difficulty faced the Germans, for the situation on the dust-clogged airstrips was chaotic. There had been no chance of despatching the second wave at 1300 hrs, even if Student had given the go-ahead. A mad dash to refuel the transports by hand in the swirling dust clouds and heat, compounded by colliding planes and men under increasing stress, persuaded the transport commander to try and obtain a postponement of take-off time until 1500 hrs. The same idea had been forced on the Corps staff, but when both sides tried to make contact the telephone lines appeared to be out of order.

Now, even greater confusion overtook the Germans. For, whatever the problems on the transport bases and the lack of news at HQ Athens, the fighter and bomber units on the airfields of 8th Air Corps were being prepared for the next round of blitz attacks on Crete which were scheduled to go in before the second wave of airborne troops took off at 1300. The air attacks were timed to end just as the first Junkers arrived off Crete, but nobody at Athens had thought of informing the 8th Air Corps commanders of the change of plan — at least, that appears to be the picture, unless of course a similar breakdown of communications had occurred through 'phone lines suddenly going out of order. Was it pure bad luck, sabotage, or just the bad Greek telephone system?

As a result of this latest error, Dorniers, Heinkels, Stukas and Messerschmitts began taking off again in the early afternoon, bound for the target areas of Retimo and Heraklion, their crews completely unaware that most of the transports had not even begun to take off. And when they did, owing to the renewed chaos on the ground, many Junkers pilots found themselves flying not in squadrons or even flights but singly or small packets and well strung out across the sea. Only some of the transports had managed to get away at the scheduled time, but most didn't; so that when the crews and occupants approached the island they failed to meet a single plane returning, as they should have done. Worse followed, for when the planes of this group reached their objective, briefed to drop on Heraklion as reserve troops, they found instead no sign of German troops below them and were met by heavy defensive fire.

The wave originally scheduled as a second sortie of 493 Ju's, which should have arrived in more or less one great formation to swamp the objectives with paratroops, in fact took three and a half hours to arrive. This meant that the paratroops were delivered in dribs and drabs, a fatal error and one which should have cost them the battle. As the paras floated down on Heraklion, at their most vulnerable and without arms, they were met by British tanks, Matildas, which, despite their inadequate anti-tank armament, were quite sufficient to annihilate the weak parachute infantry. The German troops had nothing to hand with which to penetrate the four-inch-thick frontal hide of the Matildas.

Three companies of the 2nd Battalion, 1st Parachute Regiment, were annihilated, and both the target airfields remained in British hands.

Yet, despite all the terror and slaughter that the German airborne suffered, the remaining troops held on and made such an impression on the defenders that General Freyberg was moved to record that his men were barely hanging on. Indeed, a report to his superiors now showed a marked lack of optimism, in great contrast to his earlier pronouncements.

In the circumstances few airborne troops of any nation could have survived the hell on Crete, yet by evening of the first day the Germans were able to chalk up some success against the defenders. Two sections of the Assault Regiment which had somehow survived all the New Zealand fire throughout the day on Hill 107 stormed the summit armed only with pistols and hand grenades and established themselves, even though, as the regimental physician reported afterwards, they were down to their last rounds. Had the New Zealanders and the few British tanks counter-attacked Hill 107 the Germans would have been wiped out or forced to surrender; but they didn't and by next morning the *Luftwaffe* swept in again, still entirely unopposed, to bomb and strafe the Allied troops around Maleme.

When the darkness came that first evening Kurt Seiler was at last able to raise his head:

"And when I did I saw New Zealand soldiers (as I later found out they were) searching the wrecks of our gliders and the bodies. I felt sick and afraid, and then one of the enemy soldiers saw me and ran over to me with his rifle and bayonet and demanded that I put my hands up. I was forced to give up my Schmeisser and all of my equipment and marched to their positions, and now I saw that the surrounding hills were full of rifle and machine-gun pits, and could see that we had been seriously misled.

"I sat down and they gave me a cup of tea which I was very glad to get, a few biscuits and a piece of bacon. Then I was taken to a dugout and questioned in very good German, but I said nothing, so they took me away to their HQ inland, where I was again questioned with no result. But my impression was that they already had the answers as they did not seem too worried when I told them nothing. Then I was obliged to sleep with my hands tied and guarded, and a few more Germans came in as prisoners and we had a chat. Our morale was not good but we still hoped to be rescued."

Konrad Seibert managed with a few surviving comrades to scout around after dark and collect up some rations and weapons from the dead:

"We felt our best chance was to move out of the area as in

daylight we would be pinned down again. If we could get on to one of the hills we could then see what was happening and be of some use; on the flat ground we were useless and completely at the mercy of enemy fire. By a very slow effort we managed to crawl towards the nearest hill and get round it. We could hear the New Zealanders not far away having their tea. But they did not see us or ignored us, so that by dawn we had managed to find a kind of arbor under some small trees where we dug a few holes."

Likewise, Karl Pickert and his comrades were resolved not to be caught in the open in daylight, so began moving out at nightfall, just a few inches at a time.

"We wanted to reach some point of cover and then decide on our next move. But we had not gone far when a voice challenged us in English. We lay absolutely still and then to my amazement one of our party called out 'Friend!' The Englishmen, or whatever he was, shouted again, and this bold fellow in our lot actually stood up with his hand waving. He had taken off his helmet, hoping not to be seen as German in the darkness. He then started walking towards the enemy sentry and we were all agog, wondering what would happen next. Then we heard a scuffle and a shot and we rushed forward and into a group of the enemy, but some were too sleepy and we captured them, along with rations of biscuits and water which we were very grateful for."

Pickert's group were amazed that the Allied dugout had been so close to them, but it was so well camouflaged that they had never suspected it. They decided to stay put for the night, taking turns to keep watch.

Karel Weise came to in darkness, to find his head bandaged and a comrade asking him if he could crawl:

"I found that I could, so three of us managed to crawl away into the darkness. It took hours to reach a gully and there we found some wounded paras but no rations or water. We were in a very bad situation and I thought that if we were not relieved by next day we would be captured or would even have to surrender in order to get help for the wounded."

The officer Heinrich Pabst led his men out of their hopeless position as soon as it was dark:

"One man stayed behind as he was too ill to move. We made very slow progress, but no one challenged us. But then we ran into some wire and had to divert to another route. At times we heard enemy soldiers talking and crawled on, hoping not to be seen. But then the worst happened, a machine gun opened fire. I yelled to my men to run, and we did, but two men were hit and we left them behind in a mad scramble for cover. There were now three of us including a Sergeant, who I knew well as a tough Berliner.

"We lay still for a while until we thought it safe to go on, and when we did we had a stroke of good fortune. We found one of our containers containing rifles and ammunition. We moved on quietly and by dawn had reached a small gully covered by trees."

Karl Baumer also waited until dark and then rolled over and over until he reached the wounded men who by then were dead. Rolling on, he encountered more paratroops including some of his own unit:

"We held a council of war. We could be caught again in daylight, so we had to escape that trap. I decided to lead the men towards our target, the airfield, where we might be able to kill off some of the many flak crews before more of our planes arrived next morning. We accordingly set out, down towards the field which was quite near us. It took a long time, for the enemy were very alert. We set up a little fire point near what we believed to be a flak post; from that position we hoped to open a devastating fire with our few rifles and one machine gun."

By the second day many of the German airborne troops around Maleme — those still capable of action, that is — were out of ammunition. But then a special flight of Junkers carrying ammunition zoomed in and tried to land on the airfield. Although he saw that the field was under artillery fire, the first pilot set his plane down on the beach, managing to brake to a halt just short of the rocks. The cases of ammunition were unloaded successfully and smuggled to the combat troops nearby.

General Student had decided during the night that the attack on Maleme had to be reinforced and the 5th Mountain Division flown in. He sent in the parachute General Ramcke to assume command in place of General Meindl; with fresh supplies of ammunition the parachutists attacked again and again. Then, at 1600 hrs the first Ju's carrying the 100th Regiment of the Mountain Division began to arrive and touch down on Maleme airfield from the west. The first plane to land was struck by artillery shells and caught fire, others were damaged or lost their axles; but more and more Junkers came in despite the Allied shellfire, the troops disgorging into a hail of bullets and shellbursts, but most racing away to seek cover around the field, or even among the wrecks of their own transports.

"Like the gates of hell," was how the Mountain Division's

Commander, General Ringel, described the scene at Maleme. One in three Junkers 52s was hit by Allied fire which blew off wings, engines, undercarriages, until a great park of wrecked planes littered the field. Eventually, a captured British tank was used to tow away the remains until one runway was cleared; the resulting dump contained eighty wrecked planes.

"When full daylight came the battle resumed," says Konrad Seibert, "with a lot of firing, and some Ju's came over and dropped parachutists, only some of whom got down alive. We knew that some glider troops had come down before us, but we had seen nothing of them. Our only hope was to join up with some of our comrades when we had eaten a little. We wanted to move out and around the hill in a rush. But we had not got very far when we were stopped by machine-gun fire and fell to the ground again. We had a Corporal with us and he demanded that we rush the gun, which we could see as an isolated post. We were frightened but felt obliged to try. So some of us wriggled around and then rushed straight at the machine-post, firing our weapons. Two men went down hit, but then we were upon them and the crew were killed by our fire. I had never been in close combat before, and the sight of the dead men was far from pretty.

"Then we all moved on, leaving one man dead and one wounded of our little party. Then we found another group of our paras so we had about 20 men under an officer who told us that things were very serious because the strength of the enemy had been completely underestimated. But we were paras and there was no question of defeat! This sounded very grand, but we could not see how we could proceed, as the enemy seemed to be all around us. But the officer was keen and insisted that we now split up into two parties and advance, wiping out any opposition! It seemed suicidal, but off we went. I remember I was chewing some British chocolate which was very good, but as we made our way round the same hill we saw some more of our men calling to us. They were wounded. As we went towards them all hell broke loose, and bullets were flying everywhere. I felt something hit my face and fell down. I had no idea if I had been hit by a bullet or a piece of stone. You see, the ground was covered in stones and small rocks, and every ricochet sent splinters flying. Our officer yelled at us to get on, to keep moving, so we jumped up and rushed towards the spot where we had seen our wounded − and only a few of us got there. I leapt forward and fell into a big hole with the wounded who were all in a bad way. I and two others seemed to be the only ones left of our party. I found later that several had survived, but the officer and NCO were dead.

"We helped the wounded as best we could, but we had no proper medical supplies and these lads really needed a doctor. The enemy fire continued around us and we felt helpless. The wounded seemed to be past aid. But we did not know that much heavy fighting had been going on elsewhere and that the enemy themselves were hard pressed. At one point we thought we heard tanks and many explosions, and then German planes came over again, fighters and bombers, and all hell erupted, with the flak and strafing. The heat was a big factor in driving down our morale, for we had run out of water, and could not survive without it. We were unfortunately pinned down without cover, with no trees or bushes near us. In fact, we had been far better off where we were. However, we were not giving up, and we drew lots to see who should go to try and find help. One of our comrades went off and that was the last we saw of him."

When the battle resumed that morning Karl Pickert realized that he and his comrades were with a batch of Allied prisoners but had no swastika flag to identify themselves when the German Me's came over again on their strafing runs, so they kept their heads down with the prisoners.

"Then more paratroops were dropped, and this time less of them were shot and some landed near us so we were able to link up with them and even get a machine gun, ammunition and rations from them. But when we tried to move on to contribute something to the battle we were fired on, so we were forced to stay still for another day and a half."

That morning of the second day of the battle Karel Weise was able to see the many Allied positions, which, although well camouflaged, were betrayed by the flashes of their weapons:

"But there was nothing we could do. We lay there and watched more Ju's and more paras dropping and some of the wounded died with us. We were helpless to do a thing for them."

Heinrich Pabst had managed to survive with his handful of troops:

"Our position was precarious, as we seemed to be in the middle of the enemy defence area. I set up a system of watch and sleep as we were exhausted, and by daylight tried to make out where we were and who were our nearest neighbours. I could see enemy activity and the battle resumed. More of our planes came and began bombing and strafing in a hell of flak fire, and then Ju's were dropping paratroops – obviously the situation on the island was unknown in Greece. We watched helplessly as the same performance was repeated. Many men were killed or wounded before they hit the ground. We were sickened and demoralized, but we would not give in, and decided to try and go out and make some contribution to the battle.

"I led our tiny party out of our position and towards an enemy post, where we could see that the one machine gun was not trained in our direction. At my signal we rushed forward, hurled grenades and killed the crew. In a moment we had scooped up the machine gun and some rations and fled back to our old position, where we ate some of the captured food and set up the machine gun. But the little skirmish had attracted attention and soon a patrol of the enemy came to our area. We waited until they were close and then fired at them, hitting several while the rest ran back. I felt we should try to move in case a heavier enemy attack came, so we at once rushed away to another hole – Crete was full of gullies and groves – and there we waited.

"There was a lot of shooting and more bombing by our planes. I felt we were making some contribution by being a thorn in the enemy's side, but apart from this there was little we could do. There were paratroops in our area but in isolated pockets; if only they could have been rallied together. Unfortunately, we were not close to the one or two larger bodies who had attempted to attack the airfields. Our own target had been Maleme, and it had been a disaster. However, some progress must have been made, as we saw enemy troops withdrawing to new positions and heard German voices nearer to us. We then saw Ju's coming in to the airfield, and although many were hit, others managed to land in the inferno, so we guessed the Mountain Division had arrived. We tried to make a reconnaissance, but it was too dangerous, so we waited until once again we saw enemy movement and opened fire, inflicting casualties.

"Then the Ju's came over again and the paratroops began dropping and the slaughter began again. We had a grandstand view of it all from the ground. It was sickening as many of the paras were coming in over our heads and were killed or wounded before hitting the ground. A few of those hit managed to reach us and we did our best to help those lads. Our problem was one of water and food, for we had long used up our own. The battle went on hour after hour.

"An officer reached us and insisted that we try to get at the airfield defences and neutralize them before the mountain troops arrived. But we were too few to do much good. Then the Ju's came and sure enough all hell broke loose once again, as we fired on all the enemy we could see who were firing on the landing planes which were mostly going up in flames and smoke. But some of the infantry were escaping from them and reaching cover under fire. My own feelings were that we would be lucky to win this battle. The odds were heavily against us.

"We managed to move on and find more weapons and supplies, but the area was littered with our dead. We attacked several enemy posts and neutralized them, though losing a few of our own men in the process, and by the second night felt that some progress had been made."

The battle continued on the western end of Crete, and in the early hours of sunrise on 22 May the combat planes of the 8th Air Corps took off again in droves, their crews now aware that the Royal Navy's warships were reported in the northern and western waters around the island. Reconnaissance aircraft had spotted the warships of the Mediterranean Fleet out of range of German bombers. The British sailors were determined to do all they could in the defence of Crete, but had a healthy respect for the *Luftwaffe*, especially the Stukas, and in daylight preferred to stay out of range. But when the ships ventured nearer the island they were caught by Stukas. The destroyer *Juno* was sunk on 21 May, and the cruisers *Ajax* and *Orion* slightly damaged. Next day the losses were more serious: the destroyer *Greyhound* was sent to the bottom, the cruiser *Naiad* seriously damaged, the old cruiser *Gloucester* was sunk, as was the cruiser *Fiji*; the battleship *Warspite* was seriously damaged, the battleship *Valiant* slightly so, and the flak cruiser *Carlisle* suffered light damage.

The Navy's first losses had occurred through the Germans trying to run a squadron of caiques — Greek sailing vessels fitted with motors — from the island of Milos to Crete, packed with heavy weapons, stores and troops. Halfway the ships were ordered to turn back, but then sent off again. The indecision cost them dear, for by midnight the little ships had still not reached their destination and were intercepted by the Royal Navy battle groups which at once swept among them, illuminating their targets with searchlights before closing to ram and shoot them up. Two of the German vessels caught fire, a steamer full of ammunition blew up, while the remaining seventeen or so tried to turn tail. After two and a half hours Rear-Admiral Glennie, the British commander, broke off the action so as to retire his ships to safer waters before daylight and the *Luftwaffe* came. The British reckoned that 4000 Germans had drowned. But by daylight ten of the German ships had regained the sanctuary of Milos, and after a big rescue operation it was found that only 297 men were missing.

But the new day brought out the German dive bombers and they scored the damage mentioned. The bulk of the British fleet now remained out of range to the south, but a smaller force of four cruisers and three destroyers were ordered to risk cruising into the northern slot off Crete in case the enemy tried again to reinforce by sea. In fact the Germans had indeed despatched another small fleet of supply ships and these too were spotted by the British warships, at which point the Germans turned back, defended by a solitary Italian torpedo boat, the *Sagittario*, which fired torpedos and laid a smoke screen to shield the Germans' withdrawal.

Then a group of Junkers 88s appeared overhead and were soon joined by some Dornier 17s in a sustained attack on the British ships which lasted three hours, the bombers returning to their bases to re-arm and re-fuel before setting out again after the enemy warships, which had by now used up much of their flak ammunition, calling on the main fleet for help. When the second British fleet came into range it too came under air attack, and the contest continued through much of 22 May. The Royal Navy ships, though running dangerously low on AA shells, were to remain in the vicinity around Crete for as long as possible. The Naval chiefs were determined not to abandon the embattled troops on the island.

But the German planes came over again and again, singly, in flights or larger formations, diving and releasing their bombs and flying home for more. The *Gloucester* had its whole deck set afire and the ship ran out of control in circles, until at 1600 hrs an explosion finally sank it. It was left to the Germans to rescue over 500 British sailors.

The *Fiji* had somehow survived continuous attacks, hour after hour, but finally succumbed while en route to Alexandria, struck by an extraordinary piece of bombing when a single Me 109 dropped a 500-lb bomb against the ship's side. Then a second 109 completed its destruction. That a mere two single-engined fighter-bombers should have been capable of sinking a cruiser must have been a salutary lesson for the British Admiralty.

That evening the British sent five modern destroyers including the *Kelly*, commanded by Lord Louis Mountbatten, to patrol the slot and search for British survivors. By dawn they were hurrying out of the area, but they had left it too late. 24 Stukas fell on them and the *Kelly* and *Kashmir* were sunk with the loss of 210 lives.

The commander of 8th Air Corps, General Freiherr Wolfram von Richthofen, who was a cousin of the late more famous First War air ace, recorded that the loss of six cruisers and three destroyers by the British had proved the great vulnerability of a fleet at sea within range of the *Luftwaffe*, given the right weather conditions. The actual Royal Navy losses were not quite as stated, but Richthofen was right in assessing that the British were 'out on a limb' so to speak, in these circumstances. Admiral Cunningham had made a great name for himself in bottling up the Italian fleet, but now he refused to risk his ships further and the fleet departed for its base at Alexandria.

Because of the norms of wartime propaganda and the constant need to bolster morale, neither the British nor German public were told the true state of affairs on Crete. The Germans at home heard of a continuous *Luftwaffe* blitz on the island and the gradual pushing back of the Empire troops, but naturally no hint of the slaughter of their young airborne élite. As for the British, although learning through the press and wireless of the seriousness of the situation at the very end of May, they had no idea that an evacuation had already begun on the night of 28-29th.

As usual, the reports by war correspondents were a mixture of truth and fiction. On Saturday 31 May the "Desert War" reporter Alan Moorehead's cabled despatch from Cairo was headlined:

"Decisive Battle Rages in Crete" followed by the ominous — "Freyberg's position very delicate, very serious":

"At this eleventh hour of the eleventh day of the Battle of Crete heavy fighting continues," and "little news is coming out of the island now, but it is stated that we still hold Candia (Heraklion), despite the German claim to have occupied it."

"Heavy raids" were being made on the enemy by Blenheim bombers, Moorehead claimed, though admitting that General Freyberg had been forced to "readjust" his lines because of new German reinforcements and incessant dive-bomber attacks. Our position, he wrote, "resembled the last days in Greece." But the Greek government (in exile) claimed that so far 7000 Germans had been killed on the island with a further 5000 drowned at sea. The same news columns reported in muddled fashion that the 30,000 "Nazis" who had reached Crete to date consisted of two divisions of paratroops and "glidatroops" (a new word coined by the *Daily Express*), one airborne division, and two regiments of shock troops who had been part of the division "largely lost at sea." It was further explained that Allied losses in heavy equipment such as tanks were much less because there were few on the island, which meant that "losses were lower than in any other previous expeditionary force."

Greek fishermen, it was stated, had been forced by the Germans at gunpoint to ferry the enemy across the sea to Suda Bay, but on arrival had deliberately smashed their boats onto the rocks, "spilling thousands of Nazis into deep water." The following somewhat irrelevant snippet appeared in the middle of a column describing the part played by Greek civilians in the battle:

"I have heard this startling-gratifying-story from one of the Nazi flyers captured. 'All I wanted,' he said, 'was to get command of a bomber and attack England. I have just been to Berlin on leave and seen what the RAF has done there, done to friends of mine too. Now I just want to get at London'."

British newspaper reports of the time seem to confirm what the Germans claimed later − the involvement of Cretan civilians in the struggle. Power and water plants were sabotaged, every fit monk was said to have turned out from a monastery to fight the enemy, and:

"Womenfolk, children and fathers of the dead soldiers have been taking their revenge with such fury that German planes for the past four days have been dropping pamphlets on the towns and villages saying that 'under International Law any Cretan civilian found fighting or helping the Allied Army in any way will be shot.'

"The bitter anger of the civilians' fight seems to spring largely from the fact that the Cretans supplied the crack division which was wiped out in Greece."

One tall tale emanated from Rome and Berlin radio, telling of the Empire defenders "demoralized" by a new Nazi weapon, an "artificial fog." But the German communiqué of late Friday (30 May) stated:

"The fight has been decided. Their stubborn resistance broken, the British are in full retreat. Operations begun on May 20 for possession of the British bulwark of Crete are approaching their end. The enemy has collapsed."

The British press also reported that German bulletins threatened reprisals for the maiming of wounded German troops; the Germans said that soldiers or civilians found responsible would be severely punished.*

From the propaganda viewpoint it was fortunate for the British that they had just sunk the "unsinkable" *Bismarck*, this fact enabling newspapers to devote even more front-page column inches to that success and even a good deal of the inside space of the meagre four pages allowed them.

Churchill to Wavell, 23 May:

"Crete battle must be won."

The Prime Minister asserted that even if the Germans managed to establish themselves on Crete, the struggle must go on, for it was tying down German forces, destroying their best soldiers, and helping to protect Cyprus. To General Freyberg he exhorted that the whole world was watching the battle "on which great events turn."

While the air-sea contest had been in progress the remainder of the German Mountain Division was successfully ferried across by Ju 52s, while British reinforcements brought in by sea suffered heavily from *Luftwaffe* attacks on Suda Bay and Canea. Obviously, without any air cover whatever, the Allied troops were completely at the mercy of the *Luftwaffe*.

On the island General Ringel sent his 85th Mountain Regiment from Maleme into the mountainous region to outflank the New Zealand position west of Canea, then made a frontal attack south of the coast road, using Ramcke's paratroops and the 100th Mountain Regiment. On 26 May the Germans broke through the New Zealand defences and captured Canea, which meant that Suda Bay now fell under their control. General Freyberg reported that his troops had reached the limit of their endurance and that the position was hopeless, due mostly to the incessant bombing raids. He had ordered the withdrawal of his troops to the south of the island, this in the face of heavy German assaults intended to relieve the beleaguered, battered remnants of airborne at Retimo and Heraklion. These latter troops had tied down numbers of British and Australian soldiers.

On this day, 26 May, the Germans gained the upper hand, for as soon as the Allied forces withdrew from the airfields the island

* see Appendix 3, p.111

battle was lost. The decision to evacuate the island was the only course open to the British, unless they decided to order the men to fight on to the bitter end; but the Middle East Command could not afford to throw troops away uselessly. Two complete Commando units were landed that night by minelayer, and these, together with the remains of the 5th New Zealand Brigade and the 7th and 8th Australian Battalions, acted as rearguards so that the surviving Allied forces in the north of the island could be withdrawn to the south. At Retimo the remaining Allied troops were surrounded and running out of supplies, and when these finally gave out they were forced to surrender, but this did not occur until 30 May, by which time it was reckoned they had killed about 300 of the enemy; 140 Allied soldiers managed to escape the German ring.

At Heraklion the Allied defenders had been reinforced by men of the Argyll and Sutherland Highlanders who were landed at Timbaki and fought their way through to them, but all were evacuated by sea before the Germans destroyed or captured them.

The dice had fallen in the Germans' favour and on 27 May the *Kriegsmarine* managed to land two tanks on the island, having ferried them across on an open barge. General Wavell wired Churchill that Crete was no longer tenable, and by that night the enemy forces were pursuing the British as they withdrew southwards.

"It had grown very quiet," Konrad Seibert found. "I hoped the enemy had withdrawn or forgotten us. I found a parachute and beside it a container, which was empty. I thought the 'chute would be useful in the heat of the next day, but when I picked it up I found a dead paratrooper beneath it. I took his rations and ammunition pouches and was on my way back to my hole when I saw some British watching me from not far away. I stopped dead and dropped flat, and in a moment they came over and told me to put my hands up. I was crestfallen to be captured after all I had been through.

"These were two New Zealanders and I did not understand what they said, but I was searched and taken away to their positions. They confiscated all I had, including the watch my mother had given me, which I treasured. An officer came and I noticed that these men were in as bad a way as we were. He asked me some questions in a mixture of bad German and English, but I said nothing so he went away. I asked for help for our wounded, and they did, I believe, intend trying to do something with what little they had. But it all changed, because then a big German blitz started and we all had to lay low. It was very frightening to be strafed by your own planes. Then quite suddenly all my captors vanished. One moment they were there, talking seriously, the next they had gone, leaving me with a few scraps of rations which I at once rushed back to my hole where I found just one man still alive. All the rest were dead, and those I had left unwounded had vanished.

"Soon after that I saw a German unit of mountain troops and I waved my arms and in a few moments I was in good hands. That day was a very hard one, for I went back to where parties of paras were gathering. The officers were busy counting men and trying to find out who was missing. And then we were told to collect weapons from a large heap and some rations and were sent off to chase the retreating Allies who were trying to escape to the coast and evacuation. I was very surprised by all this but did as I was told. I must mention that I had not seen any of my own comrades since jumping from the plane, so it had all been an ordeal. The men I was now with were from various battalions of the 1st Parachute Regiment, of which I was not even a member as I had come in later into the 2nd. However, we were all good comrades and followed our orders. We felt the sooner we finished the job the sooner we would go home."

But, despite all the arduous trekking that Konrad Seibert did, all they found and took prisoner were a few Allied stragglers. Attempted questioning of Cretans yielded nothing.

"Practically all the Allied troops got away by night with the help of your Navy. It was a masterly evacuation. For myself, I did not care, I had seen more than enough of the island."

Karl Pickert was one of those rallied together by an officer for a general advance to clear up the island:

"It was then, when we could finally emerge on our feet, that we began to see all our dead and wounded. Many of the latter had not been tended to as it was impossible to reach them. They died like flies and I'm sorry to say as we moved inland we found more who had been attacked by Cretan civilians and killed and stripped. You will understand that we were very shocked and angry and when later certain reprisals were taken it could be seen why. I myself saw literally hundreds of dead German troops, both lying in the folds of that wretched landscape or hanging from trees and later collected for burial in trucks. We did, I'm afraid, have to participate in helping to clear up the island battlefield, and it was a terribly gruesome task."

Karel Weise felt that as an officer cadet he should try to do something, so he crawled out of his gully and spent two hours foraging for food and water, but found nothing. He finally lay, exhausted by his efforts, in a hole with two dead men for company and the enemy not far away:

"They saw me and eventually came over and captured me. I was very well treated. They bandaged my leg wound and gave me some tablets and tea, examined my head and bandaged it too and left me sitting up under some cover. I was absolutely exhausted and thankful to be left alone. The battle went on through the day and I almost lost track of time as another night came. In fact I am no longer sure if it was that night or the next, as I seemed to be only semi-conscious part of the time, but all grew very quiet as dawn came around again, and I lay in a stupor. Then I heard German voices and found myself lifted up and found I was in the hands of some paras and mountain troops.

"They took me down the hill near Suda Bay and I passed out completely. When I next came round I was lying in a truck with many other wounded including some New Zealanders in a bad way, and after a long delay we were taken onto the airfield at Maleme in great heat and discomfort and put aboard a Ju ambulance plane. I thanked God for my delivery from that hell as we took off, landing back in Greece perhaps an hour later."

Kurt Seiler spent two days as a prisoner, until, after a great deal of shooting, all went quiet and his captors left:

"Soon after that we were found by German mountain troops, given a meal and shown how to get back to our paras. It was quite a trek and we felt very weak. We were counted after assembling near the sea, I think it was near Suda Bay, and then had a long wait until a Ju could take us back to Greece."

On his second night Heinrich Pabst and his men were desperate for food and water, so he led them out on a foraging expedition and managed to find a few scraps in an abandoned British dugout:

"We spent the night there, and next day the battle resumed, so we did what we could to observe and snipe at the enemy, and by that night we had accounted for a number of them. Early next morning we were overjoyed to see German paras and mountain troops advancing towards us, and it was a great relief to join up with them. We were not in good condition but marched down to the area near the Bay to receive some rations and try to join up with other paras. It was a very sad day, for the ranks had been thinned greatly. Later we joined a patrol and made a sweep of the island and caught quite a few prisoners, though not the main body of the enemy who had escaped to the south and were evacuated.

"When we got back to the Bay it was decided that all men in need of treatment would be evacuated, the fit men would remain on the island for a while to hunt for stragglers and secure our position until more troops arrived as a permanent garrison. It became my lot to lead forays across the island with men I mostly did not know, attempting to catch any enemy soldiers in hiding, and in this we were obliged to search the Cretan dwellings which stank horribly. The population were very hostile and committed many atrocities against our dead or indeed any unguarded men who allowed themselves to be stalked or whisked away from our positions. It was a very hard time for us, for our orders were to deal ruthlessly with all such hostile acts. A number of hostages were taken and I can tell you that having seen the results of some Cretan acts we were in no mood to use kid glove tactics. Their behaviour sickened us. I'm glad to say that after a few weeks of this we were relieved and only too happy to get away from Crete back to Greece and then back to our own homeland for a good rest."

Karl Baumer had watched the battle to the east where British tanks had initially gained success:

"I learned later that the British themselves were in a bad way, while we ourselves were being reduced to a pitiful state through lack of water. The heat was terrible and we were not acclimatized to it. We had no tropical clothing and suffered accordingly."

Nevertheless, when eventually found by mountain troops Baumer and some of his comrades were sufficiently recovered to join in an attack on some British positions near Maleme airfield. But by then they were completely spent and the fresher troops had to go on without them.

"That night we rested, and the next day more and more transports came in and we witnessed all the chaos and confusion on the airfield as they tried to get down. I believe some progress was made in clearing the wrecks so that more infantry could get down, and then the tide turned. The hill positions of the enemy were outflanked and progress made inland. We received water and rations from the infantrymen and were obliged to join in some small actions, but we were truly done for and not of much use.

"At long last we were ordered to move down to the Bay, and

there a lot of counting and reorganizing took place while the surviving commanders tried to assess our losses which were very heavy. Those fit men were re-equipped and despatched with the mountain troops to clear up the island, while the wounded and unfit were sent back to Greece and eventually Germany."

The 100th Mountain Regiment took 10,000 prisoners, so it was claimed. The shore and inlets of southern Crete were filled with Allied personnel hoping for rescue by the Royal Navy, and they were not abandoned. As one German historian put it: "The British Navy pulled off a master stroke by evacuating about 17,000 men out of Sfakia in just a few nights, transporting them back to Egypt. It had saved more than half the British Expeditionary Corps."

One British source states that over 5,000 Allied personnel were left behind on the island after the Royal Navy was finally forced to call off further evacuation attempts and these men were authorized by General Wavell to surrender. How many received such permission is unknown, but many individuals and small parties went into hiding in the hills and were aided by the Cretan inhabitants. This led to the widespread security sweeps by the Germans, as mentioned by those who took part in them, the Germans searching not only for Allied evaders but locals guilty of atrocities. Arrests, interrogations and reprisals were carried out against the civilian population and it must be said that a very one-sided picture was always painted in the British Press on this question. An influx of British and Allied agents and the kidnapping of the garrison commander, General Kreipe, did little but exacerbate a difficult situation for both the occupiers and inhabitants and in due course, after the retaking of the island, prosecutions were made against the then German commander and others for war crimes, though as usual it is doubtful if any proceedings were taken against Cretans who, according to the Germans, had violated the international rules of war.

An island, well fortified and garrisoned, had been conquered from the air, though it must be seen as a victory which could not have been won without decisive *Luftwaffe* air superiority. Before considering the human profit and loss account, what were the implications of this biggest-ever airborne operation?

In the broader sense, and whatever terrible losses the British believed they had in fact caused, the German airborne success on Crete led to the fear that a similar invasion could still occur in

Britain. The British did not at that time know the actual strength of the German airborne weapon, and, as Churchill was to admit later, the Government and War Office were obliged to review and make preparation for a possible landing by four or even five airborne divisions. In view of all the amazing disclosures in later years concerning the extent of British knowledge of enemy secrets via Ultra it seems extraordinary that such a gross over-estimate of German capability in this direction should have been made. It certainly came as a considerable surprise to the British when they later discovered that Göring had but one airborne division, or at least, a single parachute division, at that time. After the war the British counted over 4,000 graves of Germans killed in the Suda Bay and Maleme areas alone; a further thousand were discovered at Retimo and Heraklion. Churchill estimated in post-war years that the Germans must have suffered over 15,000 casualties in all in the Crete operation, plus 170 troop-carrying planes lost or damaged, and when he came to examine captured German records and critiques on the battle he discovered that the enemy had underestimated the strength of the Allied garrison by two-thirds:

"The island had been prepared for defence with the greatest care and by every possible means...all works were camouflaged with great skill...The failure, owing to lack of information, to appreciate correctly the enemy situation endangered the attack of the XIth Air Corps and resulted in exceptionally high and bloody losses."

On the morale of the Allied forces, the German report had this to say:

"As regards the spirit and morale of the British troops, it is worth mentioning that in spite of the many setbacks to the conduct of the war there remains, generally, absolute confidence in Churchill."

In mid-July the airborne troops returned to Germany as conquering heroes, leaving behind them the mass graves with the plain crosses of their comrades killed in the action. On their train carriages the Germans scrawled slogans, *Fallschirmjäger kommen von Kreta*, and in the streets of their base towns like Halberstadt, Quedlinburg and Braunschweig the grateful citizens greeted them with garlands of flowers. In their original base at Stendahl the airborne held a grand march-past wearing camouflage smocks, while in Braunschweig the bands played as the broad columns of paratroopers goose-stepped past the rows of officers taking the salute.

"We had a grand homecoming," commented Konrad Seibert,

"but before long all the civilians knew perfectly well what a terrible thing had happened. All that propaganda about our great victory! Well, it was paid for in young blood. But my parents were overjoyed and so relieved to see me. I had changed. I had a good leave but it was very depressing to go back and see so many new faces."

Karl Pickert:

"When the survivors finally got back to Germany we were garlanded and given a heroes' welcome, but the scars of that terrible battle remained, so that when the new recruits began arriving we did not really feel like talking about it. We could only do our best to advise and train them and above all teach them self-survival."

Kurt Seiler:

"When we got back to Greece we were told that we glider men would probably be transferred to the infantry — unless we wished to volunteer for the paras! This was the end of my war as an airborne soldier, for the disaster on Crete put an end to the German glider troops and I had no wish to participate in airborne operations again. I was soon transferred to an ordinary infantry unit and saw the war out in comparative safety."

Heinrich Pabst:

"We had many discussions on the failure in Crete, for we saw it as a failure. At least the ordinary soldiers realized that when so heavy a price is paid then it is a failure. We had secured the island but at such terrible cost that never again was a sizeable airborne operation contemplated. I know that many 'parachute' divisions were organized later, and as a Captain I helped to train them, but most of them were either given a short jump course or none at all. In no way did they measure up to the old *Fallschirmjäger*, although most fought as best they could. I'm afraid that a soldier who has not jumped from a plane a few times is not the same as one who has. The spirit of the parachute soldier is unquenchable. I ended the war with a few medals and a great deal to talk about!"

Karl Baumer:

"When we had re-armed we paraded in Braunschweig and a few other bases and were hailed as heroes. But we were too shaken by our terrible losses to think of ourselves in those terms. I was promoted to Sergeant-Major and sent back to Stendahl where I spent much of the rest of the war on instructional duties. I was alerted for the Ardennes [offensive] but in the event took no part in it. I ended up in an American POW cage."

Karel Weise was flown back to Germany after a week in Greece but took six months to recover, after which he took up a post as a combat instructor at Stendahl:

"I can tell you that Crete was a terrible battle and for many of us completely one-sided, but the great bravery and perseverance of my other comrades − those who survived − won the day. But in my opinion, on balance, it was a victory we could not afford."

The operations of 1940 had brought the airborne forces 24 Knight's Crosses, the year 1941 brought them a further 30. The heroes of Crete received their awards from Hitler at his HQ in the East on 19 August. But General Student was shattered by the losses suffered by his men, Hitler even more so, but perhaps from the point of view that one of his trump cards had been so bent that it was no longer usable:

"Crete has shown that the days of the paratrooper are finished," he told Student. "The paratrooper force is pure and simple a weapon of surprise. The factor of surprise has now been used up."

The effect in Britain and America was quite the opposite, for while laying emphasis on the pyrrhic victory the enemy had won, in secret Churchill ordered the sole British parachute battalion enlarged into a force ten times as great. The Americans now expanded their "test platoons" into regiments which would, as in Britain, be expanded later into divisions.

By the autumn of 1941 the grand German offensive in Russia had become bogged down in mud and snow, and at this point the German paratroops were again called to action, but from then on they would almost exclusively be engaged as "fire brigade" infantry.

In April, 1942, the Italian and German High Commands conceived a big operation to eliminate Malta as a British base and Hitler called in General Student, who had by then recovered his nerve and waxed enthusiastic about airborne participation. But quite suddenly Hitler changed his mind, for he envisaged the Italian Fleet scuttling back to Italy as soon as the Royal Navy set sail from Egypt, leaving his paratroops stranded on Malta. By then the XIth Air Corps had assembled a huge force of 1000 gliders of all types, but Operation "Hercules" never got off the ground.

In August, 1942, the Ramcke Brigade, comprising four battalions, went into the line under Rommel in Africa, but were forced to withdraw in November after the Battle of Alamein.

The next action of the German paratroops against the Allies also began in this period when the British and Americans landed in

Tunisia, and in this campaign they came up against British paras on a static front, both sides taking casualties and losing prisoners. On the German side some British paras taken prisoner were treated almost like brothers of the same fraternity, being allowed to remain with the German airborne for some days until finally sent back to Germany as POWs.

The battle for Sicily in July-August, 1943, again involved an air drop by the 3rd Parachute Regiment of the 1st Parachute Division. This unit, with other airborne troops in support, came under control of the "Schmaltz Brigade" which was in turn part of the *Hermann Göring Panzer Division*. Once again the German paras came up against their opposite numbers in the British airborne. Some years later one German officer commented in his memoirs that the red beret prisoners he took in Sicily at the start of the battle (following the disastrous Allied airdrop), were pathetically armed and did not know what they were fighting for.

In Italy the German paratroops mostly fought as ordinary infantry, their stand at Cassino being the most notable of their defensive battles, though there were some small airborne operations of interest. Major Gericke, a veteran from 1936, led the 6th Battalion of the 6th Parachute Regiment in an attempt to capture the entire Italian General Staff in September, 1943, after Italy had defected to the Allies, and succeeded in taking many officers but not the Commander-in-Chief who had already escaped to the Allies.

On 12 September the 1st Company of the Parachute Demonstration Battalion took off in gliders under the command of Otto Skorzeny of the SS to snatch Mussolini from his hotel prison on Gran Sasso. A mountain-top hideaway, it was nevertheless accessible to the German airborne who carried off a remarkable coup and delivered the deposed Italian dictator to Hitler.

German paratroopers fought on as infantry on all the battlefronts for the rest of the war, the only other airborne operations worthy of mention being the attempt to capture the Yugoslav communist partisan leader Marshal Tito by SS paratroops. It failed, but by a narrow margin. The second and last of the war was the paratroop element of the Ardennes offensive of December, 1944, which was a failure.

By 1945 the so-called 'parachute' divisions numbered ten, plus various other corps troops, and were, as indicated earlier, airborne in name only. It is not easy to understand the purpose of re-titling the *Hermann Göring Division* "Parachute-Panzer" even if its infantry element was garbed in para-type outfits.

The German parachute forces served as a model for the Allies' own airborne corps, and made a powerful impression on their opponents on all fronts. But it was their earlier operations of 1940-41 which made them best known as audacious troops, daring in attack and resolutely tough in defence and always a force to be reckoned with.

Appendix 1

The German invasion of Crete cost the British 15,743 men, according to one source, whereas Winston Churchill quoted some 13,000 in killed, wounded and taken prisoner, to which he added 2,000 naval casualties (the actual figure was 2011). 16,500 men were rescued from the island. In addition to those losses mentioned in the text the Royal Navy lost a further two destroyers and the flak cruiser *Calcutta*, while two more cruisers were seriously damaged; the carrier *Formidable*, the destroyer *Nubian*, the battleship *Barham*, the cruisers *Ajax* and *Dido* plus two more destroyers were all slightly damaged. The *Barham* was later torpedoed and sunk by a U-boat, the only British battleship lost to a submarine in the war.

These losses put the whole British position in the Eastern Mediterranean in peril.

Appendix 2

For the Crete operation the Germans deployed the following forces:
Command: XI Air Corps
Corps reconnaissance, transport, machine-gun and medical units
Airborne Assault Regiment:
Four battalions of glider and parachute troops
7th Air Division:
Divisional troops: transport, 7th Parachute Engineer Battalion, 7th Parachute Artillery, 7th Parachute Machine-gun Battalion, 7th Parachute Anti-tank detachment
1st Parachute Rifle Regiment: three battalions
2nd Parachute Rifle Regiment: three battalions
3rd Parachute Rifle Regiment: three battalions
5th Mountain Division:
Divisional troops: 95th Signals Detachment
95th Mountain Artillery (two dets), 95th Mountain Engineer Battalion, 95th Anti-tank Detachment, 95th Reconnaissance Detachment, 85th Mountain Rifle Regiment, 100th Mountain Rifle Regiment (each rifle regiment comprised three battalions)
The airborne component numbered some 13,000 men, the mountain division 9000. Losses: these vary according to source. According to *The Luftwaffe War Diaries* they were as follows:

Killed, missing or wounded including transport aircrew

Officers	Other ranks
368	6,085

A different source gives: airborne − 3,250 dead or missing, 3,400 wounded, the number missing the same as those killed in action owing to the intervention of Cretan civilians. Mountain division losses are stated as 1,510, giving a total for the operation of 6,650 (or 6,453 by the *Diaries*). The Germans also lost 271 Junkers 52 transport planes.

Awards

In the period 1940-1945 the German Airborne Forces won 201

Knights Crosses, 27 Oakleaves, 7 Swords and 1 Diamonds, this last awarded to Bernhard-Hermann Ramcke as commander of the fortress of Brest in 1944.

Interestingly, the number of Knights Crosses awarded peaked at the rank of Captain (47), falling to its lowest at Corporal (2).

Appendix 3

**To the population and the
military forces on Crete**

It has been brought to the notice of the German Supreme Command
that German soldiers who fell into the hands of the enemy on the
island of Crete have been ill-treated and even mutilated in a most
infamous and inhuman manner.
As a punishment and reprisal therefore is announced as follows:
1) Whosoever commits such crimes against international laws on
   German prisoners of war will be punished in the manner of his
   own cruel actions, no matter be he a man or a woman.
2) Localities near which such crimes have been perpetrated will be
   burned down. The population will be held responsible.
3) Beyond these measures further and sharper reprisals will be held
   in store.

The German Supreme Command

RED DEVILS

I

Striking Companies

The actions of the German airborne troops in Holland and Belgium so impressed the new Prime Minister, Winston Churchill, that soon after he took office he began pressing the War Office to form a unit of British paratroops, or at least bands of "striking companies" able to inflict lightning raids on the enemy-held coastline across the Channel. Churchill was always a man of great energy and ideas, though some of his notions ran into purest fantasy: he envisaged armed columns which, having been landed on the French coast, would strike deep inland and kill Germans, causing mayhem before withdrawing to the craft which would ferry them safely back to England.

The Prime Minister was not alone in wanting to hit back at the enemy who had so recently thrown the British off the continent; at least one other officer in the Army establishment had hit on similar notions. But the General Staff were much too preoccupied with scraping enough forces and weapons together to face the probable German invasion to devote time to such ideas, and in any case were by tradition and thinking totally opposed to "special" forces in any shape or form. In this they were really very much on a par with their opposite numbers in the German Army, which had its own long-established hierarchy of conservatism.

In view of the considerable opposition met at all levels throughout the British Army, it is surprising that so much was achieved so early, for during the early summer of 1940 the first unit of volunteers was formed which would become known as "commandos", and from these the early paratroops drew their recruits. Churchill wanted a corps of at least 5,000 paratroopers, but lack of equipment and enthusiasm in higher quarters, not the least the Air Ministry which was called upon to supply the aircraft, meant that only a small battalion was raised by the time summer ended. The parachute school set up at Manchester's Ringway airport was staffed by Army Physical Training Corps instructors and parachute tutors from the RAF. The first 'live' jump was made on 13 July and after two months 21 officers and 321 other ranks had completed the course, with two killed, thirteen badly injured and thirty men refusing to jump. At the training stage any man who opted out was returned without disgrace to his unit − 'RTU'd' as the saying goes − but, once a trained paratrooper, any further refusals entailed a charge and possible court martial.

By September Churchill had been forced to whittle down his ideas, but now a fresh 'airborne' scheme came up by which troops could be transported by glider, as an alternative to parachuting, which the Prime Minister saw as "experimental and doubtful". But it is clear from a minute he sent to General Ismay at the General Staff on 2 September that he had already witnessed a parachute drop, for he commented that some of the men's knuckles seemed "terribly cut". Had the question of protecting their hands and giving them kneecaps been considered? Churchill's technical knowledge in military matters was never very great, his forte lay in a broader sweep and grand ideas in strategy, quite the opposite to Adolf Hitler, who had an astonishing memory for technical data.

The forming and training of British paratroop units continued at a slow pace, but by February, 1941, it was felt that some kind of trial should take place, and as a result a very modest experiment was carried out. One troop of X Commando of the 11th SAS Battalion (as it was then called) was flown to Malta and then to Italy where in Operation Colossus an attempt was made to blow up an aqueduct. The operation was only a part-success and the men were unable to make the planned rendezvous with a submarine on the coast to achieve their escape. After capture by the Italians, their Italian interpreter was shot by a fascist firing squad as a traitor.

It was the German airborne success, costly as it was, that finally prodded Churchill into further action, with the subsequent expansion of the British airborne forces. The concept of 'combined operations' led in February, 1942, to the operation at Bruneval on the French coast, whereby a small force of paratroopers led by Captain John Frost would drop beside a German radar installation to allow an RAF expert technician taken along with them to remove certain parts for examination. The paras would be evacuated by sea, their withdrawal aided by a troop of infantrymen. In the event this audacious raid was a success, carried out at small loss and the prize radar parts brought back to England.

By 1942 the Army had also formed glider-borne units, impressing

21. The bridge vital to British and Germans at Arnhem, with knocked-out SS vehicles at top end.

Right: Arnhem — the end. A soldier e Border Regiment uses his sven gun nst unequal odds.

Below: British wounded in German ls.

Below Right: The principal cause of British defeat — the armoured assault

25. Captured British glidermen are interrogated by General der Waffen-SS Harmel of 10th SS Division Frundsberg.

26. **Below:** A 6-pounder anti-tank gun in place with men of 6th Airborne at Haminkeln, March 1945.

27. **Bottom:** Once the initial difficulties had been overcome men of 6th Airborne artillery got down to some 'fratting' with the Soviet troops, Wismar, May 1945.

ordinary infantry-of-the-line from county regiments and utilizing at first Hotspur gliders and then the larger Horsas. Two of the latter were used in an abortive and tragic raid on a heavy-water plant in Norway, used by the Germans in their efforts to make an atomic bomb. The troops involved were from two airborne engineer companies and were towed in their Horsas by Halifax bombers.

Despite good forecasts the planes encountered a blizzard on reaching Norway and one Halifax turned back after failing to make contact with a beacon set up by agents on the ground. But the tow rope snapped and the glider crashed on a mountainside, killing three of the men. The rest were captured by the Germans and shot; the Halifax struck a mountain top and the crew were killed.

In impossible weather the glider towed by the other Halifax cast off too soon and crashed into high ground, killing eight, four being injured and five surviving to be caught and murdered by poison in hospital by the Gestapo.

Having concentrated almost exclusively on combat plane production, the Air Ministry was obliged to "buy American" in order to equip its airborne transport squadrons, so Dakotas were used by the 1st Parachute Brigade for its operations in Tunisia in November 1942. Lessons were learned from this campaign, the paras unfortunately having been used mostly as line troops in static warfare, and encountering their opposite numbers of the German airborne. When some of the British were captured by the German paras they were treated like brothers, which in a sense they were.

Despite the shambles encountered in the Sicily operation of July, 1943, some success was attained, notably the capture of the Primosole bridge to secure a line of advance to Catania. Once again German paras were encountered, and from the post-war memoirs of one somewhat arrogant officer, as mentioned earlier, came the comment that his British prisoners were pathetically equipped and did not know what they were fighting for. Despite this dismal pronouncement, the Red Berets on Sicily gave a good account of themselves and took part in the hop across the water into Italy, but fortunately were withdrawn before becoming too embroiled in more infantry combat.

Back in England both British airborne divisions were made ready for the invasion of Europe, but in the event only the 6th was used to drop on Normandy where once again they were ensnared into a long, ground-slogging campaign which their commanders saw as a waste of special troops. Meanwhile, their comrades of the 1st

Airborne trained and fretted and prepared for one operation after another, all being cancelled until the grand slam at Arnhem, about which so much has been written. It was tragic that, when the 1st was at last used as a full and powerful division, it should meet destruction, and at that late stage of the war could not be reformed.

Lieutenant-Colonel John Rock was one of those Army officers outside the usual mould who seized on Winston Churchill's inspiration derived from the Germans' efforts, but with his fellow pioneers had to draw on the existing commandos for recruits. These were a tough bunch but contained a few misfits who disliked discipline; some even had criminal records, which the Germans discovered and made use of in their propaganda. Those men who could not shake off their old habits had to go, for their officers were intent on forming an élite force of soldiers dedicated to one end — beating the 'Jerries' at a game they excelled at.

Rock himself never lived to join his protégés on ops, dying from injuries sustained in a glider crash in August, 1942.

Military parachute training in those early days was far more dangerous than today. There were no reserve 'chutes for the British (or the Germans, for that matter), and even the instructors were novices in the matter of despatching troops. Fatalities were inevitable, yet, considering the lack of equipment, remarkably few. Despite its own difficulties the RAF did its utmost to cooperate, providing both the planes and parachute jumping instructors for the new school at Ringway, and in a comparatively short time the first airborne troops were in training. Strangely enough, one of the worst and most persistent problems was not connected with the actual training, for, as one ex-airborne pioneer was to comment later:

"There was always one thing that bothered me: not the Germans — but the ruddy Army themselves!"

The diehards in the British Army were a force to be reckoned with. Some were entrenched in high places and were inherently hostile to anything innovative, particularly if it involved 'private armies' or any kind of autonomy outside War Office control. Fortunately such people were prevented from causing fatal damage, but not without Prime Minister Churchill's intervention.

The early airborne operations were a little amateurish, partly due to lack of strength, but also due to a lack of targets and of course experienced officers to direct such efforts. The 1st Parachute Brigade dropped in Tunisia in November, 1942, and had a hard time, chiefly from the terrain, but then through misuse as ordinary line infantry where they came up against some of the best the enemy could muster – the Germans' own paras. For the first time an Allied parachute unit faced its enemy counterparts.

As with most who joined the airborne in this period, Tom Smith's beginnings in the army were far from parachuting:

"I was born in Birmingham and as a youth had no special trade, and when the war came I volunteered at once. I went into the Army, and as it happened I had an interest in cooking of all things, so after my initial training I was sent to a school of cookery. It wasn't a bad life, but I'm afraid I soon got bored with mass catering.

"By 1941 and after the fall of France and the Dunkirk disaster the Army was trying hard to patch things together and all sorts of new things were coming along. We used to read the bulletin boards and see this and that invitation to volunteer for various things, and one day I was surprised to see a call for 'hazardous duties', with no details at all. I was not a particularly brave sort of chap, but it sounded very hush-hush and we were all wondering what it could be about. I think I stuck my neck out from sheer boredom and volunteered. My CO laughed at me and said 'You may live to regret it!' I won't comment on that remark, but it has stuck in my mind ever since!

"I was sent away at once to a camp in the wilds of Scotland where I met some more volunteers, and then we were told that it was one of the new commando units, and that if we wished to enter training we would begin at once, but that the ops we did could be very dangerous and possibly mean getting behind enemy lines. It really did sound very exciting, but a bit scary too. But the officer told us that although we had volunteered and would be put to the test we could drop out whenever we liked. Well, nobody said anything, so we at once got to work.

"I'd had nothing like it before. I don't think any of us had. It was all very new then, the assault courses and roughing it out in the wilds. Learning to use explosives, dodging all over the place, with Home Guards and regular troops trying to catch us. We felt more like a bunch of crooks and saboteurs. We even wondered if in fact we'd be sent into Germany on secret missions. We had no idea at all what was coming. One or two soldiers did drop out or were scrubbed as they weren't up to the training, or just lost interest. We got very tough after a few weeks and felt we could take on anything. We knew that we were not the first blokes to join this bunch and that we were now called 'Commandos', and felt that we were something very special.

"We were then amazed to hear of the first raids on the French coast and wondered when it would be our turn. We waited and waited, but nothing happened, so we wondered what was going on. The next thing was even more amazing as an officer came to our base and asked if we'd like to volunteer for a 'special unit' — even more 'special' than we were. We'd never heard of British paratroops, but of course knew that the Jerries had used them earlier in the war. The chap said they were a new thing and the British Army was forming its first units and they would get the very best training and become the finest. He thought that by looking at us we would be the best men available. How would we like to give it a go?"

It is recorded that the first "independent companies" of British troops were raised as early as April, 1940, to harry and delay the Germans in Norway, and on 4 June Churchill minuted:

"We should immediately set to work to organize raiding forces on these coasts where the population is friendly."

Two days later the Prime Minister was urging his military hierarchy to get it out of their minds that the Channel ports and all the territory between them was enemy territory: it was Allied even if occupied by the enemy and therefore ripe for raiding. He wished to know what arrangements were being made to organize good agents in all the occupied countries; "Enterprises must be prepared, with specially trained troops of the hunter class, who can develop a reign of terror down these Coasts, first of all on the 'butcher and bolt' policy; but later on, or perhaps as soon as we are organized, we could surprise Calais or Boulogne, kill and capture the Hun garrison, and hold the place until all the preparations to reduce it by siege or heavy storm have been made, and then away. The passive resistance war, in which we have acquitted ourselves so well, must come to an end."

Churchill's mastery of language tended at times to override the simple message within.

Despite Britain's parlous state, with the enemy knocking on the door and nothing but difficulties in view, the first commando raid was launched within three weeks of the unit being formed. It was an amateur effort, of value only for the learning of lessons, an experiment. But the British genius for eccentricity and improvisation always threw up the right men for the job. There was no lack of those in army uniform who leapt at the chance to escape bureaucracy, red tape, lethargy and doing things by the book. One such character, named Geoffrey Appleyard, recorded it as being 'absolutely terrific', it was the greatest job that anyone could possibly get in the Army, one of enormous value, no red tape or paper work, just pure operations that enabled a man to act on his own initiative: "It's revolutionary".

There were men adept at stalking and killing an enemy, perhaps skilled poacher types, the 'hunter' class that Churchill had in mind, extraordinary characters whose great love was to pass on all they knew to others, instructing them to keep the sun behind them, to merge with their own shadow, avoid fruit trees which harboured birds which could set up an alarm. Cattle in need of milking tended to lick one's face; the only solution was to "milk the damn thing"; they should dirty their hands and face with soot or burnt cork (but not earth). They learned how to stop a sneeze, and "We killed several Germans because they always went to the same latrine and we noticed it".

The raid on Guernsey "achieved very little, but we learnt a good deal," was the verdict of Major Durnford-Slater, one of the first commandos.

But by August, 1940, the doubters had begun to intervene again and Churchill was moved to record that the whole position of the special troops was being questioned, that someone had decreed "no more recruiting"; he also disclosed that he had asked for 5000 parachutists, "and we must also have ten thousand of these small 'band of brothers' who will be capable of lightning war".

The initial commando raids were written off to experience and were insignificant pinpricks on the Germans' periphery of Europe, but after some months of inactivity a successful raid was carried out on the Lofoten Islands off Norway which brought some German prisoners, caused damage to enemy-held installations and sank a few small ships. Above all, it netted the British and the commandos some very valuable propaganda publicity.

Tom Smith was one of those from B and C Troop, No 2 Commando, who stepped out to become the first British paratroopers:

"Well, I'd never had any such ideas of jumping out of a plane, it all sounded very, very dangerous; but we were a bit of a mad bunch, daredevil youths, so quite a few of us stepped forward, me among them. As soon as I did I thought better of it, but by then it was too late. I didn't want to make a fool of myself in front of the lads. The officer was well pleased and said we'd be getting our orders soon to move to a special camp for training. We were very excited and, I can tell you, scared! I think we all had butterflies in our tummies.

"After a week all of the volunteers were despatched to the parachute school at Ringway near Manchester to start training. Although we were scared, the first part was very interesting and quite easy, and of course there was no question of jumping out of a plane then. We had to learn how to hit the ground in a roll, jump off a platform with a harness holding us. We were then shown parachutes and how they were expertly packed. We learned how to fit one on and jump off a platform with it already open. So nothing could go wrong and it was good fun."

Unlike the Germans, the British had WAAFs to attend to the packing of 'chutes, under the watchful eyes of an RAF Flight Sergeant, and with this notice prominently displayed:

REMEMBER A MAN'S LIFE DEPENDS ON EVERY
PARACHUTE YOU PACK.

Smith:

"The bad part came when we had to start jumping from a damned balloon, and this was terrible, I was scared stiff, even though we had a cord fixed to the 'chute and didn't have to pull anything, just jump off the basket through a hole and everything was automatic. I felt so sick I really thought I couldn't do it, but I was so conditioned to obeying orders that when the RAF Flight Sergeant said 'Go!' I jumped at once with my breath sucked out of me and my heart in my mouth. For a few seconds I was in great terror, but suddenly the 'chute opened and I was hanging and floating in space. It was a fantastic feeling and I thought, 'Christ! This is marvellous!' but the officer on the ground started yelling at me: 'Feet together – watch your legs!' Then I hit the ground with a big bang. I was OK and felt on top of the world."

Tom Smith records that when he next went up in the balloon basket to 800 ft he was scared all over again. In a couple of days it was better, "though none of us ever liked the balloon jumps".

Indeed, the universal feeling for this part of the training, which remained part of the Ringway curriculum, was one of hatred. Jim Carter was a London orphan but as a youth was found a job in the docks and, as he says, "learnt the facts of life the hard way". He lived in a men's hostel for a few years, but then met a girl and after a struggle had managed to save up a few pounds to get married:

"It was bad at first as we lived in two rooms over a pub, but we were happy. Then we had a child, a little boy, but he died at birth. We were heartbroken. And then the war came and changed everything. I was already tired of dock work as so many of us were not in work much of the time as things were then, so I jumped at the chance to get a regular wage and enough to eat. I joined the Army."

In those lean years this was a good move. It was possible to get free board and clothing yet stay in one piece, for only a proportion of the soldiers were trained for combat and would enter a danger zone. For many the life was comparatively easy and certainly far more secure than in 'civvy street', especially if one signed on as a regular soldier, which in reality could simply mean a trade engagement for life − or very nearly.

"I went through basic training but had no special skills so went into the infantry. I didn't have the brains to become an officer or even an NCO, but I believe I was good soldier material, quick to obey orders and easy to get on with. I did not smoke and only drank moderately."

Jim Carter was in one of the first units to go to France in 1939 and says that it "wasn't too bad, but when the Jerries attacked it got more and more difficult, as whatever we decided to do they always seemed to get around us. The French near us were no good and soon gave up and we were left in the lurch. In the end we got back to Calais and were among the last to leave. The rest had to stay as rearguard and were killed or captured."

Back in England Jim enjoyed a rest and received new equipment, but before long was among those rushed to the south coast to start building defences against the expected invasion:

"We had quite a good time and used to watch the aerial dogfights every day during the Battle of Britain. Nothing happened, and as it got quiet again we began to get bored. Sometime early in 1941 I think we saw a notice asking for volunteers for the new commandos and paratroops. It was all new to us and we reckoned they would be sent on dangerous jobs. I must tell you that I was no longer seeing my poor wife. We seemed to have drifted apart after the nipper arrived. It was very sad but I didn't seem to care any more. I decided that I would try for the new paratroops. It was, I reckoned, a chance to get away from where we were. I was of course stupid, as it was a pretty easy life down in the south. We had inspections, did training and went on manoeuvres, but nobody really thought the Germans would come, so we could have gone on like that for years. But when you're young you do get restless and hate sitting around doing nothing. The Army really was a boring, dull occupation, even though we felt safe. Of course, we might have been sent overseas, but it didn't seem likely at the time.

"Several of us volunteered, not many mind you, as few chaps wanted to get killed and we did think that élite troops got the worst jobs. When it came to jumping out of a plane I didn't fancy it, I suppose I really hadn't thought about it too much, and may even have thought that it would be a bit glamorous and have some sort of special uniform. As I said, it was all new and we didn't have any real idea what to expect."

Jim found it all right at first, as they all did, but the balloon jumps were terrible:

"I never liked that, but by the time I jumped out of a plane I was not nearly so frightened. I just did it almost without thinking. I'm not a sensitive type and didn't dwell on things much. Stupid may be the right word! I had learned to obey orders and did as I was told.

"We had one bloke killed, but that was his own silly fault as he twisted about coming out of the planc and he got his rigging lines all fouled up, came down much too fast and that was that. Otherwise only the occasional bruises."

Ken Norman was a regular soldier, unlike most who volunteered for parachuting, came from a military family and attended the pukka Army college at Sandhurst. When war came he was an infantry Second Lieutenant and saw some action in France in Montgomery's 3rd Infantry Division, which was supposed to be the best-trained of the lot. After Dunkirk Ken arrived back in England in one piece to start reorganizing and training to meet the expected invasion, but when it failed to materialize was sent off on a promotion course and while at college heard about the new paratroops:

"I decided to have a go. The trouble was that my old CO did not want to lose me, but he had no option other than to forward my application, so in due course I was packed off to Ringway to start parachute training. It was pretty easy and very interesting, though I expect you've heard that the balloon jumps were the worst. But when we got to the planes it was better. Although I had not qualified, I had some charge over the men and as an officer was expected to set an example.

"I did get butterflies, of course, jumping out of a plane for the first time, but soon got over my nerves and began to enjoy it immensely. We did not have a great deal of idea how to use such troops and the officers used to hold discussions on what the Germans had achieved."

Alfred Turner was a hostilities only soldier and first called to the colours in 1940. With no special aptitude, he elected to become a driver, but after a year in the Army decided that Britain was not going to lose the war after all; "not that I ever thought of a German occupation".

"Then we heard of certain special offensive units being formed, and, always willing to have a go at something new, I volunteered for the paras. At Ringway I went through the basic training and saw two men killed which was pretty frightening to those of us about to go up in a plane for the first time. What happened was this: we were on the ground watching two Whitley bombers full of recruits lumbering across the airfield. The lads started jumping, but somehow two of them got their 'chutes tangled up together, so the pair came down much too fast and hit the ground a hell of a wallop. Our RAF instructors tried to make light of this, but you can guess how we felt. One or two blokes dropped out there and then and I myself had a mind to pack it in. But I decided to stick, and since we'd already done the balloon jumps which everyone said were the worst part of it over we felt we might be OK.

"And it was. Everything went like clockwork, and our terrors turned to joy as we made our first plane jumps."

Jumping fatalities occurred to the German and American para forces, usually during the early days of military parachuting. The American "test platoons" began training in the summer of 1940, being more lavishly equipped, with every jumper carrying a reserve 'chute. The first platoon spent several weeks in ground training and the first demonstration provided them with a dummy thrown from a plane with a 'chute that failed to function.

Tom Burgess had already absorbed some of the military atmosphere through his father who was a Sergeant-Major, so he entered the Army as a boy entrant to begin appropriate training at the big camp at Catterick in Yorkshire, following which he was despatched as a cadet to Sandhurst, where it was usual to take gentlemen and turn them into officers, though exceptions were made, some recruits being transformed, it was hoped, into both officers and gentlemen:

"This was a new kind of world but very interesting, with so much to learn. I knew very well that most there were from very different backgrounds. I came from Nottingham and I suppose would have been classified as lower middle class. We were working people and my father was always very good to me. He always taught me that if I behaved myself the Army would always provide a good, secure home for life. With all the depression and unemployment it didn't seem a bad idea for a lad of fifteen. By the time I got to Sandhurst I was past seventeen and anxious to become an officer, preferably in the artillery, but things turned out differently.

"After a few months of training and past my eighteenth birthday I saw a poster for the paratroops and decided that it would be good for me − just like that. I'd always been mad on guns − artillery − so I hoped that they would have some in the paras of whom I knew next to nothing. But I was in the middle of officer training and although very keen to get into the paras I was held back until I had done a year at Sandhurst. In fact, by the time I got away it was 1942 and I was nearly nineteen. I went up to Hardwick Hall and entered into the training as just another candidate who was addressed roughly but as 'sir' by the training NCOs. It was quite an experience, very tough indeed, and I never knew until then just how tough one could get, given the right conditioning. I survived to get selected and go on to Ringway where the really interesting part began."

Hardwick Hall, near Chesterfield, was set up as the Airborne Forces seeding centre, its object to select the best candidates from the volunteers by putting them through a very tough PT course under the Army instructors who had previously served at Ringway. Those who passed were to become paratroopers in the new 1st Parachute Brigade.

Reg Andrews joined the Army straight from high school by lying about his age, finding that in wartime the authorities could overlook such things. He told the recruiting Sergeant that he was seventeen, when in fact he was a year younger:

"I went through the standard infantry training at Aldershot and also did a special toughening up course at Pirbright, the Guards Depot. It was really a discipline thing, not so much the assault type of course. I was then posted to the East Yorks and stuck in a God-forsaken hole in the wilderness of Yorkshire and it was awful, especially in winter. I was a Londoner from East Ham and had two brothers. All of us managed to get to high school though none of us was brilliant. In fact I just scraped through and never regretted it.

"In Yorkshire the weather was always cold and coming from the south I certainly noticed the difference. I heard about the paras fairly early in 1941, and being a boy and quite brave I kidded myself I fancied such a job. My CO thought I was a bit young, but didn't try to stop me, so within a few weeks I went off to the selection centre at Hardwick Hall and there it was really tough. Somehow, I don't know how, I got through it all and was still keen. The Sergeant used to look at my young face and shake his head, 'You should have stayed in school, boy!' he said.

"Those selected went up to Ringway and saw what we were in for. I enjoyed all the training until we got to the damned balloon and that was a pig. No one liked it. In fact we all hated it, but most went through with it. Funnily enough, it was the one thing which most tested your nerve. Jumping from a plane really didn't seem so bad after that.

"The first time I went up in a Whitley I forgot I was easily seasick, and the flying was at times like that; but I surprised myself and was not sick once. When the time came to jump out of the hole I said to myself, 'Reg, you will either die young or be a hero!' I was a bit of a fool but I didn't die and neither did I become a hero."

John Holmes was also an East Londoner, from Leytonstone, and at the tender age of fifteen had already decided to join the RAF, but after seeing a neighbour in his Army uniform he changed his mind. Despite this enthusiasm he did not volunteer but waited for his call-up which came in 1940. Having gone through the usual "square-bashing" course he opted for the infantry rather than a specialist trade, finding as a youth that he enjoyed the military life and "especially the shooting bit".

"I was posted to the Ox and Bucks [Oxfordshire and Buckinghamshire Light Infantry], and did all the usual drill and exercises, and after a while I began to realize that it was not all it was cracked up to be. It could be very boring indeed, but, as I was to realize later on, at that time we were not in a danger zone, though we never knew whether or not we would be sent to Africa or the Far East."

John Holmes was suddenly to experience a totally unexpected change.

Jimmy White lived in Bradford until he was called up into the

Army in 1941 at the usual age of eighteen and, following basic training, volunteered for the paratroops. Surviving the course at Hardwick Hall and selected for parachute training, he passed this hurdle also and was posted to the 1st Parachute Brigade where yet more training ensued. He was to look back on his first jump as 'the ultimate test of nerve'.

Bill Marshall was a boy soldier before the war and later entered a battalion of the Middlesex Regiment, known for its large complement of machine guns. Bill missed the Battle of France and after Dunkirk found his unit acting as a cadre for a new intake:

"So we had to show them the ropes. It was very interesting, but there was a rush on with the threatened invasion. But by 1941 we had settled down and things become much quieter. In fact, I got very bored. By that time I was a Lance Corporal and I used to go home to Durham where I had some relatives but no parents. They had died when I was very young. I did not tell them at home that I was getting a bit fed up with it, and that there was no action, nothing but drill, drill and exercises. So, when I saw the call for volunteers for the paras I at once applied. I knew nothing about planes or parachutes, but it looked special and exciting. The CO was very sorry to lose me and I think he would have blocked it if he could, but I got away and found myself in yet more training, but of a rather different sort. It was tougher, more interesting and varied. We did a lot of cross-country runs to build up our stamina, heaving logs, unarmed combat and lots of firing with live ammunition from various weapons. And then we were either passed out or 'RTU'd' as they called it. I was glad to get through it and was at once sent with a batch to Ringway to start the parachute course. This too was far more interesting and I knew that as an NCO, even a junior one, I was expected to set an example. So I listened very carefully to what I was told and did my utmost to succeed.

"The balloon jumping was a very severe test and we all hated it. But it came and went and I was still in the running and I found I was gaining confidence. When the plane jumps came I was not very nervous. Even so, it was another great test of nerve and I imagine I was as scared as the next man. When it was my turn to go out the hole in the Whitley I gritted my teeth and said 'Hallelujah!' and out I went. It was a very frightening, weird sensation until the wind caught me and I went sideways and over, but the 'chute came open with a crack and I was then floating and enjoying it greatly. There's nothing like parachuting for a thrill and we got to like it a great deal — at least, I did."

Having survived the tests the qualified parachutist did indeed feel on top of the world, and he wanted everyone to note the brand new winged parachute in white and pale blue on his upper right arm; so, at first, in his pride, he often took pains to find a seat on the left-hand side of buses and trams. The early airborne troops retained their original unit title flashes on their shoulder; then came Bellerophon seated astride a winged horse, coloured pale blue on a maroon background and designed by the artist Edward Seago and posted on both upper arms of the battledress. The maroon beret was not adopted until November, 1942, having been chosen by the commander, ex-Guardsman General 'Boy' Browning. When it became the Parachute Regiment in August, 1942, the unit discarded the old Army Air Corps cap badge in favour of a new winged parachute badge in silver metal topped by the Royal crown and lion and worn only on the red beret.

At first the three parachute battalions wore the simple title "Parachute" in pale blue on their shoulders, with the appropriate battalion number beneath it. Later this was altered to Parachute Regiment only, and this remained in use. The various regimental units seconded to the Army Air Corps retained their parent unit insignia, but added the Pegasus and word "Airborne". The South Staffordshires, transferred to the glider component, used their own badge, the silhouette of a Horsa glider with the legend "South Stafford" above. The glider pilots were later formed into their own Regiment and wore their own style of wings on the left tunic breast. When independent parachute companies were formed (the 21st and 22nd) as pathfinders they wore their identification as Roman numerals beneath their shoulder titles. Coloured shoulder lanyards were also adopted by battalions in green, yellow, red, black and light blue to represent the 1st, 2nd, 3rd, 4th and 12th battalions. Someone said that only the Parachute Regiment and Tank Corps were allowed to paint their webbing black, but the distinction is only recorded as being allowed the 4th (Wessex) Battalion in the paras. The 5th Battalion was raised from the Camerons and allowed a Balmoral bonnet with the Army Air Corps badge on a Hunting Stewart tartan until September, 1944, while the 6th Battalion wore the Royal Welch black flash behind its collar.

The first British Army paras who qualified were awarded miniature wings to be worn above the left breast pocket, this later being superseded by the better-known type already mentioned. The same (later) winged parachute sewn above the left pocket denoted a secret agent or SOE operative who had undergone a jump course for the express purpose of dropping into enemy-held territory, though the same badge worn on the left sleeve denoted a qualified parachutist not posted to an airborne unit.

Tom Smith:

"We had round rubber helmets [actually canvas-covered sorbo-rubber] and smocks."

The first British paras wore black or brown leather flying helmets with grey-green smocks based on the German model and minus insignia; various high jump boots were tried until finally none were issued, only the standard Army boot.

Tom Smith completed his course and saw no deaths: "But I know a few were killed by 'chutes that didn't open or twisted up − the 'Roman candle' cases. There was no chance of survival from a failed 'chute. When we left Ringway we were even bigger than Commandos! We now had contempt for the ordinary soldiers, believe it or not. They were all right − but soft. They had no spine compared to us. We felt we could do anything. This was the effect that successful parachuting had on you. You had faced the greatest test of courage and come through it with flying colours. I'm sure the Jerries were the same as any other soldiers who become paratroopers.

"We then went on hard manoeuvres and gave demonstrations and received lectures on the theory of airborne assault. Mind you, it was all theory as the officers didn't know very much and had never been on a paradrop. All they knew was what they had heard of the Jerries' successes, and they thought the Germans had made some mistakes, such as in Crete where the poor devils were slaughtered. By then there had been one or two small-scale jobs, nothing very much, so we just went on training as the companies became regiments, and then they were planning whole divisions."

Jim Carter:

"When we got our wings we felt terrific and could take on anyone. We went off on manoeuvres and had all sorts of big-wigs visit and watch us, all the Army brass and blimps, all the old boys from the War Office. We would do our stuff, be inspected, then go to the nearest town for a good sing-song and drink. We used to have a few fights with the other soldiers − the softies as we called them, but we weren't really a wild bunch. Some chaps got sent back to their units in disgrace, but by and large we turned into a good bunch and knew our stuff.'

Ken Norman:

"By the time I had qualified, the Crete business was all over and we knew the terrible losses the enemy had suffered, and could see that when paratroops were used improperly they could prove a very expensive flop.

"The training was long and hard. We held manoeuvres with the regular army and then the first Yank troops and ran rings round them all. We really were very fit indeed and enjoyed it all."

Alf Turner was another who was very pleased to sew the wings on to his tunic:

"It was all new and we had to go through all sorts of schemes with the Army as the staff tried to formulate some working ideas for the best use of the new paras. We knew the Germans had had some success, but our people felt that a lot more could be achieved if only we had the proper equipment and opportunities. Then of course we kept coming up against those in the Army who were against the whole idea, and this situation was not helped by the early ops which were not at all what we had hoped for."

Tom Burgess had also found the training at Ringway very interesting – until the "balloon bit" – which he found awful, and it was during one such ascent that one man refused to jump. The Flight Sergeant in charge ordered the unfortunate soldier to sit down in the basket and keep quiet, which he did. But later the man offered to go on and jump from a plane, but was refused this chance and 'RTU'd.'

"When I jumped for the first time I knew I had to go through with it, not just to satisfy myself, but because I knew that the other lads were well aware that I was an officer under training, so I had to prove myself. I must say I was full of terrible nerves but it was not as bad as the balloon. We did six to nine jumps and then entered into training in full rig using all kinds of weapons and extra gear and before long we were fully trained. By that time they had two divisions and I was sent to the 1st with a Sergeant who was a regular. He took over a platoon and I was given a company as a new boy on approval!

"We did a lot of hard training during which I felt I was under instruction from some of the old hands, and I must say I learned a lot. By then I had rather given up the idea of artillery, but we were given a section of 75mm pack howitzers and although I was very interested I decided to stay with the infantry. There were many exercises including some with the Americans, and we always came out on top. Those days were very good as we had some good places to visit on off-duty times and enjoyed ourselves, though with growing numbers of troops in southern England discipline was becoming a problem. It was my lot to keep the lads under me in line and this was becoming increasingly difficult, but we had high hopes that D-Day would soon come and give us some action."

Reg Andrews got through the para course at Ringway:

"I'll never forget the great day when we received our wings. We felt on top of the world and ready for anything. I'll never forget the looks on my brothers' faces when I went home in my paratrooper's uniform. They really thought I was the tops and a bit of a daredevil. Both brothers were called up soon after that: one went into the gunners, the other RAF ground crew."

After reaching a para unit Reg entered yet more training but this was far more interesting – especially as they did no drill, only combat manoeuvres and parachuting. The mock battles sometimes included American and Canadian troops, with the paras usually winning the day:

"Our great advantage was our speed, we were trained to move fast and light, and this we always did. We also had some very interesting initiative tests, and had to go off on our own in twos and threes around the country and try to get back without being caught by the police or Army. That was great fun. We used to steal bikes, hitch lifts, and get up to all sorts of dodges to get where we wanted to go.

"We had a few fatalities in the course of training. I saw one chap killed and I must say it was his own fault. He came out of the Whitley, and instead of staying right way up he tried to show off and do a somersault. We were always taught to jump feet first and stay that way, and we never had any problems. But this chap was a bit of a show-off and had done as many jumps as we had. I think his name was Nick, and he tried to do a head over heels, but as he did so his 'chute lines got caught up in his feet and caused a terrible tangle. I had just got down and saw him rolling over and over and struggling like mad. I only heard later how it had come about. He hit the ground not too far away from me with a terrific 'plop' and bounced, and of course it was the end of him. But as it was a self-induced accident it didn't affect our morale.

"I saw another chap get hit by the tail of a plane and that knocked him silly, so that he wasn't able to land properly and broke almost everything, but he survived."

In October, 1941, the decision was made to set up a force of glider-borne infantry. The 1st (Air Landing) Brigade Group consisted originally of the four battalions mentioned, plus a reconnaissance company, an anti-tank battery and other small ancillary units. The Glider Pilot Regiment was formed before the year was out and consisted of soldier volunteers trained in elementary flying by RAF instructors. The infantrymen who suddenly found themselves 'fliers', and not very willing ones, at first wore no special uniforms but were given para-style helmets, but soon they were allowed to use the Airborne flash and red beret, and finally issued with the standard camouflage smocks.

John Holmes:

"Then, when I suppose we had settled down to a comparatively quiet life we were suddenly told that the whole lot of us were to become glider troops. To say we were amazed is an understatement; there was no question of volunteers, we were thrust into it. Some of the lads were far from pleased and threatened to write to their MPs about it. Not that it would have done them any good. For myself, I thought, well, it looks as if you'll get your wish after all; you're going up into the sky!

"We went off to this airfield, I think it was at Netheravon in Wiltshire, and there we saw our first gliders. They were quite small, Hotspurs, and would not hold many men — about ten I think. We were fitted out with para helmets, but apart from that just had the usual Army gear. It was rather exciting of course to climb into one of those things, but when we finally went up not so funny, as there was a lot of up and down motion and some chaps were sick. That, I can tell you, in a confined space is not very pleasant. Some chaps wanted to transfer out of it, but you needed a very good excuse! The pure malingerers were given jankers. I managed to cope all right, and then we got the Horsas which were much better, but still prone to the same movements, especially when the weather was a bit breezy, which it usually was."

Henry Lambert was another glider soldier, but a volunteer, one of the few:

"I was born in Hull of a small family with one brother who was a year older than myself. He grew up to become a solicitor, in great contrast to myself. I never amounted to anything much in civilian life, but when the war came I volunteered for the Army and after a while was called up and did the usual squarebashing and went on into the Royal Artillery. They taught that they were the 'Queen of the Battlefield' and in a sense they were correct. I learned to become a gunner on the 25-pounder after doing a spell on the old 18-pounder."

Henry Lambert was about to be shipped to France, but the evacuation prevented this, so like thousands of other troops was despatched to the south coast to set up anti-invasion positions, waiting for the enemy who never came and watching the air battles overhead in the meantime.

"It was in a way a very exciting time as we were on watch for hours, looking out for the German invasion fleet. But it all passed off and after a while it became very uncomfortable living in a hutted camp with nothing to do. We sometimes went off on manoeuvres, but we were not a mobile unit, but part of the beach defences only a few hundred yards inland and not far from Folkestone. Eventually, when I heard about the new volunteer commandos and paratroops in 1941 I decided to give it a go, as I felt I could always return to my old unit if it didn't work out."

Which is precisely what happened to Private Lambert (or more accurately most likely Bombardier or Gunner). He teamed up with other volunteers en route to Manchester and on arrival at Ringway entered training at once:

"But I hated it! I just didn't care for heights at all. I had never really thought much about it, though I did like the idea of flying in a plane. I suppose I was pretty stupid really, but young and full of bravado. At last the instructor took me aside and said, 'If you can't stand heights what the hell did you volunteer for?'

"I felt a bit of an idiot as I had to stand aside while the rest of the lads went through their paces. In the end I felt so bad I asked the Sergeant if I could have another shot at it. But it was no use, I just couldn't jump off anything at height, so I was sent packing straight away."

Lambert was returned to his old unit in Kent and forced to suffer the taunts and humiliations of his chums and felt an idiot. But apart from this he could not stand the boredom:

"Then I heard about the glider troops. Some regiments were being transferred wholesale into airborne. All you had to do was get into the gliders and away you went, there was no jumping from heights, and what's more you were given the Airborne badge. I saw the CO and asked to be transferred to a glider unit, and he said he'd see what he could do, though it really wasn't on to transfer to another regiment of the line without good reason. Some weeks went by and finally my posting came through, so off I went to join the Staffords. I wasn't sorry to leave and soon made some pals in the new unit. They were not all from the Midlands as I'd expected.

"We began to learn all about glider troop techniques and had some fun practising in the early little wooden gliders. These could only hold a few men — ten or twelve — and wouldn't have been much good in a real battle. Then the much bigger Horsas came along and these were a lot better."

Jules Couvain was a Lieutenant in the Ox and Bucks when they received orders to go over to the new air-landing force and moved off to Netheravon to begin training:

"As a Lieutenant, I was responsible for helping to make the transition a smooth one, but it was not easy as a number of the lads were not at all keen; in fact they wanted to leave the unit. I had to persuade them otherwise, but in two or three cases it led to, shall I say, disagreement, and disciplinary measures had to be taken.

"At last we met our 'steeds', not very big Hotspur gliders, and we, as officers, received lectures on glider landing and the theory of envelopment from the air. It was very interesting, but the gliders seemed very vulnerable to me."

They were also nowhere near as structurally sound as ordinary aircraft, for obvious reasons, and in sudden stress or turbulence could break up in mid-air. A sequence of photographs in *Life* magazine once showed an American Waco glider breaking up some two hundred feet up. The occupants were the Mayor and a party from a local town 'enjoying' a demonstration flight.

"We had one or two accidents which were fatal to a few men, but gradually the unit came together and I felt the men were getting the hang of things. We went into exercises using live ammunition and it became a lot more lively. Our problem was lack of experience and expertise, but we were learning fast and whatever needed to be done was done. When the Horsas came they were a very great improvement in capacity and we all felt a lot safer in them, or as safe as one could be in one of those things."

The troops receiving lectures on the practice and use of gliderborne troops had good reason to feel that their instructors were themselves learners:

John Holmes:

"I don't think those giving them knew all that much about it.

We were learning as we went along and had a few accidents. I remember one day a pilot tried to land too steeply in his rush to get down, so he hit the ground nose first with a heck of a crack and killed himself and a few others. After that the pilots took more care, but the whole idea always was to get down and unloaded as rapidly as possible. We had some big exercises with the army and lots of brasshats came and asked us questions, some of them stupid. Then we received our camouflage jackets and the airborne badge so began to feel we were something special. We used to meet the real paras sometimes and have good-natured conversations with them, but they liked to kid us that we were not real airborne soldiers at all, but we knew that in a battle we would be in much greater danger than ordinary soldiers."

Henry Lambert:

"We did a great deal of training and manoeuvres, but nothing came along in the way of ops, and we did get bored stiff as we had no barrack life, living in tents or at best wooden huts. There didn't seem any way in which we could be used, and such a long time went by that I began to wonder if I'd made a mistake in bothering. But I realized that some men were being killed in overseas battles, so I thought I should count my lucky stars. We were safe and eating well and not in a real war. I was very proud of my new insignia. Even though we were not paras we felt we were much better than the ordinary soldiers. I will describe one of our manoeuvres:

"We were lifted up by Albemarles of the RAF and taken over Salisbury Plain and released into a mock battle. It was very realistic and we dived down very steeply, ready to leap out and start blazing away at the 'enemy'. The gliders were crude and only wooden, and I saw one or two turn over in bad landings and break up completely. There were casualties, some of them fatal."

Jules Couvain:

"There was a great deal of delay before we finally got into action, and we had a few problems with discipline. This always happens with active young men trained for war when no action is given them."

In fact, only some of the British glider troops were to see any action in Sicily, the rest would have to wait until D-Day, 6 June, 1944, and the invasion of France.

Before then the paratroopers had encountered their German counterparts in North Africa, and it is alleged that the enemy were the first to coin the term 'red devils' (rote teufeln) when referring to the British paras; this may have seeped back to Germany where someone in the media decided to counter it by calling the German *fallschirmjäger* 'green devils', or *grüne teufeln*, though one source mentions the term first being coined by an American correspondent.

The British glider troops did indeed have a long wait for action, and not until July, 1943, did some of them participate with their para comrades in Operation "Husky", the invasion of Sicily. Meantime, men of the 1st Parachute Brigade had their first taste of action in Tunisia in November, 1942. For most of the men it was their first trip overseas:

"Then came our first op. We were briefed for the drop in Tunisia," Tom Smith recalls. "This was quite a fantastic affair as none of us had been out of the country before; in fact, most of the lads didn't even know much about their own country! So we were very excited and felt that at last we were getting into action. You see, we were becoming really fed up by then: Monty had beaten Rommel across Africa and it looked as if the business there was coming to an end. We thought they would have used us by then."

Jim Carter:

"Our training went on too long though, and we did get brassed off. Then we heard an exciting announcement: we would help to invade Africa. This sounded fantastic. It was all a bit of a let-down, but I quite enjoyed the sea voyage, though we half-expected to be sunk by U-boats. The North African thing was bad and we did not enjoy it, but I was glad to see another country and to come out of it in one piece."

Lieutenant Ken Norman was left behind with some men in reserve while the Tunisian operation went on, but was later sent out with a batch of reinforcements, ready for the invasion of Sicily. Another left behind in England was Alfred Turner:

"As it happened, I did not go on the Tunisian thing, and I was glad in a way, although the experience would have been worthwhile. I had by then been promoted from Corporal to Sergeant and selected with others to go on a scheme. We did protest at the time as we wanted to go with the rest of the lads, but eventually, when we heard what a shambles it had been we were glad in a way that we'd stayed in England. But then we were flown out as replacements on the Sicily business and were not too keen on that either. We were complete newcomers out there, pale compared to our veterans and eager to learn what had gone wrong."

What indeed had gone wrong?

The 3rd Parachute Battalion were flown to Gibraltar on 9 November under command of Lt.-Colonel Geoffrey Pine-Coffin, and then on to the airfield at Maison Blanche twelve miles from Algiers. This force comprised two companies, plus a mortar platoon, HQ company and field ambulance. The rest of the Brigade, including the balance of the 3rd Battalion, plus 1st and 2nd, had left for their destination by sea on 1 November and after arriving at Algiers eleven days later were subjected to a heavy bombing attack by the Luftwaffe. The 3rd Battalion element, being air-lifted from Gibraltar, lost one Dakota into the sea en route, but all the occupants were rescued by an American ship. By the morning of 11 November the weak force of 360 paratroopers were ready for action, detailed to seize the airfield at Bône near the coast and the frontier with Tunisia.

By this time the enemy had been rushing in troops by air, including paratroops, who it was thought may well have also been briefed to fly from their own base at Tunis to capture the same objective. As the Dakota pilots were American and inexperienced in dropping paratroops, a night drop was cancelled and the planes flew off early on the morning of the 12th, and at this point things began to go badly wrong. One Dakota crashed into the sea, killing three men, but the pilots turned in over land and managed to drop their loads accurately. But once again disaster struck: one soldier was killed through a 'chute failure, while the completely different atmospheric conditions affected the behaviour of the 'chutes and twelve men were seriously injured on landing.

A farcical situation now developed as the paratroops rallied and set up all-round defence on the airfield. The men encountered for the first time the 'friendly' Arabs who invaded the area and at once set about purloining anything they could lay their hands on. Meantime, the German paratroops of the 5th Parachute Regiment had arrived in the vicinity in Junkers 52s, but, on observing the British drop, had flown back to Tunis. Like the British paras, these German élite would be thrown into the ground warfare in Tunisia for several months until the Axis army surrendered in May, 1943. Very few Germans escaped.

Tom Smith and his chums became more and more dispirited as the ship bearing them swung out into the Atlantic for security reasons, before moving east again and finally unloading the paras at Oran.

"It was a big let-down and we were very dispirited. There was much of interest to see, but we felt like tourists, while the fighting was going on and we knew that the 1st Army had just landed with the Yanks and they were trying to get the whole country occupied before the Jerries could react. But they were much too slow in the beginning.

"Then we had great news. We were going to drop to capture an airfield. It was all a rush job and we went off in Yank Dakotas and dropped all right, but it was all a bit of a dead loss in the end. We started marching across wastelands and had a bad time from the climate and German patrols. We lost a few men and then the worst happened. We were put in the firing line as ordinary infantry! We were thoroughly cheesed off, as the RAF chaps used to say. The only thing that made it more interesting was the fact that those opposing us were also paras. We had a hard time, but I reckon we gave as good as we got. We lost a few men and all in all I was thankful to get away from there. I was slightly wounded in the hand, and by the time I had finished with hospital it was all over. The Jerries had surrendered. I rejoined my unit and before long learned that we were going to invade Sicily with the Yanks. We did more jump training and by then I was no longer scared, just anxious to get on with it. We were very fit but not happy with the climate or the country."

Following the considerable losses incurred by the British parachute brigade in Tunisia, men were impressed into the force as a stopgap measure which meant they were no longer a band of volunteers. John Frost has related in his memoirs* how two hundred men surplus to AA Command in Britain were supplied as replacements, even though they were part or even untrained at all as infantrymen. These unwilling 'paras' were handed red berets, given some training and put into the line against Germany's finest, most becoming absorbed into the battalion and even going through parachute training later on.

"Sicily was, if I can use such an expression, a complete balls-up. Apart from one or two small but important actions we were not much use and soon left before getting too entwined with the 8th Army. They were a very good body of men, but as paras we had a very high opinion of ourselves, and tended to look down on all others as lesser mortals."

* *Nearly There* by Maj.-General John D. Frost (Leo Cooper, London, 1991)

This was how Alf Turner saw the operation in Sicily. It was the weather and Navy shooting which most upset the Allied action.

Tom Smith:

"The Navy were shooting us down in droves. I was very bitter about that, but we recovered. We took off in Yank planes in windy darkness. When we had crossed the Med things began to go badly wrong. It was a shambles. We saw AA fire and planes going down in flames. We didn't know what was happening and got really scared. We didn't mind being killed in action, but not shot down into the sea! We would have stood no chance with all the gear we were carrying. But our pilot was quite good, though we had a hell of a bumpy ride and jumped into the night. As I came down I could see the fireworks still going on. The idiots of the two Navies shot off everything they had into the sky. I saw a few planes burning on the ground and wondered if I'd be killed or captured as I hit the ground.

"I came down heavily among some rocks not far from some more of our blokes and soon teamed up with them. One or two had broken bones and we had to leave them to try and find out where we were. We knew we were in the wrong place but with no officer in sight had to do the best we could. A Sergeant took charge and we followed him. He used a compass to try and steer us in the right direction.

"At last we heard voices and stopped to investigate and found some more paras, so we then had about twenty men altogether. We plunged on over rocky terrain and as it began to get light we stopped to eat some of our hard rations and take a rest. The Sergeant thought we must be somewhere near the main dropping zone, and we did hear some firing. At least we had gone forward and reached a place where we hoped to find our original objectives, but found they had already been taken after some stiff fighting. This had all been a bit of a shambles and disappointing. Within a few days we had been withdrawn and still I had not fired a single bullet."

For Operation Husky the 1st Airborne Division was supplemented by Brigadier 'Shan' Hackett's 4th Parachute Brigade from Libya. The British airborne formations were detailed to capture two important bridges at Primosole and Ponte Grande, which would, it was hoped, enable the main body of the 8th Army landing by sea to advance and capture Catania and Syracuse. The American 505th Parachute Infantry under General Gavin was allotted an objective further west. The British air-landing brigade under Brigadier Hicks was to seize the canal bridge at Ponte Grande; the bridge was to be seized by C Company of the 2nd Battalion South Staffords, who would land on two LZs near the canal, while most of the battalion came down on a third landing zone south of the canal, to move north in consolidation. Reinforcing the Staffs was the 1st Battalion of the Border Regiment, who would also move on to the nearby harbour.

As in all airborne operations, surprise was the key to success, so the 2000 men of the British gliderborne element were towed in their mostly American Waco gliders towards Malta in order to avoid enemy radar detection. Seven gliders went down as they crossed the North African coastline, but as the rest changed course towards Sicily they found they were battling a south-easterly gale. Disaster ensued, for as the towplanes and their precious charges approached the Sicilian coastline all landmarks ashore were obliterated by dust clouds. Sixty per cent of the gliders were released too soon, many crashed into the sea, their human cargoes drowning under the weight of their equipment. The light of a pale moon enabled a very few survivors to cling to wreckage until they were rescued by assault ships. Some 252 soldiers and glider pilots were drowned off Cap Passero, over 20 miles short of their objective; of the 52 gliders which made landfall, only 12 were anywhere near the objective. The assault commander, Major Ballinger, was killed by defensive fire as he clambered out of his glider, yet a dozen men under a Lieutenant took the bridge and removed the German demolition charges.

By dawn the small British force had swelled to 80 men with 7 officers, and this unit held on under increasing enemy shellfire until by 1500 hours only fifteen remained unwounded. At this point, with all ammunition gone, they were overwhelmed by the enemy. But within the hour a Border officer who had escaped met an advancing unit of the 17th Infantry Brigade and the vital bridge was recaptured.

The parachute element of the plan had depended on successful outcomes of the glider landings, so the design was changed and the drop of 2nd Para Brigade near Augusta was cancelled. The drop of the 1st, 2nd and 3rd Para Battalions on Primosole near Catania went ahead, using 105 Dakotas, 11 Albemarles, with four-engined Halifaxes and Stirlings towing Wacos and Horsas containing gunners for the anti-tank guns, engineers and medics. In command was General Lathbury, his plan ("Fustian") was to use six drop zones west of the Syracuse-Catania road, the vital bridge lying between the towns. The formation flew the same route as the glider train had taken via Malta, but on approaching Sicily were fired on by US and Royal Navy warships who had been alerted to German torpedo-carrying planes. In this initial fusillade from the sea two British planes were shot down and nine forced to turn back through heavy damage. The close formations, having been broken up by Allied fire, now came under German and Italian flak, with the result that ten more planes were forced to turn back, while thirty-seven went into the sea or crashed on the beaches. Some 1900 men had taken off from North Africa. Only 250 reached the Primosole bridge.

German paratroops under Major Heidrich had already dropped to reinforce the area earlier in the day, and it was these men who, with the aid of armour and self-propelled guns, forced Lt-Colonel Pearson's small force to retire. Meanwhile John Frost's 2nd Parachute Battalion was in occupation of hilly terrain south of the Simeto River, and made contact with the 4th Armoured Brigade moving up the road and the bridge. Montgomery had already shifted the point of his attack by the 8th Army further west to join up with the Americans, but a 'bloody battle' (to quote one German source) ensued for the bridge over the Simeto and all enemy attempts to destroy it failed. Two more German parachute regiments tried with the Herman Göring Division to hold Sicily but in the end were forced to retreat. The last Germans to fight a rearguard and escape across the Straits of Messina were paratroops. Their commanders, incidentally, had been the veterans of Eben Emael — Messrs Koch and Witzig.

One more operation was carried out by the 1st Airborne before it returned to England to prepare for the invasion of Europe.

Following the defection of Italy to the Allied cause on 3 September the American and British forces landed in Italy, the vanguard of the British being the 2nd and 4th Parachute Brigades, with the 1st following them to land at Taranto. An advance by Shan Hackett's 4th Brigade led to the capture of Moltala, but when the 10th Battalion went into action against Germans at Castellaneta the Divisional Commander, Major-General Hopkinson, was killed. His place was taken by Major-General Eric Down.

The 4th Brigade was relieved by the Air-Landing Brigade who captured Foggia, but by 1 November the 1st Airborne Division was being withdrawn from Italy, with the exception of the 2nd Brigade, whose unhappy fate was to be declared 'independent', to remain in Italy as available for airborne operations under command of the 8th Army. The 2nd spent four months on the coastal sector of the Army's left flank; after a rest period it entered the line again with the New Zealanders at Cassino. In June, 1944, the Brigade was in a rest camp at Salerno when it was alerted to take part in the invasion of southern France following the D-Day landings in Normandy. In the event this operation did not take place until August, so the paras were frustrated. A small operation did come their way, however, when 57 men and three officers were dropped in the German rear near Torricella to assist Italian partisans to block an important supply road.

II

"Go To It!"

The prime role allotted the airborne divisions on D-Day, 6 June, 1944, was to secure a lodgement area free from German interference, and in the American case to enable their forces to cut off and occupy the Cherbourg peninsula. Specifically, the 6th Airborne Division was to occupy an area some 24 square miles to defend the British left flank of the invasion forces. The operations have been exhaustively covered in many publications, and will only be outlined here as a prelude to following the experiences of our witnesses in the battle.

The 5th Parachute Brigade was ordered to capture the bridges over the Caen Canal and River Orne; the bridges were less than a mile apart on the river and canal that met on the coast at Ouistreham. The 6th Air-Landing Brigade would reinforce this drop that afternoon, 6 June.

The 3rd Parachute Brigade were assigned the destruction of the German coastal battery at Merville, plus four bridges, to seal off the exposed left flank and deny access to enemy forces.

The airborne drops and landings would be succeeded by the coming ashore of the main force of the British and Canadian army − three divisions, plus British and French Commandos.

Facing the Allies in France were two German Armies, the 7th and 15th, with the famous Field-Marshal Erwin Rommel in command, though it was only the former which actually faced the invasion beaches. The Germans' best troops and armour were held behind the coast, ready to be switched to whichever zone posed the greatest threat, and included some of the very best Panzer and SS troops.

For the airborne operation Nos 38 and 46 groups of the RAF possessed 450 planes − Dakotas, Albemarles, Halifaxes and Stirlings − to transport 6000 parachute and glider troops to France between midnight and dawn on 6 June. A further 3000 glider troops would be ferried across later in the day.

Sixty men of the 22nd Independent Parachute Company (the Pathfinders) took off at 2303 hrs on the night of 5 June from Harwell, quickly followed by troops of the Ox and Bucks, including engineers in six gliders bound for the bridges at Caen and the Orne. The two parachute brigades too off at 2357 hrs, these followed by the assault group of 9th Paras to attack the battery at Merville, the men carried in three Horsas.

Over one thousand planes flooded the night sky over southern England with the roar of their engines, carrying the 6th, and American 82nd and 101st Airborne Divisions. The weather was not ideal; low cloud and some rain obscured the aircrews' vision. The heavier equipment for the British airborne followed the infantry force, some carried in huge Hamilcar gliders.

By twenty minutes past midnight the first British pathfinders had landed in northern France, and it is claimed that these were the first Allied troops to land — Captains Tate, Medwood, and Lieutenants Latour and Vischer — but the Americans claim that their Pathfinders of the 101st Airborne landed five minutes earlier.

Like his comrades, Reg Andrews had spent month after month in training and heard all the current rumours concerning 'the date' — when the Second Front would be launched:

"We had lots of briefings and when the 6th finally came we were raring to go and all keyed up and excited. That night I didn't get any sleep, most men were the same. We had to get up very early as we were due off in the early hours. We were loaded up with lots of gear and looked quite comical really. I had a Bren gun in a valise and some spare magazines and could only get into the plane with help. We heard some flak as we went in over France and were soon lining up to jump.

"It was absolutely black outside on the ground and hard to see a thing, but it's amazing just how much you can hear from that height, all sorts of noises, especially on that night with so much going on. I was a bit scared that I'd make a hard landing in the dark and with all that gear on. As I came down the flak guns were firing and more planes were coming over.

"I saw the ground in time to brace myself and landed OK but winded. I got to my feet and could hear other chaps not far away stumbling about in the dark. I heard one or two whistles and calls and before long I had joined up with a few more lads. We marched off, following a lane until we came to a small house and skirted round it, watching out for some sign of Jerries or our own chaps.

We had not come together as hoped so there was a lot of independent action that night. Then we heard firing and our Sergeant told us to double forward towards the action. We hadn't gone far before we bumped into a bunch of Jerries moving along the road in the same direction. We had stuck to the fields on either side of the road.

"We dropped down and opened fire on them, but couldn't see how many we hit and the noise stopped as if both sides were sweating it out and waiting for the other to start up again. Our Sergeant told us to move on, so we doubled up, still keeping to the fields, and before long we met quite a few red berets and formed a perimeter. Our job was to block the roads and stop any reinforcements reaching the beachhead.

"When it began to get light all hell broke loose with the naval bombardment on the coast which wasn't too far away. We heard a lot of planes come over and then saw gliders and also heard Germans moving towards us on the road at speed."

Jim White from Bradford had been anxious to prove himself in action, and like many 'green' troops, wondered how he would react under fire. He got his chance to find out on D-Day:

"I went over that night in one of the first waves and we dropped into the darkness. On the way down I somehow lost my Sten gun and felt very foolish, but it didn't matter as when I got down there was a fair amount of confusion in the darkness and by the time I had got organized with a handful of other blokes I had found myself another gun.

"Off we went in what we hoped was the right direction. We were under orders to get together with as many others and form a perimeter to block German access to the beachhead. Well, we heard a fair amount of noise but saw no action until daybreak when we joined up with another group and were able to intercept a German convoy, and that was when I got my first action. It was a perfect ambush and we really clobbered them."

Bill Marshall had, like the rest of the paras of the 6th, been trained to as near perfection as non-combat situations would allow; they had seen all there was to see in the manoeuvring fields of southern England and felt they could beat any who opposed them. They had seen their bad days, such as when two men collided in a drop and another when a paratrooper got himself fatally tangled up coming down. It was bad on their nerves to see such sights, but being young and resilient they soon recovered. The paras tried to liven up the manoeuvres. They were used to giving the regular troops shocks by their lightning tactics, but sometimes had fun by foxing the umpires, the officers appointed to oversee the 'games' whose job it was at the end to decide which side had won the day. The paras would simply melt away into concealment, so that nobody but themselves and certainly not the harassed umpires knew where they were. This meant that the game could not really be concluded and a winner declared.

The boredom resulted in fights in the local pubs, with military police endeavouring to quell and arrest the troublemakers among the British paras, the Canadians and Americans.

"So it was a good thing when D-Day came. I think some of the local folk were glad to see the back of us," Bill comments.

Indeed, there were those among the civilian population who grew tired of the masses of military crowding the streets and pubs. Beer was rationed, and as one fine writer who experienced it all was to record later, some pubs gave only a frosty reception to soldiers, refusing them drinks, even on the very eve of D-Day.

"We blacked our faces and some made out their wills. I didn't. I had nothing to give anyone! All I did was write one or two short letters to my relatives and sort of say goodbye in case I didn't come back."

Bill Marshall landed in France, having seen some flak and one plane on fire. By then he was a Sergeant and confesses to feeling a fool as, after setting foot on the soil of Hitler's *Festung Europa*, he found he had but one man under his command:

"Blundering about in the darkness, blowing short blasts on a whistle until at last I had managed to gather about a dozen men around me and made off in what I thought was the right direction. We lined up near a small road in case the Jerries came to investigate; they must have known by then what was happening. But it was fairly quiet until daylight when shooting broke out not far away. We stayed put and ate some rations and saw all the gliders coming over and cheered. Then things began to liven up as the Jerries finally decided to act. They sent a number of probing columns in our direction, and one came along the road we were watching. We gave them a real pasting. They were of course the first Germans we'd seen, and we were not too impressed: they stuck to the road in vehicles, with a few on foot and made a lot of noise so you could hear them from way off. We reckoned they were not Jerry's best."

Reg Andrews:

"We waited until they were in view and then let them have it and that caused a shambles. Some Germans were marching but they had some vehicles and these tried to back off, but we'd taken care of that by getting the rearmost one which caught fire, so they all got into a big muddle. The Jerry infantry tried to get off the road and into the fields, but we were already in occupation and gave them a terrible pasting. They all melted away, killed or wounded, only a few managed to escape.

"At full daylight we had consolidated our position and dominated it."

Bill Marshall:

"The first vehicle was an armoured car, behind that a lorry load of infantry, then another armoured car, then another truck, and so on. The column was perhaps a mile long and well strung out and we ambushed them in such a way that the whole column was blocked."

It is not certain if this is the same action as that described by Reg Andrews, as Bill states that the rearmost vehicles of the German column managed to escape.

"After that it was quiet for a while until they started shelling us. They had 88s and one or two tanks, but by then we had dug in and took no casualties."

Jim White:

"Then we had to dig in as the Germans started shelling us and bringing up tanks and we had a bigger battle on our hands."

Bill Marshall:

"By the time we had eaten and cleaned up a little the bigger battle had started with a lot more shellfire which was nasty, but our planes were terrific and gave them a pasting. I can't speak too highly of the RAF in that battle. They were everywhere and gave the Germans hell."

Reg Andrews:

"The Germans now made a more determined effort to get through to the coast with tanks, armoured cars and infantry coming along the roads and fields in open order. By then we had a small number of 6-pounders and some PIATs and quite a battle developed, but as we were very well dug in suffered very few casualties. The Jerries retreated away again out of sight.

"I recall that at one moment a French farmer came along the road with a cart, smoking a pipe and looking as if he hadn't a care in the world, yet not far away a ding-dong battle was in progress and a far bigger one pending. We watched him in amazement and he almost ignored us. I don't think the French thereabouts cared a hang for the Germans or the British; we were all just a nuisance to them. Then the Germans started to use their artillery, but they then had to learn a terrible lesson from our forces, for they'd no experience of our great air support. There was hardly a moment in those days when our planes were not overhead just waiting for some German to show himself — Typhoons, Spits, all sorts — they gave the Germans no rest at all. Even so, they were very, very good at camouflage, and we did take some incoming shells from hidden guns, including 88s. Then, after a few days the Army boys came along with lots of Shermans and artillery and the main battle started."

Apart from the landing, the glider troops' experience in Normandy was similar to that of their para comrades, except at the Merville battery. The hazardous nature of using gliders was once again exposed when one of the three gliders lost its tow over the English coast, and when the two survivors reached French airspace it was found that no contact could be made with the Eureka beacon placed by the advance reconnaissance party already dropped near Merville. This was almost certainly because of a disastrous raid by Lancaster bombers which had only succeeded in wiping out most of the British recon party and flattening the nearby village. One glider came down 200 yards from the battery but its occupants became involved at once with a German patrol.

The men given the job of spiking the German guns were of the 9th Parachute Battalion commanded by Lt-Colonel T. B. Otway and had rehearsed their task in great secrecy near Newbury, Berkshire. But, as so often in war, the most carefully laid plans often go awry, so at Merville Otway could only rally some 25% of his force, who, with the remains of the recce troops, blew holes in the wire surrounding the gun battery and rushed in with weapons blazing. In the fight that followed 70 of the British airborne were lost, while 100 of the German garrison of 130 were killed.

Both bridges assigned to the glider assault troops of the Ox & Bucks were taken, the six gliders splitting into two units, and once the defenders had been killed or captured their commander, Major R. J. Howard, dispersed them into a defensive perimeter covering both bridges.

The glider force which took off as the second wave suffered five lost over England and three more were shot down by heavy German flak on reaching France. Forty-seven Horsas and two Hamilcars arrived over their landing zone west of Ranville, by which time fifteen of the original seventy-two were missing. Such was the thoroughness of the British plans that engineers had already dropped ahead of the force to clear landing sites of the German obstacles and place illuminated flarepaths. Once landed, the glider troops moved to assist their comrades at the Benouville and Ranville bridges.

John Holmes:

"All our training came to a head on 6 June when we landed in Normandy. It was not an experience you could easily forget. We lost a few chaps through accidents, bad landings mostly, but in some cases they had the bad luck to come down near Germans and had to fight. In my case I and my pals were lucky; we came down bang on target and got out in one piece. We were very alert but saw no Germans at all until after the real fighting started when they tried to break through to the beachhead. By then we were well ready for them with 6-pounders and machine guns and PIATs.

"I'll never forget the first Jerry I saw. He was wearing one of those high, peaked caps, an officer, and riding in a truck with a load of men behind him. I believe he had a pistol in his hand. It soon became the possession of a pal of mine who killed him from close range with a Sten. We massacred those Germans from ambush; they didn't stand a chance."

Jules Cauvain was in charge of troops ordered to take care of some suspected German fortifications:

"When we came down we found they were deserted. Our landing was not too good and we had some bruises and damage, but were soon set up for all-round defence. When we found the enemy were not in occupation we took over their positions and awaited events which came next day in a number of small counter-attacks that we easily repelled. We had a holding brief and did our best to keep the Germans away from the beachhead build-up, but the biggest actions over the following weeks took place to the north of us, so we didn't have much trouble. What German attacks that came in were mostly broken up by our air force and artillery fire which was terrific. We took a few prisoners including some very young SS kids who were very insolent but soon quietened down."

General Gale had issued a slogan to his men of the 6th Airborne soon after taking command which was abbreviated to GO TO IT! and soon after D-Day the formation published its own news sheet called *Pegasus Goes To It*; an early copy contained an alleged complaint from a German officer of the 346th Infantry Division to the effect that he did not consider it fair that troops of his unit should have to be pitted against British airborne soldiers. Other items contained in the news bulletins recorded the German doodle-bug raids on England, humorous references to their Commando rivals' habit of digging deep and the second worst enemy of the troops living rough in Normandy — the mosquitoes.

But, once the stalemate and very severe positional fighting was over after the break-out and annihilation of the German 7th Army, the airborne of the 6th fully expected that they would be returned to Britain for rest, re-equipping and made ready for the next airborne op. In fact the division went on fighting across France until September, when it had completed three months of ground combat. It was then withdrawn and returned to its bases at Bulford and Netheravon, but only for a well-earned respite, for to the men's consternation they were returned to the continent as ground troops in the winter.

INTERLUDE

When the 6th Airborne Division next held a formal mustering parade in England it was minus 821 men killed in action, 2,709 seriously wounded, and 927 missing. The term 'missing' must always strike a baffling chord in the layman. What exactly does it mean? Did all those hundreds of men run away, never to be seen again? Were they purely and simply deserters from the field of battle, men who could not face the awfulness of war and who left it to those who could? There are always those 'missing' in war; the RAF had them in quantity among its aircrews, and men in air combat do not get a chance to run away.

Unhappily, it usually means that the men concerned simply disappeared in an explosion, and in such a way that no identifiable remains were found. If a soldier sees or knows that his pal or 'oppo' was beside him one moment and gone the next instant, in such an occurrence little or no problem exists regarding identification, even though the graves registration section usually prefer some kind of remains to label. However, everyone in the field of combat knows that desertions do occur, men crack under the strain, sometimes running away, as did the eventual hero in *The Red Badge of Courage*. But élite troops do not generally experience that kind of thing, certainly not paratroops.

Over the next three months the 6th Airborne's losses were largely made good, even though at that stage of the war a manpower crisis was happening, with reluctant airmen from the RAF being transferred to the infantry. Just before Christmas Hitler launched his offensive in the Ardennes that was intended to drive a wedge between the American and British armies and capture Antwerp. The 6th Airborne was rushed back to the Continent, across Belgium, to help stiffen the line at the River Meuse crossings; but by then the Germans had shot their bolt and were in retreat and by 24 February the Division was back in England. By that time three other airborne operations involving British troops had taken place.

THE CHAMPAGNE INVASION

Operation "Anvil", the Allied invasion of southern France, took place on 15 August, 1944, involving three US Army divisions and a French armoured force which landed around the fashionable resort of St Tropez, which was why it came to be dubbed the 'champagne invasion'. Also taking part was a US-British airborne force which flew from bases around Rome to drop inland, their task to interrupt German road traffic and generally cause mayhem.

The British contingent was the 2nd Independent Parachute Brigade which had been left behind under command of the 8th Army in Italy. The parachutists were scattered about in a haphazard drop by the 51 US Troop Carrier Wing, but the glider landings carried out in two sorties were more concentrated, the troops involved being the 6th Royal (Welch) Battalion.

The 2nd Paras secured their objectives, linking up with the American airborne, and by 26 August were back in Italy.

III

Arnhem

Perhaps no one military operation has been so written up and filmed as Operation "Market Garden", the battle which has become indelibly etched into the public mind as 'The bridge too far' — the epic Battle of Arnhem. The Battle of El Alamein has long been eclipsed by the contest in Holland in September, 1944, and in these terms has itself perhaps only been pushed into second place by the Battle of Britain, though for obvious reasons there is little or no comparison from either the viewpoint of importance or duration.

It was General Browning who, it is alleged, first coined the phrase a 'bridge too far', this being his not too optimistic view of the Arnhem plan. The phrase was taken up by the late American writer Cornelius Ryan for his book on the battle and then picked for a mammoth movie version, a blockbuster in the genre still appearing almost yearly on TV screens as, incidentally, is the far lesser known Crown Film Unit production called *Theirs is the Glory*, made in 1946. The latter is well worth seeing for its original footage and participation of real paras and Panther tanks. For obvious reasons it has never had and never will have the same impact in the public mind as the multi-million-dollar colour production which, although embedding and immortalizing the heroism of the airborne troops at Arnhem as well as the American achievements elsewhere, does in some respects fall into the modern category of "faction". Because of the film's wide dissemination and impact on the modern public's view of recent history it is worth mentioning here.

Though excellently made and with the expert help of Major-General John Frost for some superlatively done battle scenes, surely few Britishers can watch it without feelings of unease which stem from the apparent examples of British incompetence, bungling and lethargy. John Frost probably had fun helping out with the film, but of course he had no sway over the script and direction the story would take. There are serious omissions from the historian's point of view, distortions and portrayals which add up to a twisted picture.

Obviously it is impossible to make a film of the actual battle *in toto*, but when dealing with a serious subject it is galling to find quite lengthy fictional episodes apparently written in merely to provide vehicles for box office stars. Here we see top names playing square-jawed heroes in the American mould who get things done with get-up-and-go vigour, while most of the British leading roles are portrayed by actors apparently intent on going over the top to delineate almost comic characters of the kind most derided overseas as typical British asses. Errors and situations are reduced by absurd performances for the sake of entertainment and again, one is left with an impression of almost total British incompetence. To be specific:

The communications breakdown at Arnhem was bad but not unique, radio failures were commonplace throughout the war, and often caused by the nature of the terrain which at Arnhem, being a built-up area, hindered contact greatly. Some of the sets in use were also of short range; to put this failure down to one individual is an error. There was one lamentable lapse not mentioned in the film, when a ground controller was prevented, through radio failure, from contacting Typhoons waiting overhead during Second Army's battle to reach the airborne.

One American writer has quoted an instance where the tanks of the Guards Armoured Division stood waiting for almost two days while the men in Arnhem were being annihilated, and something like this is shown in the film. It is certainly a gross over-simplification and most probably a slur on a fine body of men who fought hard and suffered in that drive to Arnhem.

When a British para POW was freed by an advancing American column in Germany in 1945 one of the young officer liberators is alleged to have said, in relation to Arnhem, "We would have done it". The Britisher, on consideration, seems to have decided that they would have.

No one error caused the British defeat at Arnhem, and the mistakes made have been whittled down in the main to an error of judgement in the first place, which is to say that the original fault lay at the top, with the Commander-in-Chief, Field-Marshal Bernard Montgomery. The buck has to stop there because, not only was it his responsibility, it was his plan.

By September, 1944, Monty, as he was affectionately known to the public, was riding high on a wave of public and self-esteem gained by his victories over the enemy from Alamein onwards. He had enjoyed two years of triumph and, as is now well known, was basking in it. Because of his earlier experiences and nature Montgomery never moved in the military (or private) sense without careful consideration. He had become well-known for caution and thoroughness, which makes his failure at Arnhem the more extraordinary.

Military criticism of Monty began soon after D-Day, mostly by the Americans, who, despite the Field-Marshal's briefings in England, either ignored or simply did not understand his strategy in Normandy. True, his forces had failed to capture such objectives as Caen, the reasons for which need not be entered into here. They do not affect the outcome of his plan which was to pivot the Allied front on the British-Canadian sector and allow the Americans to swing south and west to cut off the Cherbourg peninsula. There have been those who refute this, but it is plain that this was his intention at least from June onwards, even if not before. This plan did indeed draw off most of the German armoured forces, including their top-notch Army and SS troops on to the British and Canadians who bore the brunt of blood-letting battles and it was their sacrifice that enabled the eventual American breakout — eventual because of repeated American failures to get started or crash through the comparatively weaker forces facing them. It was the great pressure and engaging of the best of the German panzers that enabled General Patton's 3rd Army to make its breakthrough in the south. They did this in great style and were lauded thereafter as the most dangerous of the Allied formations, though it is perfectly obvious that their triumph was achieved against negligible opposition. Patton's army was essentially a pursuit corps. When they found a soft chink in the enemy's armour they exploited it brilliantly, but when up against really tough opposition in a set-to battle the General tended to give up at once and take another tack. The British too could move fast — the dash to Brussels proved that.

By September the Allies had swept across the continent to the German border and a difficult supply situation resulted. Montgomery had failed to give sufficient priority to the capture of Antwerp, but a good flow of petrol and other essentials was flowing to the front from the ports in Allied hands, especially Dieppe. But the American 'red ball express' convoys did not help the British. Montgomery had rightly seen a great opportunity to thrust powerfully into Germany. He had suggested to Bradley that they combine their two armies of 40 divisions for this purpose in a concentrated thrust northwards. This would mean a priority of supplies and bring Patton's 3rd Army in the south to a halt. Patton would never countenance this — and, thought Ike − neither would the American public. 'Victories are won by public opinion', he told Monty, an astonishing assertion but indicative of American thinking. But Monty came back with the truism that given the victories the public at home would soon show its opinion. Montgomery pressed for his single-thrust policy but this was out of keeping with Eisenhower's and American doctrine which tended to see the broad front as an American football field: whichever player got the ball was allowed to run with it. Patton felt he had it and was determined to keep it. A flamboyant, ambitious man, but with a strong emotional side, he contrived to grab all the fuel he could to maintain his troops' momentum, concealing the fact that his men had captured 100,000 gallons of German fuel, even sending his officers masquerading as from a fellow general's army to steal petrol from their own dumps.

By then Montgomery had, by tactlessness, got up the noses of the Americans, even though, when under his orders in Normandy, Bradley had found him a considerate boss; but things had gradually soured, especially since Eisenhower had taken over control of the land forces as per plan once the break-out from Normandy had been achieved. Eisenhower had neither the experience, ideas or determination to control large field forces, though in his role as 'diplomatic overseer' he had proved brilliant. He refused to consent to what he called in his memoirs a 'pencil-like thrust' into the heart of Germany, which was certainly not what Monty had been pressing for; he had even offered to serve under an American commander if Ike would agree. When Eisenhower proposed using the airborne divisions to drop behind the Siegfried Line Bradley demurred, preferring to use the transport planes for flying up supplies, so the Supreme Commander allowed himself to be talked out of it. Bradley was too conservative, but in turn permitted his junior, Patton, to contravene Eisenhower's orders in maintaining his drive in the south; indeed, it can be said that he was prepared to overlook much in order to snub Montgomery and secure the American way.

By September it was clear that the British would have no single-drive plan approved by Eisenhower. The consequence would be a 'pencil-like' thrust along a fragile route with a mere two British battalions at the point.

The British were therefore faced with two options, and these were fairly obvious ones from the military point of view, and certainly recognized by the enemy. The Second Army could either strike north-east across the River Maas towards Wesel, or almost due north along the route Eindhoven-Nijmegen-Arnhem; both of these plans favoured an airborne drop. But while the Arnhem scheme would require the capture of three major river crossings and five minor waterways, it would be less dangerous than the Wesel route which was believed to be more flak-ridden and open to German fighter attack. The withdrawal of the Germans into Holland and Germany meant that what fighter forces remained − and these included the deadly new Messerschmitt 262 jets − could more easily be concentrated in defending western localities, and indeed at a later stage of the Arnhem battle this is what happened. Always swift to repair their battered airfields, the *Luftwaffe* mounted bombing raids and on one day put up 500 fighters over Holland.

Consideration of the few days immediately before Arnhem is vital in weighing up how the operation ever came to be mounted, and it must be seen in the overall context of the British offensive operations as a whole.

There were definite advantages to Montgomery's theme of a single, concerted thrust, a heavy punch to the north-east, for if it came off it would perhaps pay two immediate dividends − a drive round into the vital Ruhr industrial area and the outflanking of the Siegfried Line. There were more, for it could well also cut off the German forces in Holland. Again, these were fairly obvious considerations not unnoticed by the Germans. In fact Hitler himself said, during his midnight conference on the night of 17-18 September, when the British operation at Arnhem was well under way, that the situation was more serious than in the East. This was why the enemy reacted so vigorously and heavily, not merely because an enemy force had landed in its midst.

So, by early September the Allied generals were all in a sense trying to do their own thing, in today's parlance, with Monty determined to hit the Germans for six, as he would say, in the northern front, while to the south Patton was equally determined to maintain his own momentum whatever the supply situation. Bradley, as usual, was content to plod along.

But during these few days the commander of the British Second Army, General Dempsey, a quiet but competent man not given in any way to seeking the limelight, began to receive reports through his Intelligence of increased German rail and road movement in the area of Arnhem-Nijmegen, and raised this when visiting Montgomery on 10 September. But even at this stage, the latter was undecided, for the RAF had objected to any idea of an airborne drop to the north-east or Wesel route because of the flak and fighters, even though any such operation would be covered by many hundreds of Allied escorts. Dempsey said later that, when he spoke to him, Monty had just received a message from the War Office in London asking him if it was possible to swing his Army north towards the Dutch coast, this because the Germans had begun firing V2 rockets at Britain two days before, their launch sites believed to be on the coast of Holland. That seemed to clinch the matter. Monty opted for Arnhem.

Having decided on the objective, it was up to the commander to set the date, and Montgomery may have been persuaded by the War Office signal that there was no time to be lost, and so opted for an early date. This surely meant that a plan had to be rushed through, a complex operation involving his allies the Americans, plus the Poles, needed to be planned in detail and briefings made to all ranks in seven days. It is hard to believe that even the Germans would have tried to hurry through such an operation in that kind of timescale.

In truth, because of the nature of the terrain Monty's single-thrust could only be mounted along a single highway, a stretch of white concrete road which ran from the frontier into Holland. Even with additional corps following up through the terrain on either flank, it posed obvious risks and problems which should have been thoroughly assessed in appreciations before the battle was launched, and it seems obvious they were not. Otherwise, why did Montgomery himself airily inform General Browning that the Second Army would be with him in a couple of days? In fact, the airborne troops were told at briefings that they would be relieved by around midday on Tuesday, 19 September. This was the time scale repeated in the re-enactment documentary film *Theirs Is the Glory* made just after the war.

This inaccurate assessment of the situation and possible enemy reaction seems to have been based on the experiences of the previous weeks – the stunning victory in France and Belgium. Indeed, there exists a BBC recording by Montgomery allegedly made on the very day the Arnhem operation was launched, a kind of pep talk review extolling the triumphs to date, probably made for home consumption and containing no word of the airborne assault. This talk is not mentioned in Monty's memoirs or most historical accounts and includes the following:

"It is becoming problematical how much longer he [the enemy] can continue the struggle".

But Montgomery, the cautious general, should have known by that time that the Germans had a remarkable capacity for recovery given half a chance and could bounce back as tough as ever. Did he really imagine they would allow his army to motor smoothly along the highway to Arnhem? Or had the Field-Marshal by then become so immersed in self-confidence and esteem that he felt capable of achieving anything? Winston Churchill said he was insufferable in victory. Certainly, everything points to the fact that the general adopted an uncharacteristically 'un-Monty' approach to the Arnhem operation. Or was he by then well aware of criticisms of his style and determined to prove his detractors wrong?

When the Americans heard of his plan many of them were not just impressed, they were amazed by his boldness – or recklessness. Eisenhower agreed to release two American airborne divisions to assist, plus the necessary supplies to sustain them, though one source records that two US truck companies designated to re-supply their airborne arrived at the River Meuse with the wrong calibre ammunition – or empty.

Major-General Roy E. Urquhart took command of the 1st Airborne Division in December, 1943. He was a Scotsman, aged 42, had served well in Africa, Sicily and Italy, but had no experience of airborne operations, only in planning them, had never parachuted and was prone to airsickness. By September, 1944, his Division was as over-trained and restless as it could be. In the General's own words, "Battle-hungry to a degree which only those who have commanded large forces of trained soldiers can fully comprehend".

No less than sixteen operations had been drawn up for the 1st Airborne since D-Day and every one had for various reasons been cancelled, so when the Arnhem plan was put up as 'on' everyone from the Army Group Commander downwards became caught up in an irresistible tide of enthusiasm, though this was mixed with some caution or even doubts in some quarters. But in the main the troops were relieved and excited to be going into action. Yet as one officer recalled later:

"I could see that it would be a tough one and some of us objected to various facets of the plan, but were stuck with it and I will not go into the wrangling that went on. Let's say we would have done it another way. When you hit the Jerries they react with everything they've got, and boy! did we stir up a hornet's nest!"

Tom Smith:

"You can guess how we felt after D-Day and the successful invasion and the German retreat. We just hung about in England and had lots of jobs planned, but not one came off. Then, just as we thought that we'd never get back into the war we were called to yet another briefing for an op, and this is when we learned of the Arnhem plan for the first time. It all seemed very dangerous, but we were all keyed up and confident in our officers and thought it would work out OK.

"On the day I know I was very excited at the chance to jump into Europe – into the proper war. I think we all felt we would give the Jerries a hard time and hopefully win."

Jim Carter laments that every plan made after D-Day was scrapped and none they could take part in came to anything. Ken Norman comments on the disappointment felt by all when D-Day came and the 1st were left out of it:

"Then, when the Arnhem affair was mooted we were very excited and could see that we would either get great acclaim or possibly be annihilated. It all depended on how Jerry reacted – and my guess was unfortunately wrong: we thought they had taken such a beating that they could not muster the strength to stop us. However, some parts of the plan were a little disquieting, but we had no doubts that we would acquit ourselves well."

Alf Turner:

"That op to us was a bit of a shot in the dark and we knew we'd be in for a fight, as although the Germans had suffered some tremendous losses in France they were not finished by a long shot."

Henry Lambert:

"We had kicked our heels for a long time, and a lot of well-laid plans came to nothing. Then came Arnhem, and this time we were in for it, as we could see that to land gliders behind enemy lines was going to be no picnic."

The Allied plan was simple: it was to land three airborne divisions along a road route which could lead the British 30th Corps around behind the enemy northern flank and into the Ruhr, heartland of the German war industry. The US 82nd and 101st Airborne would seize the first two bridges, the British 1st the last and farthest from early assistance.

Because of his inexperience, Urquhart was obliged to rely on the advice of others, so bowed to the RAF insistence that it could not drop paras or land gliders south of the Arnhem bridge itself because of German flak posts in the vicinity, and finally agreed to the use of LZ's and DZ's seven to eight miles from the target bridge. This was the worst error of the plan, and should not have occurred because of the experience gained on D-Day. At that time the airborne drops

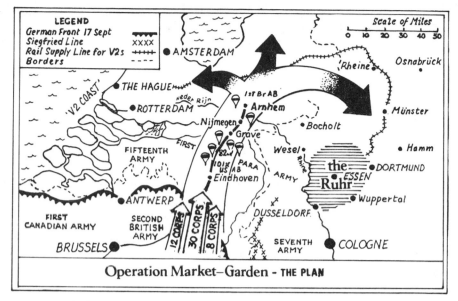

Operation Market–Garden - THE PLAN

were made in several lifts, instead of in one mass. Like the Germans, the Allies were suffering from a lack of transport aircraft for such large operations. It was the need to protect drop and landing zones for the following flights that forced Urquhart to designate the air-landing troops in part to remain where they were after arrival. Yet the RAF's reluctance to risk nothing and deposit the troops so far from the objective was ill-advised in view of the huge flak suppression programme they had laid on. As the American General Gavin observed, it was better to take some losses by landing plumb on the target. But, to offset this, the British allocated a squadron of armoured reconnaissance jeeps who, after being landed, would 'race for the bridge'.

Of the transport aircraft allocated to fly in the paratroops, only 155 of the 519 used by the 1st Airborne would be British; the rest would be provided by the Americans; most of the tug planes would be British. In the event not one of the Division's planes or gliders was hit by flak; though the Americans suffered 35 plane losses and 13 gliders shot down in their own operation further south. But 38 gliders failed to arrive of the 358 despatched owing to tow-rope failures. This lack of German flak and fighter interference could not last, and it didn't. As the Polish para General Sosabowski had forecast, German reaction and the weather interfering with air activity upset the whole programme. Only some of Sosabowski's men were volunteers, many were drafted into his parachute force who had trained for so long in the hope of returning to their own homeland in triumph.

Before relating the experiences of men who took part in the Arnhem battle it is as well to give just a mention of the enormous and unexpected difficulties which beset Second Army in its drive north.

Although this battle is usually referred to as Operation "Market Garden" to signify the air and ground components respectively, it was of course two quite separate ground battles, even four if one includes the two American airborne operations.

The white concrete highway already mentioned was flanked by boggy ground unsuitable for heavy vehicles, with pine and cypress plantations each side which provided ideal concealment for German defenders. The 20,000 vehicles of Lt-General Horrocks' 30th Corps were spearheaded by the tanks of the Irish Guards who were poised on the start line to advance at all possible speed and crash through the barrier the Germans had erected a few hundred yards along the road. Close behind the tanks rode infantry in armoured personnel carriers, while overhead the RAF had arranged for 100 Typhoons who would make rocket and cannon attacks on the enemy at five-minute intervals. The attack would be assisted by a rolling barrage provided by 400 guns of the artillery. In the woods either side of this single road route were concealed and waiting five battalions of Germans from the 6th Parachute Regiment, the 9th SS Division and 6th Penal Battalion, the latter from the Walther Division composed of military felons escaping jail by combat service.

The airborne troops had begun landing near Arnhem at about 1315, and having received word of this, Horrocks gave the signal for the assault by 30 Corps − ten minutes after the artillery barrage had begun. The tanks began to roll and the RAF Typhoons attacked the wooded areas and any German positions noted by the F00 riding below them in his armoured control vehicle. The German troops were compelled to keep their heads down or be destroyed by the British assault and the first tank squadron of the Irish Guards was able to rush along the highway and crash through the barrier without harm. But, as always, the Germans recovered in the short intervals when no planes were overhead, and in no time eight tanks of the British column had been brewed up, the whole vast cavalcade came to a halt as the following infantry debussed from their carriers and rushed into the woods to try and remove the defenders. It had really only needed a small number of Germans to impose this delay, and a few bazooka teams plus one anti-tank gun were all the British infantry dislodged. But since speed was of the essence, they told their prisoners to climb up with them in the carriers and on the tanks, for there was no time to escort them to the rear. This so shook the Germans that they at once began pointing out further defence positions which would have opened fire on both them and the British. The information was relayed to the Typhoons and artillery who proceeded to plaster the positions and enable the advance to continue.

The 30 Corps advance went according to schedule so that by the following afternoon the spearhead had reached Valkenswaard, five miles south of Eindhoven and then linked up with the troops of the US 101st Airborne. That was the promising start, but from then on things went wrong, with constant enemy attacks which cut the road many times so that at one stage the log-jam of vehicles was two deep and stretched for many miles. The spearhead force was continually having to turn back men and tanks to clear the road, and some of these combats were fierce and protracted, and hampered by the ground either side which the Germans had mined. At some points the road was elevated on an embankment, thus making the British tanks perfect skyline targets for the German units concealed in small farms and woods with anti-tank guns and machine guns. Every time a tank or other vehicle was hit it blocked the road and caused a jam. Then, to make matters worse, soon after the battle got underway the *Luftwaffe* raided Eindhoven while it was jammed with British vehicles, including an ammunition convoy which was burned and blown up. The wreckage took 24 hours to clear. These were the kind of delays which slowed down and often brought the 30 Corps attack to a standstill. In the battles to keep open both the highway and the drop zones of the American airborne the US troops were closely involved.

At one stage a German counter-attack overran the landing grounds of the 82nd Airborne and only a desperate assault by the Americans saved it in time for another fly-in of airborne.

Lieutenant Tom Burgess decided, on hearing of the Arnhem operation, that it would be "a risky thing to attempt". They were going right into enemy territory and he thought they might be biting off more than they could chew:

"It was a grand Sunday and we took off, very heavily laden and keen to get on with it; the lads were in good fettle and I thought we'd do a good job. When we got over Holland we could hear the flak, but it didn't bother us and everything went like clockwork. We jumped on target and after forming up made haste to reach Arnhem.

It was bad because the further we went the more Dutch civilians we met who held us up. Then we heard shooting, but saw no Germans. Then at last we had just reached a crossroads I believe and came under direct machine-gun fire and had to hit the deck. We tried to move on and outflank the Germans and this took precious time. We could hear shooting elsewhere and could see that things were getting bogged down. I sent a section on to get around the Germans, and at last we moved on. But the same thing happened again, so I decided we should split into groups and try to go hell for leather for Arnhem.

"We got ourselves organized and set off again, but took casualties at once from machine-gun fire. We reached an embankment and got onto this, but we were now under fire from several directions so had to withdraw. Obviously, things had gone wrong, but we were not giving up, and after a bit of consultation tried to push on again. By then it was evening and there was a lot of confused shooting in progress and a lack of communication. We moved off in sections, trying to probe the enemy to find out what we were up against, but they got behind us and we were split up. I lost my Sergeant in the confusion and things went from bad to worse. I decided it was better to wait for daylight, there were too many small parties and all kinds of disasters can occur in darkness."

Tom Smith:

"When we flew over Holland we could see that the d.z. was far from the objective. We had known this from the maps and models, but once there it seemed even further on the ground."

Jim Carter:

"We dropped outside Arnhem and I hurt my ankle, but it wasn't serious and I managed to keep up with the rest of the lads as we marched towards our objective."

Ken Norman recalls that Sunday 17 September was a fine day and that all went like clockwork:

"There was little flak over Holland and we dropped bang on target, though of course our real objective was miles away — too far as it turned out."

Alf Turner:

"We were confident though, despite some misgivings, and went off singing into the Daks on that Sunday which I'll never forget. It was a good flight with not much opposition from the enemy and we were dropped exactly where we were supposed to be, but of course miles from our objective, which was fatal."

Henry Lambert sailed across the North Sea on that fine day while millions of British Mums were preparing what passed for Sunday lunch:

"We set off in an armada, and next thing I knew we were diving down and I heard popping as the Germans opened up with their AA. We made a safe landing, unloaded our jeeps and cycles, and rushed off to the rendezvous just as planned. We could hear a bit of shooting, but it didn't bother us as [it was] too far away. It was a grand feeling to see so many airborne dropping in one place."

In fact, things began to go wrong as soon as the troops landed, for the gliders carrying the armoured jeeps never arrived. It is recorded that while no gliders were actually shot down en route, thirty-five failed to arrive at the landing zone, and among them were those containing the armoured recon jeeps. What happened to these gliders is unknown, but it meant that John Frost and his 2nd Paras were re-assigned to make their way on foot to the bridge at Arnhem. For many of the British soldiers it had turned out to be a rather pleasant hike along sunlit, leafy lanes, but their disillusionment was about to begin. Tom Smith:

"We set off at a good pace, meeting many civilians who gave us flowers and kisses and seemed delighted to see us. The poor devils really thought that liberation day had come at last.

"We had only gone about a mile when we came under fire, and to our great disappointment had to halt and lie low for a while. Then we cut across some fields off a side road, under fire the whole way from machine guns, and lost a few men. By now we felt that things were going wrong and this was a bitter disappointment to us. But we were still in good heart and were not in the least thinking of giving up."

Jim Carter:

"We'd only done a couple of miles when the Jerries opened up and we had to take cover. But we managed to get on and actually saw the bridge, our target, not too far away – but that's as far as we got. The Jerries brought up lots of SS troops and tanks and we got into a hell of a big fight. I dived into some houses with my mates and we knew we were in for it. We had not expected such opposition and knew that we could not cope with the tanks without heavier support than we ourselves had. We started to move through and behind the houses to outflank the Jerries and succeeded in doing so. But after we had opened up on them they turned everything on to us and that was when I was knocked out of the battle.

"I remember I was lying in a front garden under a hedge with my rifle poking through it trying to sight on some Germans marching along the road. But as I was going to fire a Jerry machine gun opened up and swept the whole hedge with fire. Something hit me in the eye, the pain was horrible and I passed out. I must have come to a little bit, as I heard the Jerries shouting, but there was a lot more noise and everything went black."

The 1 p.m. timing on the Sunday airdrop had given the British press ample time in which to set up the Monday front-page headlines which told of over one thousand planes and gliders disgorging thousands of airborne troops before the German flak guns had a chance to fire. The landing at least, the papers claimed, had gone 'according to plan', and several Dutch towns had already been cleared of the enemy. At this stage neither the British newspapers nor radio nor the Germans made any mention of the town of Arnhem. On the home side this was because of the usual partial news blackout when military objectives were involved, while the enemy were in some initial ignorance and made mention only of airborne landings at Nijmegen and near the river Lek.

One British war correspondent had landed in the fourth glider to touch down, finding himself in a turnip field near a house outside which a Dutch couple in their Sunday best stood ready to greet their supposed liberators. In fact, many of the Dutch folk were garbed in their black church-going clothes, as noted by one low-flying fighter pilot who also reported seeing airborne soldiers already "leaning over a garden wall talking to girls", which was not necessarily typical of the delays that occurred that afternoon.

But one reporter especially was to go down in the history of the Arnhem battle. The Canadian Stanley Maxted would escape the area, but not until he had crouched in a foxhole while making his BBC recording. "The bundles are coming down," he said, watching the re-supply planes flying over, the sound of German flak guns in the background.

Although, as might be expected, the war correspondents were cautiously optimistic in their coverage, there were the usual inaccuracies and inadvisable comments. One reporter at SHAEF stated that good radio contact had been established between the Supreme HQ and the Airborne Army: if this was the case then it could only have been with the American units. But the same correspondent stated that, "The new invasion, linked with the advance of the British 2nd and Canadian 1st Armies from Belgium, is an immediate thrust intended for the heart of the Reich."

Symptomatic of the general optimism was Field-Marshal Montgomery's own "order of the day" broadcast on Sunday night, his "triumphant cry" being "FORWARD INTO GERMANY", and containing morale-boosting praise for his soldiers' efforts so far, the capture of almost 400,000 Germans (and assorted other nationalities including Mongols), and another of those foolishly inappropriate religious phrases:

"Let us say to ourselves, 'This was the Lord's doing, and it was marvellous in our eyes'."

Since the hard news from Holland was scant, the newspaper editors were obliged to prompt their feature writers to come up with supporting items, and in the *Daily Herald* this took the form of a write-up on the two Allied airborne generals: Lt-General Lewis H. Brereton, the American Commander-in-Chief of the Allied Airborne Army, and his deputy Lt-General Frederick Browning, an ex-Guards officer who fortunately for the journalist happened to be married to the famous novelist Daphne du Maurier, whose father Gerald was also well-known as an actor. Browning was credited with having built up the British airborne forces against opposition and, unlike his subordinate Urquhart, loved flying and held a pilot's certificate.

While Browning by appearance was seen as the typical British officer, with good looks and the standard moustache, his American counterpart seems to have been one of those military types peculiar to the US forces who specialize in profanity, being known as "Cussing Brereton", a general who allegedly boasted an ability to "swear in more languages than any other senior officer in the American forces", including in his "cuss repertoire" Malayan, Hindustani, Japanese "and most European languages".

One leader writer on this Monday commenting on 'The Lessons of Holland', wrote:

"The feats recorded from Holland today therefore mark, first of all, the triumph of those who in 1940 and 1941 set about the task of training and equipping a new British Army capable of teaching the Germans how to make war." Bold words indeed.

As soon as it became evident to the Germans that the British drive was directed to Arnhem the highway became a vital factor to them also — as did the bridge itself, for they too wished to use it for transporting tanks and other reinforcements to the south.

By late afternoon on the 17th John Frost and his men of A Company, 2nd Para Battalion were battling their way towards the objective. At 1930 hours that evening they had almost reached it, what is more the bridge was unguarded, for the couple of dozen elderly German guards had fled. There was just one uniformed figure at his post on the northern end of the bridge, a Dutch policeman, and he too was apprehensive as he heard the noises of battle, having witnessed the aerial armada and parachutists coming down some hours earlier. Then, hearing shouts and vehicles, he saw a party of German soldiers arriving across the bridge, and almost at once the British too arrived and began reconnoitering the crossing, while Frost set up his command post in one of the buildings beside the bridge.

In a few moments the first firing broke out. The Dutchman vanished as a platoon of Frost's men attempted to cross the bridge and were repulsed by SS troops with an armoured car and flak gun. Frost was joined by some engineers, his HQ staff and then B Company who had been detached earlier to deal with some German opposition on the way into the town. He now had about 600 men and one 6-pdr anti-tank gun. This small force were the only British troops of the whole Division to reach the bridge, apart from a troop of six-pounders which broke through to them the next day; within 24 hours all the guns were practically out of ammunition. Not until Wednesday did Frost learn via the Dutch telephone system, which was in part manned by the Resistance, of the situation elsewhere and that his own Divisional HQ was under siege. By that night the Frost battalion was down to 140 effectives and was overwhelmed by the enemy, which meant that the Germans could now start using the bridge to reinforce their forces further south. This fact was confirmed by air reconnaisance.

Jim Carter had left his mates to "do a bit of sniping", but was seen and hit and next woke up in German care, knocked out of the battle in its early stages.

Lieutenant Norman had pressed on through the sunny lanes as fast as he could with his men, being badly delayed by the Dutch folk who insisted on shaking hands and pressing flowers on them:

"They really imagined the war was ending. I suppose we had done a mile or two when we began to get enemy fire from carefully sited machine guns and snipers. The first casualties occurred and we had to change our line of approach, but we were not downhearted. Nobody expected the Germans to present any walkover. Then we entered the Arnhem suburbs and began to scout through the streets, intending to enfilade the bridge and take the Germans by surprise. But we soon ran into fire from all sides and had to go to ground, having lost some men. I distributed the men among the houses and gardens and tried to get in touch with command to find out what was happening. So far we had made quite good progress, but I didn't like the look of things. Worst of all, we seemed to be out of touch with those above us and very much on our own.* I had around one hundred men under me, and we were now beginning to receive increasing fire, not only from small arms but heavy stuff too."

Alf Turner had set off at a good pace also, delayed by Dutch citizens who "were all over us", but they couldn't stop and pressed on. "After a couple of miles we were drawing sniper and machine-gun fire, but deployed and kept going. But then we ran into some enemy crossfire and what sounded like heavy vehicles shooting at us, and we were forced to go to ground. This is where everything started to go wrong. I was sent off with a section to probe and see what the opposition was, but we didn't get very far as the opposition was too heavy and accurate. We were halted and when we got back I found that the Germans had worked their way round to the back. This meant that our platoon was cut off from the main body. We could not contact them so were on our own.

"Things began to get sticky and we lost a few men, so I decided to try and fight our way through to one side and get out of the trap. The only solution was to reach some houses on the outskirts of Arnhem from where we could set up an all-round defence, until relieved we hoped by the Second Army. I also hoped that our main force would come up to us and then we could continue on to the objective."

The "main force" was of course even at this early stage being broken up by German fire on its flanks.

Henry Lambert:

"We set off in convoy along a nice leafy lane, and after a mile or two came to a halt, as a lot of Dutch people were holding us up with bottles of fruit juice and giving us flowers. It was all very much like a celebration, yet we could hear shooting going on, so we pushed on past these good people and soon had to deploy as we came under fire.

"The town lay before us, but we were held up for a while as the paras ahead cleared up the Germans, and then we all pushed on again until we reached the first houses. It was a good day for weather and we were in good spirits. A few men had gone missing for one reason or another, and when we got into the town we had to start splitting

* The Divisional Commander, General Urquart, who landed by glider, was in a worse situation.

169

our company because of the German fire now coming at us from several directions. I led a few men through a little alley, intending to by-pass the German machine guns that were set up at a crossroads, and were covering all the main approaches. We managed to get behind some of them and put paid to them with our fire. It was fairly easy so far, but then we came under heavy fire from some more German positions unseen by us. A couple of men went down and we had to scramble for cover. We were completely pinned down, but managed to get into a house where we took stock of our situation. I could see that the regiment was being split up into small units and this was not good."

Arnhem was a small town of some 80,000 inhabitants, with suburbs rather like an English locality, rows of small houses with neat gardens front and back. Into this peaceful Sunday town atmosphere had erupted first the rap and tap of rifle and machine-gun fire from the countryside to the west. The inhabitants had, of course, like their German occupiers, been amazed by the great fleet of low-flying aircraft and had seen the parachutes and perhaps even the gliders coming down. They were well used to the throb of warplanes, both German and Allied, by day and night, for Holland had been in the path of the raiding bombers since 1940. Four years on, with increasing difficulties over food and enemy harassment, the townspeople could be forgiven for hoping and praying that it was all coming to an end. It certainly seemed that way. The sound of firing grew nearer until the men in camouflage jackets were actually among the little roads and gardens. And then came an ever-increasing number of Germans with armoured vehicles, tanks and self-propelled guns, engines growling, clouds of blue smoke belching from their exhausts. And before long these armoured monsters were chugging through the main street and byways alike, gun barrels swinging and then firing, the grey-green SS infantrymen crouching alongside and blazing away at the hedgerows and houses, anywhere that the British soldiers might be hiding. The whole area was ablaze with an inferno of noise.

Lambert:

"I went carefully to the window, and could see Germans all over the place, with heavy stuff moving up. I could not see into the area of the bridge, but I could hear heavy firing from the centre of the town, so I guessed some of our airborne must have got there."

Tom Smith's unit tried to rush around the German flank to trap the enemy machine-gunners, but were at once pinned down and had to withdraw to try another route:

"We tried a new approach and made good headway until we were held up once more by an armoured car. But we dealt with this and I saw my first dead Jerries — not a pretty sight. At last to our relief we actually got into the suburbs and houses of Arnhem, but had to take cover at once through enemy fire. In fact we began to be split up as a unit and I knew this was not good. But I still had my pals with me and we did a bit of grumbling at our situation as we didn't know what was happening and had lost touch with our officers. This was the bad part of it, but there was no question of giving up, we just felt we had to hang on and do the best we could.

"We tried to move through the back gardens which were quite attractive and reminded us of home. It was the only way to make any progress, but the gardens were in places intersected by little paths into the streets, and the Germans were getting wise to us and covering them with men. So we had to make sudden dashes and keep our heads down."

By afternoon those British airborne who had penetrated into the town in small groups were isolated and trapped by a thickening web of Germans.

Ken Norman:

"By evening I felt we should press on in some measure before the Germans could really move in on us properly. I decided to do some infiltrating and move us by parties to better positions. The Germans didn't fight too well in darkness and at such time we would have the advantage. Having split the men up, I made sure that we all moved in the right direction, and off we went. Not long afterwards I heard heavy firing behind us, so we sent a man back to find out what was happening, and when he returned he said that all the men behind seemed to have vanished. So we pushed on, passing through the gardens at the rear of the houses and when necessary stepping across the paths which cut between them. By dawn we had only covered a few hundred yards and from a good vantage point in a house I had a good view of the area and discovered we were actually worse off than before. There were enemy troops all round us, including vehicles and tanks.

"I saw that the men ate some rations and held a council of war. There was nothing we could do but stay put. This was the Monday, and we were bottled up. I could not see how we with our meagre strength could possibly go for our objective. In fact, things seemed to be hotting up, the Germans were trying to patrol the streets, shooting wherever they suspected we might be. I organized a few scouting parties to try and probe for weak spots in the enemy ring, and of course to bring in any ammo or rations they found. I had to try and keep up their morale, and reminded them that the Second Army was on its way, and we would in any case be re-supplied by the RAF. We remained in good heart, but when the lads sent out returned they'd had no luck. The Germans had us locked in solid, and there seemed no way out. A few more boxes of ammo and some apples were all the supplies found."

One para CO observed later:

"Let's just say that errors and bad luck contributed to us being trapped like rats and we didn't stand a chance. I myself had a few narrow squeaks, and I wondered what our folks back home would be thinking of us − an élite British unit taking such a licking. I guessed that at home they'd be told what a glorious, epic of British arms it was − and this is exactly what happened."

Alf Turner says that, although they had run into trouble, there was no question of either giving up the mission or surrendering, but was not optimistic as the lack of communications was a major obstacle:

"That side of things in a battle is very important, as without knowledge of our own and the enemy's positions it is impossible to fight a cohesive battle. Well, we got ourselves together and charged across a field, making best use of what cover there was. I don't think the Jerries had too much idea of where we were or in what strength at that stage, so perhaps we were lucky."

If this was the case then it was soon to be rectified, at least in some quarters, for a map case outlining all the Allied plans was picked up by the Germans from a dead American officer in a crashed glider farther south. But in any case, with American landings from the air at two points further down the Rhine, it was quite obvious that the Allies were trying to establish a salient into the German front.

"There was plenty of stuff flying about though, and I heard a few men cry out behind me. We shot off a lot of precious ammunition at where we thought the Germans were hiding, and after a hell of a run reached the houses where we took shelter. We then set up lookouts and counted ourselves lucky. I reckoned we'd lost a dozen men in that little skirmish."

By evening Tom Smith, and most likely the rest of the British airborne, had to admit that they had failed. They had no chance of reaching their objective and would be lucky even to survive where they were:

"We had hopes that, as promised, the Second Army would soon crash into the area and save our skins. As it was, we only had supplies for a day or two. We started scrounging round in the gardens to try and pick up what few vegetables we could find, stuffing them into the pockets of our smocks. We then tried to link up with other lads, and succeeded in finding a small bunch with a Bren gun, which was something. That night we slept in gardens and sheds and heard Jerry moving up armour all around the place, and didn't get much sleep."

The Dutch had by then either fled or were hiding in their cellars, and little contact seems to have occurred between them and the British who for some reason failed to make proper use of either the Dutch underground members or the telephone system which could well have afforded them some communication. The Germans had cut off the water and fuel supplies, so there was no way the isolated parties of airborne men could find succour in the houses, apart from shelter, and this was becoming increasingly dubious as the enemy tightened its grip on every street.

Henry Lambert and his fellow glider troops tried to advance further through the back gardens, but drew heavy fire and were forced back into their 'safe' house.

"Obviously, things had not gone according to plan and we were a bit depressed, but of course intending to stick it out. That night we had to stay on the alert as we could hear movement all round us, but had no idea who they were – ours or theirs. We ate our rations and searched the empty home but found no food. Then I saw a German tank coming along the road, and as we had a PIAT with us I took a man round the side of the house to have a go at knocking it out. We waited until it was about twenty yards away and then let go. We missed it, and before we could re-load we were under machine-gun fire and had to retreat."

Disclosing their position cost Henry and his mates dearly.

"We ran back into the house, as I not only wanted some cover but thought we could have another go at the tank from upstairs. But they had got wind of us, and as soon as we set up the PIAT there was an almighty burst of firing which plastered the walls and sent debris flying. We dashed downstairs and right away there was a great crash and everything came in on us. The tank had fired point-blank at the house with us in it.

"Something hit me on the head very hard and I passed out. I half woke up and heard myself groaning loudly. The pain was very bad but then it went very quiet and I felt myself slipping away into unconsciousness."

When Henry woke up in a daze he was under German guard outside, and, between bouts of consciousness, realized he was being moved on a vehicle and reached a dressing station where there were many more wounded, British and German.

The British troops were steadily being annihilated, but the process was a long and expensive one for the Germans. In daylight the troops occupying more open ground were forced to watch helplessly as RAF transport planes flew over to drop the much needed supply canisters and panniers in the wrong place. There was no way that those in command at home could learn the true situation in Arnhem. But the airborne fought on.

"We got what rest we could," Alf Turner recalls, "but there was sporadic firing all round for much of that night, and at dawn we heard all sorts of unwelcome noises. Obviously, the Germans were bringing up heavy stuff. It sounded like tanks and self-propelled guns. I went out by myself on a recce and saw all my worst fears confirmed: the enemy were thoroughly infesting the area with lorried infantry and carriers. I could see that we'd be lucky to link up with any more of our lads, or in fact make any progress. I thought we might be in for a siege, so sent a few men out to scrounge about for food and water.

"As the day wore on we tried to improve our position and move nearer the objective, but we never got more than a hundred yards before being spotted and plastered by machine guns. It was all very disappointing, but we weren't giving up. At least we would give the Germans a great deal of trouble and help the Second Army advance. That was my feeling."

A study of more detailed histories of the Second Army's attack discloses a distinct lack of urgency and drive on the part of some commanders and men, even though it had been impressed on all that the airborne would be in need of early relief. Overall, the British Army was simply not trained to act and move fast; it was never ingrained into their mental make-up. By this stage of the war the soldiers were becoming more cautious than ever, and in any case had become used to calling up "air" and massive artillery support whenever opposition was met. One unit commander in this drive took several vital hours to mount a set-piece attack against comparatively light opposition; he was obviously not the man for the job. General Horrocks himself erred by commanding from the rear and at times had no idea that commanders in front were being so lethargic. The

Irish Guards tanks took until dusk on the first day to cover six miles — but that was the objective set them! It took them until the afternoon of D+1 to enter Eindhoven and link up with the American 101st Airborne; they still had at least forty miles to go to relieve the British airborne at Arnhem. It seems incomprehensible that such short-range objectives were set in view of the fact that Montgomery had promised a 60-mile dash in two days.

Alf Turner's third day in Holland was his last in combat:

"After midday we'd had a small bite to eat and I decided to take some men to try and find whatever airborne lads I could behind us, as I still felt we might be able to link up with them. We were not doing any good where we were.

"I set off, crouching low with a Sten gun and pistol, with a Private I knew well behind me with his pockets stuffed with grenades. We moved through the back gardens and alleys and had just reached a small road when we were surprised by a German patrol. We saw them at the same moment and I fired at once, but my chum was hit and went down. I dived backwards but felt a terrific pain in the small of my back and fell on my face. Everything went grey and then black and I yelled for a moment, but forced myself to shut up. I distinctly remember saying to myself, 'You idiot, shut your mouth and lie doggo!'"

The Germans fired again, hitting him in the foot, but Alf Turner was unconscious and when he came to found it was night and he was lying on the ground outside the German dressing centre, in pain and wondering if it was the end of everything.

Tom Smith's third day began with 'masses of firing' and he knew the battle had begun in earnest:

"We were really dying for a cup of tea, but we had nothing except some water in our bottles. One of us, a Corporal, decided to go into some of the houses to see what he could scrounge. He took one man with him and came back with some apples and some chocolate. We were pretty hungry and soon scoffed the lot, which of course we shared out.

"We now heard the Jerries making a sweep through the streets nearby with troops and heavy vehicles. They were shooting everywhere, at the houses and the hedges, as they thought that we were hidden in them. So we decided to try a bit of skirmishing and split up into small parties to stalk them from behind. As I said, the little paths led into the streets, and we used these. As soon as a bunch of Jerries went by we dashed out and shot them down from behind, then rushed back into our hiding places. We thought if we couldn't reach our target at the river then we'd damn well do as much damage to them as possible.

"This was very successful at first, but the Jerries soon wised up and sent men into the paths with machine guns and started lobbing grenades and mortar bombs over the tops of the houses into the gardens, so we had to move on. In this we lost one or two lads who vanished.

"This dodging about went on for hours, and we got very hot and tired, and thirsty as well as hungry. We went into some houses and found nothing to eat. The water was cut off and the civvies had either gone or were in hiding. The noise got worse and went on and on, but we didn't care; we were trained soldiers and knew the things that happen in a battle. But by now we were sure we were trapped and could only hope for rescue by the Second Army and some re-supply by the RAF. But, stuck in the gardens and alleys, there was no way that we could get any of the parachuted supplies as the RAF couldn't drop them on the town itself. We hoped that someone would realize what was going on. We knew that the Poles were due to reinforce us and hoped this would ease the pressure. The Germans now began going down every street with tanks and armoured cars and shooting at everything.

"After three or four days we were getting a bit weak, without any decent grub and so short of water. Some men of our party had gone off to find ammo and scrounge food and we never saw them again. I wondered if my Mum realized what sort of scrape I was in. She knew I was in the paras, but maybe thought I was safe in England.

"After five days we found we could not move at all. There were Germans stationed at every corner and dug in with machine guns sited in every direction, with tanks and self-propelled guns parading up and down, popping off whenever they thought they saw a red beret. We didn't use our helmets much, they were too damned hot. I had thrown mine away days before. No one ever thought of surrender. We would just hang on till the Army came. We saw the RAF Dakotas dropping their stuff and one or two shot down, but it seemed miles away. We could only guess that the whole Division was bottled up in small bits like us and being ground to pieces, but we thought we'd made a dent in the German defences and were doing some good, so would hang on as long as possible.

"I learned later that this terrible siege went on for nine days. But I never saw the end of it. After about six days the shooting and noise was so terrific that we decided to move into one of the houses and get some sleep while one man stood guard. We had so little ammo that we couldn't shoot unless we were directly attacked. So we dodged into the nearest house which was quite big. It was already wrecked by shellfire but still standing. We hoped we'd get a bit of peace there and perhaps find something to eat. Well, there wasn't a thing – no food, no water. We were filthy, unshaven and starving. We just flopped down and fell asleep while a bloke manned a Bren gun near the window with one mag left.

"I'm not sure what happened next, but I was rudely woken up by a terrific noise as the whole house collapsed around me. I heard shouts and saw my mates rushing about. It was all dust and smoke, and then there was a terrific flash and I passed out."

Like his comrades Tom was half-buried in the debris as the German fire demolished the house about them, and when he next gained consciousness he was in enemy hands.

Having lost some of his troops on the first evening, Lieutenant Tom Burgess had lain low, eaten some rations and tried to snatch some sleep, but there were too many noises and alarms. Next morning at first light he led his men into the Arnhem suburbs without much trouble in a confused situation. A lack of cohesion and control was evident in the British side of the battle:

"This was not at all good. As an officer I could see that the operation had gone badly wrong. We were split up into small parties, lacking central control, left to fend for ourselves, with the enemy closing in around us in greater strength. We hid in some gardens to await events and then into a couple of houses for better observation and could see German activity all round us. It seemed stupid to draw attention to ourselves and I resolved to get on into Arnhem in short dashes, hoping to hide in the gardens and houses. So far we had only penetrated the outskirts.

"But that morning we could hear more shooting and the sound of heavy weapons which were not ours. This did not bode good for us. It signified that the enemy were in strength and dominating the area. But we moved off as planned, crossing lanes and gardens in short leaps and hiding in sheds and houses when necessary. But by midday I could see that we were not getting anywhere. The Germans had blocked off the roads and crossings and in fact were enfilading all the roads. We were obliged to lay low and just assess the situation and see what developed.

"An afternoon went by and from a room upstairs in a house vacated by the Dutch occupants I could see that we were hopelessly pinned down. The Germans now controlled the whole area; the only thing we could do was surrender — or fight. I decided we had only one course which was to make things as hard for the enemy as possible. So we made ourselves ready to catch as many Germans from ambush as possible. I split my twenty or so men into two sections and sent them out on stalking expeditions, with orders to return if possible to the base.

"I set off with one section, armed with rifles and grenades. We made our way cautiously through the back gardens until we judged we had got into a favourable position, then out through two alleyways lined with thick hedges, and found we were near a German machine-gun post with several soldiers. We opened fire and threw grenades and the whole lot blew up. We raced away and took cover to await reactions. None came, so we went on carefully but more confidently and reached a crossroads which we knew would be covered by a machine gun somewhere, but we couldn't see it. So one man crept off along the pavement. He had plenty of guts and when he reached the corner he gazed all round and waved to us. At that moment he was shot and collapsed, so we dived for cover.

"It wasn't long before we heard the Germans shooting, and soon an armoured car came along the street to investigate. We let it go past and then sprang out and lobbed grenades onto the back on the engine plates. It went up at once and that was when the enemy machine gun caught us again. Two chaps went down and I was hit in the left shoulder, but I managed to get under cover while a Sergeant bandaged the wound which hurt like hell. The bullet had gone right through my shoulder and I was losing a lot of blood.

"I ordered the rest of the lads to take cover in some houses. We had about two wounded apart from two killed. We got into two houses and made ready to defend ourselves. Before long the Germans sent men along the road and through the back gardens to trap us and a grand battle started. We got several of them in the front and threw grenades at the back, but two more of my lads were hit and one killed. I decided to change our position, so everyone went downstairs and crept out the back, escaping, we hoped, from the remains of the German patrol.

"We had not gone far when a hell of a racket broke out and we found we were under fire from houses nearby. We were caught in the gardens and tried to get into the nearest house, and in doing so two more men went down. I now had about ten men or less. We got into a house and made ready to defend ourselves. We were fairly exhausted and had run out of rations but found a few scraps of bread in the house but nothing to drink as the water was cut off.

"Before long some German armoured cars and a tank began probing the street while their infantry began infiltrating the gardens. We opened fire and drove them back, but the tank and armoured cars opened fire and the whole house started to fall apart on us. We rushed downstairs as the roof and upper floors collapsed, but one or two men were caught in the mess. We were shooting out of the back and front, but the enemy armour came right up to the front and fired at point-blank range and it was over for us.

"I felt a terrific pressure on me as the ceiling came down and only just managed to get out of the back door with one or two others where we collapsed in the garden. At that point some German infantrymen rushed us firing, but soon gave up and took us prisoners. We were in a bit of a mess, covered in dust and blood, and looked quite a sight I reckon. I know the Germans looked at us in disbelief. They felt we were an élite and were very wary as they searched us and took us away.

"We were taken to a house and interrogated by an SS officer who gave us cigarettes. He had an interpreter and wanted to know what we thought we were doing. We were, he said, in no position to do any good, so the whole operation was a futile waste.

"We were taken away, with all the noise of the battle still going on, and sat in a field full of our lads. That was the end of our war. They did not give us much to eat or drink, but we survived until we reached a POW camp in Germany where we got more organized."

Ken Norman:

"I asked for volunteers to try in various directions for help, or at least to try and find out what was happening elsewhere. This was the great problem – the loss of control at Arnhem. Without news we were helpless. We would fight to the last but it had to have some cohesion if we were to have any effect.

"When I sent off more patrols I'm afraid they were all killed or captured. After five days we were down to one clip of ammo each and the last Bren gun magazine. We had hardly slept a wink since we arrived and of course it was very difficult to wash or shave. We had run out of water and food and there was no sanitation. But despite all this we remained in good heart, certain that relief was on its way. I had about twenty wounded on my hands and wanted to get help for them, and decided to put up a white flag of truce to ask the Germans to get them to hospital. At first nothing happened, but then a German officer appeared in a scout car, and one of our Sergeants spoke to him in German to arrange a truce. He said we could have a vehicle to take our wounded who would be taken care of. He also said we could have all the food and drink we wanted if we surrendered. This of course we refused.

"They sent up some lorries, and as soon as the wounded were removed the firing started up again. Now they used everything on us — self-propelled guns, tanks, machine guns, flame throwers. We beat off their rushes, but then found we were completely out of ammo. I called my NCOs together and told them the situation. By then we were down to about thirty men still on their feet, the rest dead or wounded. We decided to hang on for an hour or two and use up our very last bullet before packing it in.

"I had my pistol and six rounds so decided to make them count. I climbed up into the top storey of the nearest house still standing, intending to try and pick off any German officer I saw. I fired a couple of shots, but suddenly a tremendous bang shook the house and I felt myself falling as the floor collapsed. I hit my head on something and everything seemed to go black and I passed out. When I came to I was in a sort of coma. I could hear lots of noise and smelt burning, but could only see dimly. I thought, 'Dear God, don't let me be burnt alive'."

When Ken Norman next became conscious he was being roughly pulled out of the smoking debris by unseen hands and survived as a prisoner.

The surviving British airborne in Arnhem were in an increasingly hopeless situation. The miracle is that they never gave up hope of relief by Second Army, even though this hope could not be realized. Inevitably, over the preceding days the press at home had been forced to reflect the truth of the situation, even though the lack of communications meant delays in obtaining any real picture. But eleven days after that fateful Sunday drop, on 28 September, the newspapers were informing the British public of the great left hook towards the Ruhr that had failed so disastrously, and book-title phrases became commonplace: 'Epic of the Sky Men', 'The Agony of Arnhem', '230 Hours of Hell', and 'Break-out Order to Survivors'. Gone now were the cries of a triumphant airborne army of liberation. To speak of 'survivors' was indication enough of the extent of the disaster. An American radio report from Paris spoke of 2,000 men safe out of the 7-8,000 soldiers sent into battle, while the Germans seemed to have it all wrapped up, claiming 1,500 British airborne dead, and 1,700 wounded of the 6,450 prisoners taken. For that number of élite troops to be taken was a catastrophe for the Allies in itself.

The first-hand accounts now began to appear in print and an indication of the hell the men had gone through:

"This is the end. The most tragic and glorious battle of the war is over, and the survivors of the British airborne force can sleep soundly for the first time in eight days and nights."

One leader column stated:

"The battle of Arnhem is over. It ended when a band of heroes . . . retreated, unbeaten, from the scene which they have made immortal. Their uniforms were torn and faded and caked with mud. They were grimed with smoke. Their faces were lined with fatigue, their eyes clouded by lack of sleep. . . . These were the remnant of that company of gallant gentlemen who will forever be numbered among the foremost of their race. They have shown themselves true men of their blood — worthy of their fathers and an example to their sons. They have held high the pride and honour of their country. . . . The Airborne Army was the lever with which the Allied command planned to move and turn the great mass of the German Wehrmacht."

Along with the comments and tales of gallantry against impossible odds came the cushioning explanations for the failure which avoided the critical reasons, then to the fact that the men of Arnhem had 'given us Nijmegen' etc., as Monty was to point out years later.

After nine days the British commanders of Second Army had agreed to try and evacuate the remnants of the airborne troops from Arnhem, by which time small numbers of British infantry and Polish paras had reached the west bank of the Lower Rhine and did their utmost to bring help to their beleaguered comrades. General Sosabowski's Polish parachute brigade had been delayed in England by fog, and when it did finally drop it was into an area infested by the enemy. Only fifty Poles managed to cross the Rhine, but were forced to withdraw with the British remnants in the few small boats available, hampered by a strong current and increasing enemy fire as the Germans woke up to what was happening. The withdrawal was carried out in darkness and rain, under covering fire from artillery of the Second Army, the airborne lads guided by tapes with glider pilots acting as guides.

Not uncommonly, the Battle of Arnhem is yet another where quoted losses vary from one source to another. It is not surprising that the German figures hurriedly presented in September, 1944, were not entirely accurate. There were still bodies to be discovered among the debris of the many Dutch houses demolished.

From the total Allied force which went into combat in Operation *Market Garden*, some 20,000 men, 17,200 were killed, wounded, or missing. Of these the two American airborne divisions suffered the following casualties up to the end of the Arnhem battle: 82nd Airborne − 1,432; 101st Airborne − 2,110. But since the Americans were, much to their dismay, retained by Montgomery in the defensive fighting until mid-to-late November, they suffered a further 1,812 and 1,682 casualties for the two divisions respectively. Exactly 10,005 British troops landed at Arnhem and one British source says that, of these, 5,000 were taken prisoner, including 3,000 wounded. Earlier, only 500 were listed as killed in action, but 1,500 posted as 'missing' never returned and that number are buried in the cemetery at Oosterbeek. To put another perspective on it, an American historian lists the British killed, wounded and missing at 7,212, and also, discomfortingly, cites various instances of apparent lethargy on the part of the Second Army units in the attempt to break through to Arnhem. Yet another British source gives the following figures: Killed: over 1,300; prisoners, including wounded, over 6,000; escaped across the Rhine 2,400. To these sombre figures must be added 500 Poles of Sosabowski's ill-fated brigade (the General wrote his own bitter memoirs after the war*), plus an appalling estimated 10,000 Dutch civilians, who either died in the fighting or during the bitter winter that followed.

By that time Montgomery seems to have given up his practice of showing himself to his troops and distributing cartons of cigarettes. He was not on hand to welcome back the battered remnants of the 1st Airborne. It was only at General Urquhart's suggestion that the Field-Marshal prepared a letter dated 28 September to be read out to the survivors when they reassembled in England. In five paragraphs Monty praised the men for their efforts, including the phrases: "Few episodes more glorious than the epic at Arnhem," and "In the years to come it will be a great thing for a man to be able to say, 'I fought at Arnhem'."

It had by then become the way of politicians and commanders who had failed to trot out the traditional, obligatory terms such as 'glorious' and 'gallant' when trying to gloss over disaster; the second phrase quoted was reminiscent of one employed by Göring after

* *Parachute General*, (Kimber, London).

Stalingrad. For the airborne lads who survived, including the disabled and scarred, would come in due course a 'gratuity' after demobilization and, if they were lucky, a pittance pension from a grateful if parsimonious government. As for Monty, he kept his head down until late December and the Battle of the Bulge, popping up again as perky as ever, creating his own limelight as he helped to clear up the mess of Hitler's last gamble in the Ardennes, and by the way also stirring up yet another hornets' nest among his American allies by the same kind of boastful, irritating remarks he had issued in Normandy.

There is no doubt that Montgomery knew what he was doing as a general – apart from the lapse at Arnhem – and little if any criticism appeared in the British press regarding his military abilities, certainly not his quirks. This would come in a later era. Among the most virulent were some by a woman who served in the supply services behind the front who was of the same Irish extraction and alleges she knew him before the war. Then there were those at the sharp end in 1944 who, in suitable circumstances, gave vent to their opinions. Prisoners can often be foolishly garrulous. Such a one was a little Cockney captured by SS troops in France who amused and pleased his interrogators by referring to Monty as 'that little prick'.

After the war Monty enjoyed fame and fortune, part of his wealth derived from his memoirs which appeared in 1958*. In these he enjoined the reader to study Chester Wilmot's account of the actual battle at Arnhem, which was fair enough, while setting out the reasons why in his opinion the operation had failed, though claiming, perhaps with some justification, that the bridgehead gained into Holland proved of immense value later. However much Montgomery has been accused since in some quarters of 're-writing' the campaign in Normandy, he was candid enough to admit his own errors in these operations.

The cardinal reason for the Arnhem fiasco, Monty wrote, was Eisenhower's inability to provide him with the men and supplies, but admits that his own failure to capture Antwerp soon enough was a 'bad mistake on my part'. In belatedly diverting the Canadians to that task, plus more troops to occupy the 'V2 coast' (the V2 rocket launch sites) he left himself with insufficient strength to force through the thrust by Second British Army. By then the manpower shortage was of real concern: from the day of the invasion, 6 June, until early

* *The Memoirs of Field-Marshal Montgomery* (Collins, London.)

October, his 21st Army Group had suffered 82,318 killed and wounded, the worst losses occurring in the 3rd Canadian Infantry Division. The figure quoted did not include those incurred by the 1st Airborne at Arnhem.

However, it is possible that the benefits gained at the expense of the British airborne troops were not fully appreciated at the time. The German front was stretched ever nearer to breaking point: the 'fire brigade' general, Field-Marshal Model, complained that in the period 1-25 September his army on the western front had suffered 75,000 casualties but received only 6,500 replacements, that he had fewer guns than the British had left after Dunkirk, that he was too weak to eliminate the mile-wide corridor cut into his territory by Dempsey's Second British Army towards Arnhem, or even wipe out those American airborne troops who had remained above the Neder Rijn. The German weakness remained until mid-October, during which time Monty struggled to maintain the initiative. Thereafter it was too late: the Eisenhower Doctrine and supply problems enabled the enemy to stabilize and heavily reinforce their front.

In a remarkable scouring, Dr Goebbels and his staff supplied enough men from the Home Front, plus many redundant from the Luftwaffe and Kriegsmarine, to send Model another 600,000 soldiers. This feat was in part accomplished by simply lowering the call-up age to 16, though naturally those contributed by the two services named were mostly young and already disciplined. As a result many new divisions were formed, units the Germans felt would suffice in a defensive role after a mere 4-5 weeks' training. They were of course in no way comparable to the old, experienced divisions of the German Army and Waffen-SS.

Success at Arnhem and the left-hook drive into the Ruhr envisaged by Monty would have pre-empted the enemy's Ardennes gamble. It would also have enabled the Allies to take Berlin ahead of the Russians with all this implies for the post-war scene.

By comparison to other campaigns and battles British losses at Arnhem were small, grievous as was the loss of such an élite division; the casualties were perhaps equal to one day's fighting across the front as a whole, and of course when compared to the Russian front, miniscule. But, for the reasons given, the battle has to be seen in the broader context. And perhaps the comment by Winston Churchill concerning the clash between Britain and Germany's finest is not irrelevant.

As one American historian put it, the remains of the 1st British

Airborne returned to Britain with their heads held high. The survivors of the 1st, 2nd and 3rd Parachute Battalions were joined up with the 4th until November, 1944, and in May, 1945, elements of the division returned to North-West Europe, mainly to take over German forces surrendering in Norway and Denmark. The 1st Airborne Division was officially disbanded in November, by which time segments of it had been transferred to the 6th Airborne.

As a sidelight to this period, while the struggle for Arnhem was at its height the newspapers at home announced two government measures affecting the lot of the British soldier, one beneficial, the other punitive, for, by age-old custom, what it gave away with one hand the Treasury always somehow managed to grab back with the other.

The measures made known by the Chancellor of the Exchequer covered War Service pay increases arranged as 'increments' and intended to come into effect from 3 September, 1944, while a different segment of the same scheme directed towards the men facing the Japanese would for some reason become statutory on 1 November. Even so, the Government pointed out that 'It will be impossible for the authorities to cope with the new rates at once'. Moreover, as one political correspondent pointed out, the Chancellor in his wisdom had ruled that the increases (with the exception of those for the Far Eastern theatre) would be subject to income tax.

The weekly increases in pay would, as an example at base rate, reward a private soldier who had been 'in it from the start' (i.e. had completed five years' war service), with one shilling (5p) for his first three years service, plus two increments of sixpence for the other two years (a further 5p), which gave him an extra two shillings or 10p per week on pay parade, to be added to the existing rate of up to five shillings or 25p per day. The Far East soldier would receive a straight seven shillings or 35p a week extra.

British service pay was, for lower ranks, more or less 'spending money' since all board and clothing was provided free; it had never been subject to tax. The sums involved seem paltry, though it has to be remembered that paratroopers received extra 'jump pay', though the exact amount is not known. And whether the nation could really afford more is debatable in view of the fact that the war as a whole was bankrupting Britain. What the British squaddie would spend his extra coppers on was not hard to guess — 'tea and wads', small meals in the NAAFI canteen, perhaps better seats with his girl at the 'flicks', two-and-sixes instead of the back row at one-and-ninepence. With tea at about a penny a cup and cigarettes at ten for a shilling or so even a few shillings could cover a fair amount.

But, true to form, the Government also made it known that the wives of serving soldiers receiving grants would have their allowances cut accordingly (by proportion to the extra pay received by their menfolk). Furthermore, as if to add insult to injury, troops overseas read a Reuter report in the newspapers that all items bought abroad and sent home to kinfolk or friends as gifts would be liable to British purchase tax, the same tax which had been introduced as a 'temporary' wartime measure but which stayed on for decades until it was transformed into a vastly wider tax called VAT.

ARNHEM QUOTES

"Of course they had to put a brave face on it and all that, but the truth is of course that it was an unmitigated disaster and cost us dear. We lost around eight thousand of our very finest élite soldiers one way or another, and it meant the demise of one of our two airborne divisions. This was impossible to recover from at that stage of the war; there was a very difficult manpower situation, we had trouble getting the best men any more.

"The Arnhem operation should never have been mounted, for the intelligence was there. It was clear there were Germans in the area in strength. But the pressures to go ahead from the higher-ups was insurmountable; they were simply determined to get on with it, from Monty downwards, whatever one thought in the lower ranks. I had no great say or weight in the matter or planning; I was at the executive end of things, so in a sense had to follow orders and just do the best we could. But we did give a very good account of ourselves, and though we were beaten the Germans, I think, were full of admiration for the quality of the British airborne at Arnhem. But we never had the chance to redeem ourselves as the 1st was smashed for ever and it was the end of a very fine division.

"Montgomery was a very good general and did a lot for Britain. He had his weaknesses and faults, but overall I think he knew what he was doing. He did not have the dash or flair of Rommel or Patton, but they were a very different kind of general altogether. They too had their faults and could not always see the wood for the trees, but were very good in a battle. But Monty was of the old school who had seen so much slaughter in World War 1, and that I think coloured much of his thinking, so that he planned accordingly."

(Anonymous officer, 1st Airborne)

"They were well trained, particularly for independent fighting, and of good combat value. The officers, graded up in rank according to age, were the finest in the whole British Army, very well schooled, personally hard, persevering and brave. They made an outstanding impression."
After-battle report by SS Major Sepp Krafft.

"It is better to take landing losses and land on the objective than to have to fight after landing to reach the objective."
General James Gavin US 101st Airborne Division.

"There is no direct evidence that the area Arnhem-Nijmegen is manned by much more than the considerable flak defences already known to exist. . . . In Arnhem itself there is nothing larger than a brigade with a few guns and tanks."
1st Allied Airborne Army HQ Intelligence.

"SS Div Hohenstaufen along Ijssel; sub-units observed between Arnhem and Zutphen-Apeldoorn road!"
Dutch Resistance message not passed to 1st Airborne until 20 September.

"Expect heavy casualties."
Brigadier J. W. Hackett, 4th Parachute Brigade.

"Two days. They'll be up with you by then."
Field-Marshal Montgomery, when asked by General Browning how long the 1st would be expected to hold the bridge at Arnhem.
"We can hold it for four."
Browning's reply.

"Oh! How I wish I had such a powerful force at my disposal."
General Student, watching the Allied air armada pass over his HQ 17 September, 1944.

"An Allied airborne landing in the Arnhem area is a distinct possibility."
SS Commissar Rauter, Nazi Police Chief in Holland.

"Montgomery is tactically a very prudent man and would not use them on such a mission."
Field-Marshal Model and deputy General Krebs in response to above.

"We must remember that British soldiers do not act on their own initiative when fighting in a town, but when it consequently becomes difficult to exercise control they are amazing in defence, but we need not be afraid of their capabilities in attack."
SS General Willi Bittrich, CO 2nd SS Panzerkorps.

"The only way to draw the teeth of an airborne landing with an inferior force is to drive straight into it."
SS Major Sepp Krafft, Battalion CO.

"Some of the maps given us were wildly inaccurate, showing few of the roads that actually existed."
1st Airborne Company Commander.

"The fighting was of an indescribable fanaticism . . . the fight raged through ceilings and staircases. Hand grenades flew in every direction. Each house had to be taken this way. Some of the British offered resistance to their last breath."
German soldier after the capture of the bridge at Arnhem.

"A collection of individuals holding on."
General Urquhart.

"Almost before the British touched the ground we were ready to defeat them."
SS General Bittrich.

'The prisoners were absolutely exhausted, starving, thirsty, and in many cases wounded, and I felt very sympathetic to them. They had fought like demons and done all that could be expected of them and were only defeated by bad planning. I remember one Sergeant who was a Cockney I believe. He was cheerful but downhearted that his hopes had been dashed and so many of his comrades lost. I asked him what he wanted most out of the war, and he said to go home in one piece. Another fellow, a glider pilot, was a very good type and quite well educated. I asked him how he had come to join the airborne and he said from choice. It was the élite force of the British Army and he was proud to have been at Arnhem. I asked him if he thought his officers had let him down, and he said no, not really, 'We all make mistakes, including the Germans. What about Crete?'

"Then there was a tall officer with a leg wound who looked as if he had been through hell and I asked him how he saw the war. He said simply, 'Nearly over, thank God!' I asked him what he thought of the troops he had fought against in Arnhem, and he said they were good but they would have beaten them easily if they'd been without armour support. He was taken away grinning.

"Then there was a man who I believe had led the dash to the bridge at Arnhem. He had very little to say, but I could see the disappointment on his face. There were a lot of private soldiers who had endured much. They were in good heart and we respected them greatly. In fact I would say they were as good as our own best troops and it was a shame they were wasted.

"I saw something of the terrible effects of war on a nice little Dutch town which was ruined. I also know that certain reprisals were taken afterwards against the Dutch population who had already suffered enough."

Karl-Heinz Roberts, SS Lieutenant Interpreter with *Hohenstaufen* Division

" . . . during our battle they were a chivalrous foe. Their sympathy and kindness for us wounded, I, for one, will not forget."*

Major-General John D. Frost, CB, DSO, MC.

* (Writing in *Arnhem Spearhead* by James Sims, IWM, 1978).

IV

Spearhead

The 2nd Independent Parachute Brigade was launched in Operation "Manna" on 12 October, 1944, landing on Megara airfield in Greece, which was one of the bases used by Student's airborne troops for the assault on Crete in 1941. The paras were part of "Arkforce", and with the 23rd Armoured Brigade ordered to drive the Germans out of Greece. Unfortunately, as soon as the enemy had departed communal strife broke out among the Greeks as opposing political parties — especially the communists — tried to take over the country. Even as the red berets completed their task of chasing the Germans to the Bulgarian frontier street fighting broke out in Athens and the paras became involved against the armed communists. After four weeks of heavy street fighting the reds were driven from the city and by January, 1945, the airborne troops had been returned to the 8th Army in Italy.

By this time the end of the war was in sight, but the enemy did not surrender, and no less than thirty airborne operations were planned for the British paras on the Italian front — every one of them being cancelled. But the end of the campaign in Europe also brought an end to the fighting in Italy and by June, 1945, the 2nd Brigade had returned to England, to be disbanded on 31 August.

But the 6th Airborne Division had more battles to fight before the German surrender. After its return to England from the continent in February it was made ready for Operation "Varsity" — the Rhine crossing, one of Montgomery's large set-piece battles designed to launch the Allied armies into Germany. By then the Division had been taken over by Major-General E. L. Bols, General Browning having taken up a post under Mountbatten in the Far East, while General Gale took over as deputy Commander, 1st Allied Airborne Army; Montgomery himself took on the post of Colonel Commandant of the Parachute Regiment.

It was later considered by some in retrospect (especially by General Patton who succeeded in crossing the Rhine without any great air and artillery preparation and, on setting foot on the east bank, wired Eisenhower that he had 'pissed in the Rhine'), as an unnecessary operation which cost considerable casualties to the airborne.

A new concept had been thought up for the operation, for the airborne troops would be landed *after* the initial assault crossing by the British Second and American Ninth Armies, their object to secure ground that dominated the areas to be occupied by the regular troops. For this battle the 6th was allied with the US 17th Airborne Division with General Matthew Ridgway in overall command. The airborne troops were conveyed after daybreak on 24 March by 1,696 transport planes and 1,348 gliders taking 21,680 soldiers into enemy territory in one lift. In air support as escorts were nearly 1,000 Allied fighter planes with a similar number engaged in ground-attack sorties.

In a classic error the 5th Parachute Brigade was dropped from 1000 ft which gave the Germans on the ground ample time to let fly with all arms at the descending paratroopers who were hit by bullets and air-burst shrapnel. But the target bridges and village assigned the British glider and paras were captured.

No less than twenty-two C-46 Commando transports were lost to flak; this type was new and fitted with doors on both sides of its fuselage to enable faster exit of paratroops — but the type burned too easily when hit by fire. All told forty-four transports and eighty gliders were destroyed by flak and small arms fire. Yet the Second Army swept across and onward from the Rhine in an almost unopposed assault, and apart from the plane losses forty-one aircrew were killed, 153 wounded and 163 missing. The 6th Airborne lost 347 killed, 731 wounded and the Americans 681 in all. At the time 1000 Allied airborne soldiers were reported missing, but most returned later.

The rest of the 6th Airborne's actions were to be a slow, steady and always costly slog across Germany.

Reg Andrews:

"It was a very hard slog and we lost some good men in many small actions. In one of these around the border area I and my mates were advancing in single file, hopping across fences and ditches to get behind some village houses where we expected to find German opposition. There was a tremendous bang, and one of my mates literally vanished in a puff of smoke as he stepped on a mine. We went to ground at once, and only later were we able to search and find a few bits of him. He was a very good man I'd known a long time.

"We captured that village, however, without a fight, but the mines weren't finished with us. Another of our section trod on an S mine and lost both his legs and bled to death before he could be evacuated, a terrible sight and one to turn your stomach, specially when an old pal.

"When we crossed the Rhine in our big drop it was worse than expected and we had quite a few casualties from various causes, mostly ground fire. But once down it was easy. There were few Jerries about; they'd mostly run away, but as we went on it was the old slog: the Germans had a way of extracting a heavy price if they decided to defend a place. They would use 88s and mines and only risk close combat if all else failed. We were usually on foot and had a rough time and were fed up being used as spearhead infantry, but that's the way it was.

"We came up against Jerry paras and they were damned good. We gave them a hard time too as we had learned a few tricks by then and in any case they couldn't stand up to our terrific artillery and air power. Once we got into Germany we didn't care what we knocked down so long as it saved lives. So many a pretty hamlet or town was ruined, but only when the Germans defended them, and they mostly did. When we reached the bigger towns and cities in Germany and could have a rest we would choose the best-looking houses and have a damned good lie up on the beds and loot the places, and look for anything to make our lives more comfortable. I know we all had our pockets filled with a few trinkets and Nazi souvenirs, but a lot of it was dumped later to make room for more essential items."

John Holmes:

"Some of our battles were hard, others easy. I guess we lost half our chaps from various reasons, usually the cursed mines, but also in accidents. I had a few narrow escapes in various ways.

"I was walking in a line of men one morning. It was raining and we had our capes on and I think we were all pretty brassed off. The Sergeant was in the lead with a Bren slung from his shoulder. We had just gone through a village we thought secure when a burst of fire opened up on us from behind. We hit the deck but not fast enough, the men behind were all hit, mostly killed. In fact the man nearest me got a bullet through the neck and died soon after. He was quite young, about eighteen I think.

"We had to detour back and comb through the village, but whoever had got our blokes had got away and we found nobody, so we had a bad morning. A truck took away the bodies and we plodded on, after taking a meal break in one of the houses. This was just over the border into Germany, and although many of the towns and cities were full of white bunting, some of the villages were full of mines and a few suicide squads, though the Germans relied a lot on booby traps and a few 88s to make us pay."

This was the reality of much of the slog across the beaten Reich. When the 6th began its spearhead drive it had little transport and many odd vehicles and carts were confiscated, but most of the time the troops footed it through increasing cold and rain. Supporting them were two regiments of artillery and tanks. There were no great mass attacks in this war, just thin lines of weary men who, being paratroops and glider men of the airborne, were less than enthusiastic about the kind of role they had been given.

A "lot of small nasty actions" was how Jim White recalled his experience in Germany:

"We entered a small town in single file and very alert. Some of us had put our berets out of sight, some wore their helmets, but some just bareheaded, as I was. We suddenly came under fire from houses and went to ground while some of the lads went round the back to break in and get at the Germans. There was quite a fight and a few of the enemy came out with their hands up. I took charge of the prisoners and eventually a truck came for them. These Germans were very mucky and worn out, but I would say in good spirits.

"At the next block, a small village, the Germans had 88s and some paras and we had a proper set-piece battle. We had some Churchills, but the 88s took care of them. We tried to get around the fields to outflank the guns, but the German paras had us zeroed in and we were pinned down. We called up some air support and some Tempests came over and gave the place a real going-over and we were able to advance. The Germans did not leave any of their dead or wounded paras behind, but there were some German dead in very well-camouflaged positions, but the planes had got them all."

Jim White had missed the Rhine crossing drop owing to a virus infection, and glad of it because, as he recalls, the casualties were worse than on D-Day.

Jules Couvain survived the Rhine crossing and with his men

neutralized what small opposition they found, but taking casualties in the process, including two men killed, he himself getting a scratch on one arm:

"We had a hard slog into Germany in the autumn and winter, and it was bad. It was one small battle after another, but the greatest danger was from mines and the ever present spandaus*. The Germans would liberally sprinkle all approaches to a locality with various types of anti-tank and anti-personnel mine and cover the whole with machine guns from very well-concealed positions. There were never any great numbers of men involved. We stayed off the roads and kept to the fields, trying to envelop the villages, but they were aware of our intentions so laid mines across the fields too. We did not always have tanks to clear the way as they stayed on the road unless German tanks appeared, and when they did they were always holed up in defensive positions and out of sight, so the Churchills were picked off by 88s or tanks and we would be alone in trying to get across the fields covered in mines.

"I had one man blown up right in front of me and there was nothing I could do for him at all. We had to lie flat and inch our way forward, probing for the mines and especially watching out for the damned S mine with two prongs sticking out of the ground which was very easily missed in a field of stubble.

"I recall one day we were taking a breather in a house in a German village when someone yelled 'Tigers!' and we rushed to the window in time to see this damned great giant thing lumbering along the street of the village. We lay flat and got our bombs ready and hoped the anti-tank guns were near us. We did not usually get tank attacks of this kind. The Tiger was a superb defensive tank, but in attack it was vulnerable.

"We were well concealed down by the windows, or rather the holes of them, when this great thing went by all battened down and with no infantry and very vulnerable. At the right moment we leapt out and stuck our bombs on the engine plates and ran back into the houses. There was a hell of a bang and the Tiger went up in flames. The crew tried to bail out but got no chance in our fire so that was the end of them.

"We resumed our tea then advanced again."

Bill Marshall recalls the Rhine crossing by bad flak and quite a few casualties – much worse than D-Day. After some fighting the men were taken forward in trucks and jeeps:

* machine-guns.

194

"From then on it was small nasty actions right across Germany in a rotten winter. I remember one village we occupied after driving out the Germans, the people were mostly gone, but there was a family in our billet which we took over for the night. This was an old couple with a young daughter and we had a sort of argument with them which I'll never forget. The old man spoke English and told us that he had been a prisoner in England in the first war and was very well treated. He seemed to like us, but the daughter was more of a Nazi type and very hostile. In fact at one point we wondered if she'd been left behind to spy on us and we might have to lock her up. She said a great deal, the old boy laughing as he translated to us. It was all anti-British propaganda and mostly rubbish. When we left the next day she spat at us so I gave her a kick up the backside.

"We used that billet because it was intact. The rest of the houses were damaged with leaking roofs. But we were glad to get out of the rain for a bit.

"In another small town we fought an action against an 88mm gun and a bunch of German paras, and I recall one of the Germans calling out to us, 'You English red berets. We will show you how real parachutists fight!' Well, we had a ding-dong battle and gave as good as we got and drove them out. They lost a few but took them with them. We saw no dead German paras.

"One of my chums was killed just after that by a sniper in a house we had thought cleared. There was one shot and my old mucker Tom fell dead, shot in the back. We were very put out by this and went back to find the culprit. We shot up the houses and combed through them and found this young sniper in a camouflaged suit and gave him a real beating, I can tell you, before sending him back. I don't know why we didn't kill him, but he had surrendered and looked so pathetic, but he'd killed my mate and I really gave him a pasting. It sounds brutal but that's the way it was in the war."

Many soldiers wanted to take home something for friends and loved ones at home − souvenirs − though naturally there was the conquerer's loot and something for nothing element in it. John Holmes:

"I always wanted to take home a few souvenirs for my parents, silver ashtrays and that sort of thing, and we did usually get what we wanted. I had some sympathy for the German civilians as they had suffered far worse than our own people from the air raids, but just the same we'd had our mates killed by Germans and had no time at all for sentiment. When you see so much death at close hand it does harden you and you can lose all the softer feelings. But really it was them or us − and too many of our boys had copped it. So when we entered Germany we had no thought of being nice to the enemy − quite the reverse. But this does not mean at all that we had malice for the civilians, and certainly not the kids. We saw plenty of good kids there and sometimes offered them sweets, which, when they got over the fact that we weren't going to eat them, they took!

"But the German people contained a few who hated us, and it showed in their faces. We were very wary of them as we'd been warned to watch out for the so-called 'National Redoubt' and 'Werewolves' behind our lines. We saw Hitler Youth kids, but they mostly just stared at us. I did see one kid who swore viciously at one of our lads and spat at him. This chap was from Lancashire and gave him quite a mouthful in return and followed that up with a slap on the face, which soon shut up that brat, I can tell you.

"We had a lot of trouble with German paras who of course we respected, but when we had our tanks and the air boys have a go they got out quick. There were bad moments when we were hit by rockets − the 'Moaning Minnies' as we called them. The noise they made was a terrible, screeching sound and the explosions were deafening. Once again we were near a small village, just about to enter it from the fields on each side. We hit the deck as all hell broke loose around us. We lost two good men who were blown to bits − not really enough to bury. Then we rushed into the houses for cover. It was fatal to be caught in the open when the rockets came down. At least in the houses we found some shelter.

"Then I recall another rotten day in that winter of 44-45. We had so many of them. The cold and rain put a real damper on our spirits. The food was surprisingly good considering the circumstances. The CO always managed to get something hot to us at least once or twice a day. We also had cold compo rations, but we never managed to find any food in the houses we entered. We took the usual souvenirs, but there wasn't much to take in the villages, but when we reached the larger localities it was a different matter. This was the enemy. They had caused the war, so anything we wanted we took!"

Jim White:

"When we reached Osnabruck there were lots of white flags and we saw a few civilians watching us. We were prepared for anything as usual, but nothing happened until we got outside the town and then they opened up on us and I was hit in the right leg. It was a splinter wound that hurt like hell and put me out of action. I was taken to the rear into a hospital, a large German house with our own medical staff, and there were a few German wounded in there too. I got chatting to one of them who happened to be a para and knew some English. He seemed a decent sort of chap and told me that he had been a para since before the war. He said the war was kaput but Hitler would not admit it. We got on quite well together, but then he was taken away to a POW camp."

Jules Couvain also found little German resistance in the larger localities. The troops had expected some heavy street fighting, but it never happened. "There were skirmishes and small fights, but we had the measure of them. It was not at all as I expected and I was very relieved, though I can tell you we were taking casualties all the time, so one was resigned to losing one's own life. That far I had come through unscathed, apart from the scratch mentioned.

"When we reached North Germany it became a race to the coast to beat the Russians. We were taking lots of prisoners and we just told them to keep on walking. There were also plenty of refugees, mostly German, but also some displaced persons. At last we reached Bremen where we went into camp while the paras went on to Wismar to meet the Russians and had some kind of brief encounter with them before peace was established." Jim White recovered to do guard duty in north Germany, reaching the north German port and city of Bremen where he dropped off with other airborne troops to watch over the thousands of German prisoners, while as mentioned, paras raced on in convoy to prevent the Russians from overreaching themselves.

John Holmes:

"When we could see it was almost over we wondered when we'd meet the Russians and when we reached Bremen and entered the port we knew the time was not far off. We set off in a convoy of jeeps and 17-pounders and the air force was on hand as ever and at last we came to a village and there we saw our first Russians. I was in a small section. Most of the lads there were paras, unlike ourselves of course. When we saw the Russians they looked quite menacing at first and didn't seem to realize we were British, and even when they did an officer had a job convincing them that they could in no way advance further. I can tell you we were ready for anything, but it all passed off peacefully. I did not relish another war, but we had our orders and would have carried them out."

One account says of this meeting between the British and Russians that as soon as the latter recognized their ally's uniforms peace reigned; it wasn't as easy as that. Bill Marshall was in the convoy which had its powerful 17-pounder tank-killer anti-tank guns ready for action:

"We reached Wismar and stopped just short of the Russian advance. They wore all sorts of leather jackets and brown caps and looked very experienced and tough types. We had an order to stop them from getting further and that was it. Our officers explained to the Russians that we were already in occupation of the town, so they could not go on. They too I believe had their orders and wanted to carry them out. But our blokes were very firm and polite and in the end the Russkis could see we meant business. Our planes were on hand not far off and armed with rockets etc. and we had no intention of allowing them to proceed. We had no love for the Germans but the Russians had to know that that was as far as they could go in Europe.

"The Germans in the town knew very well what was going on and hoped we'd start shooting. They were mostly in their houses but a few heads kept bobbing out to watch. It all passed off peacefully in the end and we were left to continue the business of rounding up German stragglers or Nazis."

Jules Couvain noticed how many of the German prisoners appeared to be in perfect health "and ready to continue the war against the bolsheviks as they called them and wanted to join us. I interrogated a few of the more interesting types and we rounded up a few suspected Nazis but no big fry. In a way this was one of the most interesting periods for me as it enabled me to get an insight into the enemy's thinking. We had of course seen very many Germans of the ordinary Wehrmacht who were beaten and only interested in getting home. But with all the U-boat men we felt something different: it was as if they had stopped fighting with their weapons but were still hating us with their minds. Even so, I got along with some of them all right. I spoke some German so was able to have some interesting conversations with them. Their general mood was that Hitler had made Germany great again and that it was the selfishness and greed of the Allies, especially the British and Americans, who wanted all the world's riches for themselves and prevented Germany from having its rightful share.

"I saw some Germans as highly intelligent, intellectuals in uniform who looked down on us as inferior beings. Well, I did my best to dispel any such notions, but this was before they really got to know about the concentration camps, and all that came about after we had left."

The battle of the British airborne forces in Europe was over. By August, 1945, the 6th Airborne Division had returned to England. But its work was not quite over, for the very next month it was despatched to the Middle East where it saw service in Palestine in the Jewish-Arab conflict then beginning in a more militant way, then into Iraq, Transjordan and the Sudan, before finally returning to England in 1948 and disbandment.

THE WAY OF A PARATROOPER

Afterthoughts:

"When I went into the Army as a regular I had no idea at all of becoming a parachutist, and most of us were the same. It seemed to be a real challenge to us to take up such a vocation; it was the ultimate test, and coupled with the soldiering gave us I suppose some inner fulfilment of course. When we were young we were apt to be foolhardy, but there is too the spirit of youth and all that. I came from a background which was in a way under-privileged, if that is the right term. I felt we had not had a fair crack of the whip, and this explains in a way my own desire to get into life in a broader context, not the best way to put it but I mean to imply that I longed in a vague sort of way to do something better in life, and I suppose the Army etc. gave me and my class that chance.

"It is probably true to say that any fighting men obtain their fulfilment in war, and in doing so find other things they had not expected. So when I went into parachuting I was in a big way fulfilling some inner desire of course, and the fighting part of it was something else; it all came together in the war, and looking back I feel that it was in a sense a kind of destiny."

Anon

Appendix

A British Airborne Division in World War II comprised:

DIV. HQ inc: Intelligence Section, Field Section, Defence & Emplaning Platoon

Two PARACHUTE BRIGADES, each with three battalions, HQ & defence platoons

One AIR-LANDING BRIGADE, with three battalions
Artillery: three batteries (18 75mm howitzers) two anti-tank batteries (12 6 pdrs) & one light AA battery (Bofors)
Reconnaissance Squadron, Engineer & Signals sections
Two Wings Army Air Corps (Glider pilots)
plus: one Pathfinder comp, one Forward Observation unit, three Royal Army Service Corps com, two Parachute Field Ambulance com, one Air-Landing Field Ambulance, one Ordnance Field park, REME Workshops, Photo Unit, RE Field Com, Field Security, Provost & Post units.

Total strength 12, 148

Divisional Weapons Allocation:

Sub-machine-guns	6504	75mm how.	18
Rifles	7171	Light AA	23
Pistols	2942	Mortars 2 in	474
Bren guns	966	Mortars 3 in	56
Vickers m.gs	46	Mortars 4.2 in	5
PIATs	392	Flame-throwers	38
6-pdr a.t. guns	84	Tanks (light)	11
17-pdr a.t. guns	16	Tanks (overland)	11*

*In tanks there is little evidence that the Tetrarch tank-cum-armoured car was used in operations though its replacement the Locust was. In weapons, variations occurred, the American .30 Carbine was a favourite.

Bibliography

The Red Beret   Hilary St George Saunders   Michael Joseph, 1950
Go To It! (6th Airborne)   Peter Harclerode   Bloomsbury, 1990
Paratrooper   Gerard M Devlin   Robson Books, 1979
Fallschirmjäger   Bohmler & Haupt   Hans Henning Verlag, 1971
Storming Eagles (German Airborne Forces)
    James Lucas   Arms & Armour Press, 1988
British Airborne Troops   Barry Gregory   Macdonald, 1974
The Struggle for Europe   Chester Wilmot   Collins, 1954
Fallschirmjäger in Action   Squadron-Signal, 1973
Arnhem Spearhead   James Sims   Imperial War Museum, 1978
Arnhem Lift   Louis Hagen   Severn House, 1977
The Luftwaffe War Diaries   Cajus Bekker   Macdonald, 1966
The Second World War Vol 3   Winston S Churchill   Cassell, 1950
Daedalus Returns   Von der Heydte
Parachute General   General Sosabowski   Kimber, 1954

Index

Göring, Gen, 11, 12, 13, 63, 103
Göring Regiment, 13, 14
Greyhound, HMS, 93

Hackett, Brig, 140, 187
Hamilcar glider, 145, 150, 187
Hardwick Hall, 126, 127, 128
Heidrich, Maj, 23
Heraklion, 76, 86, 98
Herman Göring Panzer Division, 13, 106, 107
Hess, Rudolf, 63
Heydte, Baron von der, 84
Hicks, Brig, 141
Hopkinson, Maj-Gen, 142
Horrocks, Lt-Gen, 162
Horsa glider, 135, 150
Hotspur, glider, 133
Howard, Maj, 149

Ismay, Gen, 116

Jackoby, Gen, 11
Jeschonnek, Gen, 63
Jottrand, Maj, 50, 52, 53
Juno, HMS, 93

Kashmir, HMS, 95
Keitel, Gen, 64
Kelly, HMS, 95
Kesselring, 46
Koch, Maj, 48, 51, 54, 77, 82, 142
Kreipe, Gen, 7, 102

Lathbury, Gen, 142
Leicestershire Regiment (2nd Battalion), 76
Lohr, Gen, 63

Maleme airfield, 71, 75, 76, 82, 89, 92, 101
Malta, 116, 142
Manstein, Gen, 38
Meindl, Gen, 82, 83
Milch, Gen, 11, 12
Model, Field Marsal, 184

Montgomery, Field Marshal, 124, 142, 154, 157, 167, 181, 182, 183, 186, 190
Mountain Division (German 5th), 71, 89
Mountain Regiment (German 85th), 97
Mountain Regiment (German 100th), 97, 102
Mussolini, Benito, 58, 59, 61, 64, 106

Naiad, HMS, 93
New Zealand Brigade, 75, 98
Nubian, HMS, 108

Operation Anvil, 152
Operation Barbarossa, 59
Operation Colossus, 116
Operation Husky, 140
Operation Manna, 190
Operation Market-Garden, 153, 162, 182
Operation Mercury, 65, 68
Operation Varsity, 190
Orion, HMS, 93
Otway, Lt-Col, 149
Ox & Bucks Light Infantry, 127, 135, 149

Parachute, the 1-4
Parachute Battalions, (British), 1st, 2nd, 3rd, 4th, 5th, 6th, 9th, 12th, 129, 138, 141, 149, 185
Parachute Brigade (1st), 118, 128
Parachute Brigade (2nd), 141, 142, 143
Parachute Brigade (4th), 140, 142
Parachute Brigade (5th), 191
Parachute Brigade (2nd Independent), 152, 190
Parachute Brigade (22nd Independent Company), 145
Parachute Demonstration Battalion (German), 106
Parachute Division (1st German), 106
Parachute Infantry (American 505th), 140
Patton, Gen, 155, 157
Pearson, Lt-Col, 142